AT FIVE IN THE AFTERNOON
My Battle with Male Cancer

MICHAEL MURPHY

AT FIVE IN THE AFTERNOON
My Battle with Male Cancer

Foreword by Mary Robinson

BRANDON

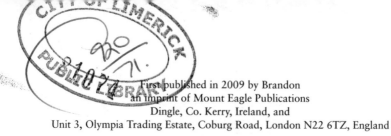

First published in 2009 by Brandon
an imprint of Mount Eagle Publications
Dingle, Co. Kerry, Ireland, and
Unit 3, Olympia Trading Estate, Coburg Road, London N22 6TZ, England

www.brandonbooks.com

Hardback ISBN 9780863224072
Paperback ISBN 9780863224140

Mount Eagle Publications/Sliabh an Fhiolar Teoranta receives support from
the Arts Council/An Chomhairle Ealaíon.

2 4 6 8 10 9 7 5 3 1

Cover design: Anú Design
Typesetting by Red Barn Publishing, Skeagh, Skibbereen

A las cinco de la tarde.
Eran las cinco en punto de la tarde.
Un niño trajo la blanca sábana
a las cinco de la tarde.
Una espuerta de cal ya prevenida
a las cinco de la tarde.
Lo demás era muerte y solo muerte
a las cinco de la tarde.

At five in the afternoon.
It was exactly five in the afternoon.
A boy brought the linen sheet
at five in the afternoon.
A basket of lime standing ready
at five in the afternoon.
Everything else was death, only death,
At five in the afternoon.

Federico García Lorca (1898–1936), "The Goring and the Death", published in *Lament for Ignacio Sánchez Mejías* (1935, translated 1995).

Permissions

I would like to thank the following for permission to include copyright material: *Llanto por Ignacio Sánchez Mejías* by Federico Garcia Lorca © Herederos de Federico Garcia Lorca from *Obras Completas* (Galaxia/Gutenberg, 1996 edition). Translation by Galway Kinnell and Herederos de Federico Garcia Lorca. All rights reserved. For information regarding rights and permissions, please contact lorca@artslaw.co.uk or William Peter Kosmas, Esq., 8 Franklin Square, London W14 9UU.

© Éditions Gallimard, Paris, for permission to quote in French from *Le Mythe de Sisyphe* and *L'Étranger* by Albert Camus, Bibliotheque de la Pléiade, publiée aux Éditions Gallimard (1967). And Penguin Books Ltd., England, for permission to quote in English from *The Myth of Sisyphus* by Albert Camus, trans. Justin O'Brien (1975) and *The Outsider* by Albert Camus, trans. Stuart Gilbert (1966).

Suhrkamp Verlag, Frankfurt a.M., to quote from *"Beim Schlafengehen"* by Hermann Hesse.

Dover Publications, Inc., New York, to quote from *The World as Will and Representation* by Arthur Schopenhauer, trans. by E.F.J. Payne, Vol. 1, 1969.

© Joan Baez/Chandos Music to quote from "Sweet Sir Galahad".

Faber & Faber Ltd., to quote from *Worstward Ho* by Samuel Beckett in *Company / IIISeenIIISaid / Worstward Ho / Stirrings Still*, ed. Dirk Van Hulle (2009).

Cambridge University Press for *The Gay Science: with a Prelude in German Rhymes and an Appendix of Songs* (Cambridge Texts in the History of Philosophy) by Friedrich Nietzsche, ed. Bernard Wiley, trans. Josefine Nauckhoff (2001).

Quotations from *Understanding Prostate Cancer* ed. Antoinette Walker, revised edition 2006, reproduced with the kind permission of the Irish Cancer Society, the national cancer care charity.

If I have neglected to mention any names or accidentally infringed any copyright, I apologise for the unintended omission.

Contents

Foreword

There is an old Irish custom of placing a light in the window. It has a three-fold purpose: to show people that they are welcome inside, to light the way forward for the stranger and to shine a light in the darkness. When I became President of Ireland, I placed a permanent light in the window of my official residence, Áras an Uachtaráin, to welcome into my home those who had not been welcomed there before, particularly the diaspora, those millions of Irish blood who have been scattered all over the world. The beacon was to encourage all of them now and in their future endeavours abroad by shining the light of memory on to our history as a people, demonstrating that the struggles of those who were dispossessed or displaced are not forgotten by us, and that we take a continuing pride in their soaring achievements. Finally, I wanted to shine a light in the darkness, a darkness of ignorance, of prejudice, violence, fear and hopelessness, all of whose spreading cancers assault us as human beings, and which attack at the roots the free flowering of the human spirit. I have tried as best I can to allow the spirit that inspired the gesture to continue to inform me and my work.

When I agreed initially to write a foreword for Michael's book, I did so on the understanding that male cancer does not receive as high a profile as female cancer. My intention was to highlight that the suffering cancer causes to victims and their families is indiscriminate, but that the isolating, physical and emotional effects of treating the disease – incontinence and erectile dysfunction – can be compounded by the fact that men are more reticent than women to speak openly about those possibilities. The subtitle of Michael's book is "My Battle with Male Cancer". *A las cinco de la tarde* is also the time of the bullfight in Spain, that single combat which Michael movingly employs as an allegory for his own battle. His book is unflinchingly honest, and he breaks down the taboo around men speaking the unspeakable, by saying so live on air on the RTÉ afternoon-radio Mooney Show:

"That question. 'You know I have to ask you this...' and brutally, 'Is there any lead in your pencil?'"

"'No, Derek – I don't have any lead in my pencil.'"

What I have realised is that in writing about all aspects of the cancer theme – traumatic assault, mortality, endurance – Michael has created a personal myth to live by. His memoir graphically treats of themes which take enormous risks of courage to put into words, but through the exceptional quality of his writing, they have become a pillar of light which has enabled him to continue on in the warmth of its lustre, despite his loss and the limits that have now been reached.

"I have told it like it is, what I have seen and what I have heard. I have said it, and my saying is true. Because of the cancer, there's no longer any space available to hide in; neither is there any time left over for being silent."

It is a freedom from the prison of silence that Michael has proven can be open to all. The welcome home in his book is for all whose lives have been touched by the many forms of cancer. It is a true house of the gathering, where the strands and themes of his narrative congregate to offer hope and a way forward out of the darkness that surrounds.

His writing can clearly be seen as an attempt to come to terms with the death of his brother Kieran, who died from cancer in his early forties. The death of a sibling is so deeply personal that it is akin to the death of the self. The emotional trauma it causes leaves a profound mark on the personality, so that, as Michael says, he has found himself living in "a beyond of death". He has already had the terrible experience of the death of a person he loved, so that the shock of having cancer intensifies and deepens that first wound. The response of those who have been touched by cancer, the mustering of bravery involved in coming to terms with mortality, with, as Michael phrases it, "the terrible understanding of not being here any more", has compelled him to seek out and to follow, in the dark, the faltering light of wisdom.

I found Michael's memoir to be a love poem to Mayo, to its landscape, its heritage, above all to its people. And I see that Michael has described me warmly as "Mayo's second citizen president", following on John Moore's short-lived presidency in 1798! Michael's battle against the diminishing yoke of cancer is counterpointed by the struggle of our ancestors for the freedom to determine our own destiny, particularly around the time of the Land League. He has told the story of his great-grandfather, who was imprisoned in Galway Gaol for his political beliefs over a hundred years ago, and whose painful sacrifice has inspired him to endure, for this day.

I was particularly struck by the shining generosity of the women who grace Michael's life. He acknowledges those women as "*deá-chroí*, good-hearted women". They are the cancer survivors, Helen, Anna and Ursula, who shared their personal life stories with Michael so that he could make a full recovery. They nourished him with their words, giving him a life-giving transfusion which has enabled Michael to survive. He writes incisively, "Always there are those valorous women whose strength is that of the true warrior, who take arms against the odds stacked against them, and who fight to the death only as a very last resort..." Ursula, the photographer, has since lost her fight against pancreatic cancer, but her spirit lives on in Michael's poetry: "I pointed out that Ursula had kept her word: she endured to keep on this side of the river Styx for as long as she was able. As in her photographs of those great trees that had fallen some millions of years before, those traces of her presence were all she had to offer in the twilight days at season's change, but Ursula had offered all, in love." That loving mediation by women, particularly in health matters, is a radiant quality which can smooth the way for men to act. There is a vignette at the end of the Mooney chapter, where Valerie, who has suffered breast cancer, is serving Michael his meal. She says, "I'm always at my husband to go to the doctor and have the test done, and he never will. But after he heard you speak about it on the radio, he agreed. We rang the doctor when you had finished, and he has an appointment for Monday morning!"

Finally, I am delighted to have the opportunity to introduce a new Irish voice to the world. While Michael Murphy's language is steeped in the culture of his native land, his writing takes its place in the wider European canvas of France, Germany and Spain; his is a voice which is born of a modern and changing Ireland, but which also draws from the well of a traditional, Irish heritage, which has reverberated for us down through the centuries. The title *At Five in the Afternoon* is from the poem by the Spanish poet, Federico García Lorca, and refers to "the inevitable ending of a final dance with God, a dance with Death". The sensibility Michael expresses, his moral and aesthetic responsiveness, is underpinned by an unremitting emphasis on the truth, culminating in his final explanation: "I have told the truth to save my life." And in that final chapter he has the young bullfighter, Ismael Cuevas, "climbing the steps of a rainbow *ar shlí na firinne*, on the pathway of truth", emphasising the redemption that Michael has found in facing the impossible reality of cancer head on, a trustworthy position woven from words that has guaranteed his footing, free from *an fóidín mearaí*, the sod of confusion. If there is an overall impression to be gleaned about the way forward out of intractable situations, surely it is about the emphasis that Michael has placed on the primacy of language and on the transcendent, transformative power of words.

His book is about more than male cancer. Michael has drawn on his unique background in psychoanalysis, in the art of constructing television programmes, and on his broadcasting experience as newscaster where the human voice is privileged, to write a beautiful, layered work about the importance of saying, about putting the world of the imagination into words that are true. As he memorably phrases it: "The word is a rose that opens slowly for me, hiding at the heart of its corolla the Latin *praedicare*, to assert or proclaim publicly. This book is a predicate, that which is said of the subject. The way forward I've chosen is to predicate upon that earlier noun and base my actions on whatever I shall say, be it wild or barbarous, before the blown petals shall fall."

Today, I am delighted to herald another golden light in the firmament, which strengthens us on our journey through life. It is shining aloft, defying the darkness of cancer, and illuminates for all of us the way forward and the way home.

Mary Robinson
May 2009

To Terry, and to all who have been touched by cancer. Out of the beautiful words that my mother gave me, I have woven you a wreath, for valour.

Part One: Origins

I've come to borrow my brother's saying since the doctor diagnosed me with prostate cancer. "And how're you now?" is what Tom says when he answers the phone. Commonplace, you may say, but he's the only one I know who does that. The rueful way he accents the "now" implies his sympathetic understanding of life's predicament, that although matters had been bad previously, the projected outcome will oftentimes be a great deal worse. And yet he's also saying, "Bring it on." For me, that's like the lethal, flourishing, blood-red gesture of a matador: the male equivalent of the tight skirt-strutting, killer-heel clacking, hand through the hair gesticulating, broadest *"Díga me"*, that "Say it to me" greeting I so much enjoy hearing and observing in Spain. Such black humour continues the family conversation: "The Murphys of The Mall" advance, swords straight, aiming for the more difficult feat of the *estocada al recibir,* when a man receives the full force of the black bull's last charge.

For the longest time now, I've been bearing in mind the valour of the matador in his costume of lights, facing death in the *corrida* at five in the afternoon. About six months after my next brother, Kieran, died from cancer at forty-two years of age, I was in Innsbruck one sunny Palm Sunday morning, searching the skyline for the spires of a church in which I could attend mass to pray for the repose of his soul. Although lined with cars, the streets were empty. There was no movement. I became aware of the absence as I walked in the centre of an avenue which seemed, straight as a Roman road, to go on for ever. I turned around, but there was nobody behind me, just a silent kiss from the wind, a stooping down to brush the cold forehead *atque in perpetuum, frater, ave atque vale* with parted lips.

I heard a shuffling sound. It was like hundreds of the softest footfalls, louder, getting louder, marching in unison. I could hear the rat-tat-tat of the snare-drum. Out from a side-street in the distance stepped the eight-wide phalanx of a Tyrolean brass band in lederhosen period costume, row after row of men with red plumes cocked in their hats, the sun glinting off their instruments and multi-coloured banners waving in the breeze. The corps was wheeling around and heading directly up towards me. Wave after wave of musicians were coming, bands from every valley in Austria preceded by their standard-bearers, hundreds of people in marching boots, with white stockings and shirts and velvet Spanish-style boleros.

I moved to the side and reached for my camera. The leader looked me in the eye, pointed over at me with his baton, then hurled it heavenwards where it shattered the sun into stars. As he caught he struck it down, and every brass band began to play. The shock of the noise beat me back against the side of a car. It was awe-inspiring. And I realised that all of these people were making music just for me: there was nobody else to hear this explosion of joy. It was Kie. It was my younger brother Kie, who was saying to me in the trumpeting music of the massed brass bands, "And how're you now?" For certain I knew that this was his way of getting through to me.

Appropriately, the photographs didn't come out. I wasn't

able to focus the camera because I was blinded with grief: the tears wouldn't stop, and my sobbing beat time with the thundering loudness of the music, which was riotous. It burst the banks of the street in a glorious, reverberating, drunken defiance of the dark. The sound of the brass bands was so overwhelming, such an archetypal noise, that I was blasted by what my ancestors must also have heard in a long-distant past, speaking to me now through the vibrancy of this present moment. And the flags were waving, the music was playing, and the men were marching through.

Overlooking it all from the golden whiteness of the highest heavens was Kie, laughing and cheering and wielding his flag in a brilliantly courageous performance, a *faena de muleta* that drew rapturous music from those glittering brass instruments, the white kerchiefs of shirt and stockings undulating before me. Each of those musicians, line after line of them, acknowledged my presence by nodding his head as he passed on, blowing his horn and banging on his drum, and putting the terrorising blackness to flight. The roar of the music was a shouted affirmation that our living continues on, no matter what. The massed ranks just brushed aside the terrible waste that was Kie's death and that any time now could be my death. Just as suddenly they were gone, nothing left but the memories, swirled about by the wind.

On the morning of my father's funeral, Kie and I went into the bank to get some money to buy wellingtons against the long grasses of the graveyard. We were preparing ourselves for that gun-carriage moment of ritual, when his five sons would carry their father's coffin up to the family plot dominated by a monumental Celtic cross, the man's wife walking directly behind leading the band of mourners. And when the bank manager spotted us, he snaked out from his office, buttoning the jacket of his shiny suit. "Ye're welcome home to Castlebar.

It's always nice to see the Murphys of the Mall walking the streets on the right side of the Shannon."

Cork accent. We're the Wexford branch of the Murphys, who emigrated after the 1798 Rebellion, which was put down by the Cork Militia. We escaped into exile at Castletown in Queen's County, from whence my grandfather, the first Thomas Murphy, migrated to Mayo. On the twenty-second of August in that same year of 1798, three gleaming, white angels with massive wingspans descended from heaven disguised as frigates in full sail and appeared out of the sea mist at Kilcummin Strand in the north of Mayo, bearing with them the subversive gifts of liberty, equality and fraternity. A French expeditionary force of eleven hundred men under General Humbert had arrived on his forty-second birthday bringing salvation for all the people. During the "Races of Castlebar," the British occupying forces were routed by my fellow townspeople at Stab-all Hill with French encouragement, and Mayo became the cradle of a short-lived republic under our first president, John Moore. The inscription upon the tombstone over his grave on the Mall in Castlebar says he was of Ashbrook and Moorehall in Mayo, but a Spaniard by birth. That mirror image is a passionate connection I value now more than ever, because then I was the cross bearer, an altar server at the funeral ceremony for his reinterment, and now I too possess a piece of Spanish earth.

Sometimes it can be difficult outside of the psychoanalyst's consulting room not to overhear what a person is really saying. And the bank manager's patronising double entendre, "It's always nice to see the Murphys of the Mall walking the streets . . .", made me recoil, but I could sense Kie's delight in being handed a justification for battle, and he moved closer to me so that we were standing shoulder to shoulder.

"I always like to keep up with the doings of our customers. And of course, we all know Michael from the television."

18

Kie said nothing, just continued writing on the withdrawal slip, but his elbow was digging into my waist.

"And how is ye'er father?"

"Not too good, actually," said Kie, writing away.

"Oh . . . And why is he not too good?"

Dad's pastime was reading cowboy books, which we borrowed for him from the library. And in a personal tribute, Kie raised his head like a sheriff, looked across the counter at this outlaw and gave him both barrels right between the eyes: "He died yesterday."

The Mall is the linden-lined walkway of fluttering leaves which cuts across the side of a large, circular park in the centre of Castlebar town. It leads from Lord Lucan's demesne and the British military barracks to Christ Church, the Protestant church. But locals have always referred to the whole of this rich expanse of grassland as the Mall. It's still surrounded by the massive chestnut trees, their large white candles standing gloriously erect above the spreading branches, which Lucan had planted. It was his cricket pitch: his soldiers and his tenantry played many's the match there once upon a time. As children we played our own games in the new-mown grass (the dogs involved were Lassie Mellett and Tatters Chambers) of what was our front garden, in those for ever summers when the light barely faded and the towering trees and a necklace of looping iron chains protected us from what was outside.

My father was born in a gracious four-storied building called Burleigh House, which abuts the Mall. The story goes that he didn't came home one particular night and that he met my grandmother at the doors on her way out to the eight o'clock morning mass – the brasses polished and the washing already drying on the line – as he unsteadily began to clamber up the eight steps to the entrance hall, evidently the worse for drink.

"And what is it this time, Thomas? Twelve hours of snooker in the Forester's Hall?"

Dad looked up in Granny's direction: "And Jesus meets his afflicted mother."

"Thomas," she reprimanded, "I asked you a question. What were you doing all night?"

Dad gave her one of the lopsided smiles that I've associated with Kie, but realise now for the first time where he got it from, and by way of a reply, he said, "Ma'am, I was walking round and round the Mall looking for the house, but I wasn't able to find it."

Embracing him in a look, she retorted, "Thrue fo' ya, Thomáisín, thrue fo' ya, as Maggie Burke would say," borrowing language from a neighbour in Ellison Street, to distance herself from the disappointment at her son's weakness. And she stepped past him on her way down to the Church of the Holy Rosary, tilting her latest Langan's hat in response to his drunken salute. As no team was bowled out, the match on the Mall ended in a draw. Honours even.

My now frail, eighty-seven-year-old mother was spotted by John Joe out in the rain last week with a bag of groceries from Shane's in her arms. John Joe is a neighbour from next door, and he holds an emergency key to her hall door in what used to be Granny's house on her retirement.

"How're you, Mrs Murphy?"

"Oh, John Joe." She recognised him. "Tommie hasn't come home for his tea. He promised me he'd give up the drink. I wonder would he be down in Tansey's?"

When it was related to her a day or two later what she'd said to John Joe, she chuckled. "Come on! I know I'm bad, but I'm not that bad. Perhaps, if the story were less far-fetched . . . You know that I'd never say anything like that to someone outside of the house."

She never spoke about her own father, so she did keep her counsel. But there must have been times when keeping silent wasn't easy. Reverting glimpses are beginning to slip out from the damp paper bag that was holding them in for so long. Like Jackie Kennedy, who marvelled that she hadn't gone mad, the wonder is that my mother didn't begin to lose it sooner, in her case as a result of the aftershocks of an explosion that was to shatter the certainties of her comfortable childhood world into smithereens.

There were seven children in my mother's family: the sepia photographs show the girls dressed in the latest flapper fashions, the boys in skinny ties, and, as in my father's upbringing, there were helpers, a housekeeper and a cook to look after them. They had a thriving business in Ballinamore, County Leitrim; to the back, a pub, and in the front, a grocery shop. Rice O'Beirnes owned the first car in Ballinamore, and the family visited Dublin regularly with their children for concerts, the operas and to conduct business; they all ate in the fashionable restaurant, Jammet's. And always there was music: everyone played piano and the violin for sing-songs, and for dancing there were the latest 78s on the wind-up gramophone. Like Granny Murphy in Castlebar, my grandmother in Ballinamore grew up in a hotel, so she was a capable organiser, who made preserves with gathered fruit from the trees and bushes she had planted in the garden, directing operations with jars and huge copper pans in the heat of the kitchen. She grew flowers which the girls carried carefully down the back way to decorate the church: larkspur and foxglove, baby's breath, phlox, bellflowers, gladioli and lilies, sweet pea and chrysanthemums. But the undertow bringing death and destruction, which was set off by the explosion that happened a generation earlier, now hit the family with full force.

My great-grandfather, Charles O'Beirne, was imprisoned in Galway Gaol by the British authorities for giving his public support to a Mayoman, Michael Davitt from Straide, who had founded the National Land League in October 1879, in the hotel across from us on the Mall. This was an organisation of tenant farmers, objecting to the exorbitant rents being charged by the British absentee landlords, who agitated under the slogan "The land of Ireland for the people of Ireland." We've the letters that my great-grandfather wrote home from prison, which have been carefully passed down the generations. They are selfless; full of concerns for his family, for the shop boys and for the business. His was a fight for liberation, for his family and for his neighbours, and he paid the ultimate price. The British broke his health after months of torture on the treadmill. When Charles was returned to his family, he lived for only the shortest time, and the explosion caused by his early death has marked all subsequent generations of the family. His four young sons were left with no father, no direction, and without a proper introduction to the outside world. Charlie, the eldest, had emigrated to America, so the business fell by default on to the shoulders of the second son, my grandfather, Rice O'Beirne, who then became the head of the family. He married Susan McGauran from the Railway Hotel on the other side of the Main Street.

But my grandmother died, and she died of cancer, a disease that lives for ever in our genes. Mama was only forty-eight, and my mother was just twelve, an incalculable loss for such a young girl. This second early death unleashed something terrible for the whole family. My grandfather, Papa, married again almost immediately, but it was a *mésalliance* which foundered; his new wife soon returned to her family home with her baby son. The first family had scattered. At the same time, the O'Beirne family home and the business that had been built up over generations was repossessed by the Ulster Bank, a neighbour from just three doors down the street, and it was auctioned off. Rice O'Beirne, without a wife, a family or a home, took to the road as a commercial traveller, and for the first time, in his fifties, he also took to the drink. The main reason for the collapse of the family business was the accumulation of individual debts that were run up by the people of Ballinamore and its environs, who were suffering hardship under Britain's Economic War. So for a second time, another generation of the O'Beirne family paid a catastrophic price for Irish freedom. When Mum took the bus home from boarding school in Castlebar on her first school holidays, she was met by her Uncle Charlie, newly returned from America, who took her into his home and who eventually was to pay for her wedding.

My grandpapa's alcoholism is another form of cancer that continues to wither generations of Irish people, because nobody speaks truthfully about the secret which everyone shares. The contagion is like a lighthouse beam that searches out replicas of itself in order to pass on down the generations the blight of the suffering to the family that it causes. My mother had five sons within the space of eight years with a husband who also suffered from that disease, and who broke out occasionally. It's thanks to the enduring lessons of her family history, allied to her intellect, that she had the resources to strike back for the emotional well-being of herself and of her fellow townspeople: it was my mother who brought Al Anon to Castlebar.

They say that Grandpapa died in an asylum in Dublin. He never visited his daughter or his grandchildren in Mayo, but the flowering of those terrible sufferings which tragically left him dispossessed and a prisoner of drink, and those of his father before him in whom they'd fatally taken root, but whose spirit was able to triumph over prison to yield a towering immortality, have seeded in me possibilities of absence and of presence, a dual heritage which I've only lately begun to examine.

It was a gentle, summer's day in Dublin, bathed in the soft yellow light of Ireland, and we were heading up to the newly opened Dundrum Shopping Centre, passing by the Central Mental Hospital. I was idly wondering in my mind whether my grandpapa had died behind those high walls, out of sight and on his own. I'd never met him, and I don't know where he died or where he's buried. Terry's mobile rang, which he passed over to me.

"Hello – who is this?"

"It's Fiona McGoldrick, Michael. The result of your PSA test has come back – that's one of the blood tests which targets the prostate gland – and the prostate specific antigen is a little raised."

The ivory fist clenched around the haft of the steel blade, held up behind the hooded head.

"There's probably nothing to worry about, but to be sure I'd like you to get in touch with a consultant."

With force he brought it forward . . .

"The surgeon's name is David Mulvin, and can I give you his number?"

. . . and down, so that the blade entered cleanly between two ribs and pierced me to the heart. I pretended to take down the figures, "987 . . .", but my concentration had evaporated.

"Thanks, Fiona – I'll get on to it right away."

I saw the sign for a post office and we pulled up outside it. I escaped from the car, dropping the mobile phone into the gutter. Inside I asked them for a telephone directory to get the number of St Vincent's University Hospital and rang it for an appointment three months hence.

Terry and I didn't speak nor look at each other. It seemed unmannerly somehow to draw attention to the fact that we were panicked by the shockingly casual nature of what had been set in train. It felt as if my skewered heart were dangling from the end of a bloodied blade, held in the terrifying immediacy of the present moment by a powerful, hooded figure dressed in black, who'd interposed his bulk between the two of us, cleaving us apart. With hindsight, it was a mercy that neither Terry nor I could give any consideration to the massive explosion ahead, when each of us would be blown apart by the reality of male cancer.

While I'm known in Ireland for the thirty-five years I've spent as a broadcaster, my university training both here and in France has been in psychoanalysis. Four days a week I work with clients at my rooms in Dublin 4; Friday is a study day. Nine months before the prostatectomy operation, I had a cancellation one morning in late spring, when the air was crisp and the daffodils were blooming. I took advantage of the break to clear my head of the statements of pain that I'd been listening to intently and fled the practice pursued by others' phantoms to walk down to Donnybrook Fair. I'd buy additions to the salad for lunch: some slices of barbecued chicken, a tub of bean salad and fresh olives from Spain. As I walked back carrying my paper bag, there was a showering down of pink and white confetti in the wind, petals shaken like droplets off the umbrellas of flowering cherries. I was admiring the various trees spreading and weeping, clusters of blooms covering the branches with five petalled flowers in pink, over there thousands of them in white. And I knew it was over. The thought arrived unannounced. I've always valued thoughts, but this one had captured me. The certainty of it was an absolute, so overwhelmingly present that there was no room for doubt. It was over.

One of the trees had almost black leaves fluttering in the sunlight, perhaps an ornamental plum. Petals had stuck to my navy jacket. Leaves of loss began to bury me, creating a cairn of leaf mould, damp with the spreading desolation. Gerard Manley Hopkins' desolation looking out over St Stephen's Green: "Margaret, are you grieving over golden-grove unleaving . . ." I realised I was listening to the closing cantata of Bach's *St Matthew Passion* playing in my mind: "*Wir setzen uns mit Tränen nieder, und rufen dir im Grabe zu: ruhe sanft, sanfte ruh . . .*" We sit down in tears and call to you in the grave: sleep softly, soft sleep . . . I questioned whether I'd picked up some unexpressed feelings from the clients I'd been working with earlier, but no, that wasn't the case. Was it Kie's death? My father's death? The knowledge of death continues to inform me, and I deepen into the terrible understanding of not being here any more, particularly as I get older, but it wasn't a perfect match with the hopeless inevitability of what I was feeling, which was a fatigue, an inability to respond to a situation that I seemed to have been overexposed to. The hooded figure had entwined his bony limbs around me in an obscene intimacy, bundling me up into the dank, smothering heaviness of his cloak, which robbed me of presence. His was an exhausting weight to drag around with me whenever I moved, blind and unseen, my skin withdrawing in revulsion from the feel of his touch.

I got back to the practice and I looked up the word in the dictionary to see what I meant. "Over" is a postpositive adjective which means finished, from the Latin *finis*, end, or boundary: to come to an end: the death or the absolute defeat of a person. The word began to access all of the memories which cluster around such a list of concepts and which clamour to be heard like the waving arms I remember from a classroom of children in St Patrick's national school in Castlebar, asking to be freed, "*Bhfuil cead agam dul amach?*" Back then our demand was to be given the time and the space to put as much of our thoughts and feelings as was possible into speech, a running to and fro with words so that we could be heard. More than all that, we wished to draw from any adult a loving smile of recognition for our wanting, which shyly held back in the words' resonances. Now I see it as a want of being, which makes a space in words for each tiny individual to become present and which has enabled me to be more in spirit than the manifest sum of all my sentences.

When eventually I sat in front of Dr Fiona and told her of the fatigue and the attendant symptoms, I was crying. I told her that something which was off to the side, that I barely saw out of the corner of my eye, that had not even registered yet, would one day take centre stage and threaten me. She listened in silence and then said that she wanted to put me on Zispin, because all the signs of depression were there: deep sadness, difficulty in performing day-to-day tasks, disturbances in sleep and feelings of anxiety. Intellectually I knew the origins of the thought had to lie in the past: there was nothing in the present I was aware of that triggered it, and the future had not yet arrived in all the baroque splendour of its horrifying pageantry. So from out of my memories, is it the fatal Freudian question that life poses for a man of how to deal with the father? Freud had a creative illness about it lasting six years, during which his father died. He concluded a hero is someone who courageously rebels against his father, and overcomes him. Jung's illness also lasted six years, which he referred to as his Nekiya, after Ulysses' journey to the Sojourn of the Dead. My odyssey in writing this book about male cancer seems to be, to overcome both death and my father. Such a banal prospect fills me with reluctance, because I shouldn't have to wait out those six years, if miserly Death were to parcel out the time for me. And I already know the answer to that question about the father: you dry your tears, and you sit to the table as though nothing had happened and stoically continue to smile. You are not to have your say. But does that impassive effacement lead on to the present moment where I break down and blubber in front of a kindly doctor, mourning something that didn't have a voice in the past, or that was unheard, not recognised, so that now it returns to haunt, stalking me like the ghost in Hamlet?

One afternoon in mid-January 2007, I was lying on my back looking at the two hundred and ten ceiling tiles in room 312 of St Vincent's Private Hospital in Dublin, my grasp on reality distorted by the injections of morphine from the pump that I was pressing for the pain. It's a room twelve paces by five, which has a panoramic view over Elm Park golf course. I wore earphones to block out the suffering of having no protection against the outside, concentrated on the Canadian musician Glenn Gould interpreting Johann Sebastian Bach's *The Well-Tempered Clavier* Book 1. At the beginning of most manuscripts by Bach, you can read the ejaculation that I was using over and over, "JJ": *Jesu Juva*, Jesus help me. Gould's mother was a music teacher like mine, and she taught him to play all of Book 1 by the time that he was ten, each note articulated clearly like the vowels of good speech so that one didn't obscure another. I had the thought that this series of preludes and fugues encompasses all you ever need to know about music. The revelation was that all of music is worked out here in these forty-eight short pieces, which is the *opus summum* of the keyboard. It's truly a book about everything, and I entered into it like a newborn soul enters into the universe.

God knocked on the door of the room, introduced himself and walked in to have a chat: "I'm cold and uncaring, so I'll only be a moment." I was amazed to meet him after so long an absence – his or mine? It's a jigsaw piece I keep coming across in the most unlikely of places. The first thing I'd say is that he's not at all as I'd expected him to be. He's very like the unconscious: playful, punning, insistent and overwhelmingly present, painting word pictures with a great sense of humour. Intellectually, I did have some idea of him being in the language of which we are dispossessed: "*Dia Dhuit.* Hello – God be with you." "*Dia 's Muire Dhuit.* Hello yourself – God and Mary be with you." An Irish formation of the unconscious deep in our psyche, a language based on being in which there's no verb "to have." My Gaelic ancestors worshipped the Supreme Being who speaks in the human voice: the English word "god" comes from a root word related to the Old Irish "*guth.*" Those Celts were so overwhelmed by the wonder of spoken expression that they shared their naming with all of the Germanic peoples, which was felt to push up beyond our threshold of experience. In the course of a conversation in which I felt grateful, I was given to understand that he'd be guided by me, that I was responsible. He also said, "Michael, we got the entire prostate; I assure you all of it was removed. However, there was one square tumour about the size of my thumbnail on the left-hand side, and that was attached."

It was out before I could help it: "*Ciotógach,* cack-handed! I've always led with my left hand in a right-handed world."

He roared laughing, and said, "Put it there." It's the first time that I shook hands *ciothóg* to *ciothóg.*

I can hear God speak through the music of Bach and also through the human presence of Glenn Gould's background but audible singing at the keyboard. I can see Bach seated at his desk, dipping his quill pen in brown ink and signing off on his manuscripts with the letters SDG: *Soli Deo Gloria,* for the glory of God alone. In the rapturous way that Glenn Gould responds, humming along to the music that Bach composed, I can hear him affirm, "I believe in Bach's God," and his faith touches me deeply. All there is really is music.

I remember studying in a stuffy classroom at St Mary's Priory in Tallaght in the days when I was a Dominican student for the priesthood. It was a metaphysics class on Thomism, and the lecturer, Fr McLoughlin, had posed the question, "What is of the highest importance?" to which the answer was self-evidently "being." I knew it instinctively. But the two or three students he pounced on seemed bewildered and gave answers which had no relevance to what he'd asked. In exasperation, the lecturer began at the back wall of the class and worked his way up student by student, row by row, to the front, but nobody knew the answer. With the tension building, I wondered whether there was a conspiracy afoot of which I was unaware to deliberately frustrate this lecturer, Fr McLoughlin, a very brilliant man. We were privileged to be in his masterclass, so why treat him like a fool? Fear stepped out of the darkness and bullied me as the questioning went on, taunting me to doubt myself, so I leafed through my notes to make sure that I had the external comfort of an answer written down. Bernard Mercier didn't have any idea; Pius Horgan gave the wrong answer. I was called after the order's founder, and my name in religion was Br Dominic.

"Br Dominic?" he called out, and his face was red from exertion and anxiety.

"*Esse est supremus:* being is supreme."

The lecturer gestured Gallic fashion, a shrug of the shoulders with both hands in the air, and sank down wearily into his chair, a long lock of white hair obscuring his spectacles. What d'you expect? That's it – *ça y est*. That was it: being is the only answer to everything.

"Feelin' That I Got It Made" is the title of a song of mine that won first prize at the Castlebar International Song Contest. I was in my early twenties, and the cheerful, ragtime music presented clearly how I felt about life beginning to blossom. My youngest brother Fintan was in the group that sang the winning entry: "Ain't got nothin' to do but die, don't give a damn if life is passin' me by . . ." As La Salle advanced upon the massive audience and launched into a key change for the final chorus, the enormous Royal Ballroom took off, sensing that this would be a first for Castlebar, and it began to soar. Ian McGarry, the RTÉ producer, was the drummer that night, and he pounded out the triple figure signalling the *rallentando* before the end. Liam Lyons from Westport snapped the photograph of Kie and me in bow ties and dress suits sitting side by side. There was just the dulled hush, and it was pleasant. We could see beyond the blue, unclouded horizon, and anxiousness dropped away like sandbags. The group on stage began to turn in slow motion for a final kick out to the left, and we saw Fintan singing his heart out, playing the guitar, but the only sound was the breath of God, a tendency. Mum and Dad were in New York that autumn, a gift for their twenty-fifth wedding anniversary. People around us were standing on chairs, cheering and clapping, hoarse that a victory was coming home. A wind of considerable force became a roaring hurricane, and we were enveloped in the thunderous ovation that broke overhead and rolled towards the stage for La Salle's final gesture, guitar hand raised, emphasising the triumph of a win. There was pandemonium. Shay Healy, one of the judges, gave a thumbs up as I walked on to the stage. Mr Howick, from Guinness's, recognising shock, reminded me to smile as he handed over the cheque. "I got everything goin' for me, I got life, I got love, and I gotta be free, I'm feelin' that I got it made!" Castlebar had won the contest. The applause went on and on for about twenty-five, maybe thirty minutes. Back then it was easy to shine from the highest heavens within the generous, supportive embrace of a gathering of my own people.

But now that I'm in my sixties, imprisoned by the thought that it's over following the doctor's deadly diagnosis of prostate cancer: "And, how're you *now*?"

Part Two: Displacement

I crept down the stairs, and there at the bottom in the hall was the biggest, sturdiest red tricycle I'd ever seen. Santy came! I clambered up on it but could barely manage the pedals if I didn't sit down. In the kitchen, the carrot for Rudolph the red-nosed reindeer on the tray that I had set was gone, and the glass was empty, so Santy drank the milk and ate the biscuits. I convinced myself that I could even see a stray white hair on the glass. I cycled that tricycle, with my friend Frank Pelly on his bicycle, miles out the Pontoon road as far as Clydagh Falls, to paint them using my paintbox; out the golf links road where we tracked a *smólach's* nest, the nest of a speckled thrush, high up in a ditch at McDonald's house; as far as Manulla Junction, to see the woman close the gates to let the Ballina train thunder through, then she gave us a spin on them, holding on tight, as she pushed one, then the other creaking open again in the sudden silence. But my favourite run was up and down the path in front of our house from the Green Bay Café down to Mellett's petrol pumps. By the time that I was born, the year of the bad winter in 1947, Granda Murphy had sold Burleigh House to a dentist, and he'd renovated two smaller houses side by side on the Mall: Granny and Granda lived in one, and they hanselled the other to my father as a wedding gift.

A crateful of long bottles of oil capped with coloured foil was placed between the two petrol pumps. We used to collect and flatten out these rejected discs once the bottles had been used: they were our money for playing shop. When I got good at the tricycle and Dad had lowered the saddle, I could loop in and out between these three objects when there was nobody around. One evening, I clipped the crate of bottles with my back wheel, which toppled them over, and some of the glass bottles broke, leaking spreading pools of oil. I was panic-stricken, but I didn't let it show. So I continued on around the second pump and back into the oil, where I upended the tricycle. This time I left it at the scene of the crime and fled. I knew that Dad would be mad, so I hid under Auntie Má's bed upstairs, terrified at the prospect of what was about to happen.

I could hear Mr Mellett talking to him through the open window on his way home for the tea, and then I heard the chain clicking as he pushed the tricycle up the path. He left it outside and started calling for me when he reached the house, and soon his flailing arm was fishing for me under the bed. He grasped at my ankle and pulled me out, dragged me protesting down the stairs to outside the turf place. The turf place is a small, rectangular atrium, with four doors leading off it: the turf-place door, where we stored the sods of turf for the fire, the door out to the yard and back garden, the door into the kitchen, and the door into the main hallway. There was to be no discussion, no room there for my words. My father held my left hand in his, and he started in to beat me with his right hand. As the blows rained down, I ran round and around on tippy toes like water disappearing down a plug hole. Every time I ran past the kitchen door, I could see Mum standing in there, looking on, and she was crying too. He continued beating me, on my legs and on my buttocks, working himself up into a *leadhair* of shame and of rage, until I was terrorised.

The beating went on and on. I was very little, three or four maybe, and to me he was a very big and heavy man. It soon seemed as if we were the ones standing still and that all of the doors and the very house itself were whirling around us, the infernal work of some demented poltergeist, angry at the ley lines being transgressed. Each time that we passed the kitchen door, I was darting an appeal to see if maybe she would come to my aid, but she stood there immobile, deferring.

Then the battering began to be a serious matter. I was crying and sobbing so much that I wasn't able to breathe. If the ferocity of the assault were to continue at this level, then I knew I was going to die. My father was beating the living daylights out of me, beating the life out of me. He wanted me gone and out of the way: I felt the certainty of his heart's intention right down his arm, in being beaten aside by his right hand, in the smothering imprint of his beating fingers. And I also knew for the first time that there was never going to be any end to this beating, no matter how short or how long that I lived. And as I caught glimpses of my mother, I also grasped with a certainty born of bitter experience that nobody was ever going to extend a hand to save me, ever. I was completely on my own. It were better if I hadn't been born; an angle on the oedipal myth, the father who's jealous of the son. He beat me so that not being born became something I'd always have to wrestle with, an object of belief in my mind, an inscription branded into my flesh, a cancerous life without end inside my body: so profound and early an initiation into an adulthood not yet developed in me that try as I might, there'd never be any possibility of escape from what was laid down for me that evening in that atrium *móin*.

From the silence of a calm place next door to me, I had the certainty that I was going to die: this beating was the definitive one that I remember, and it was to be to the death. *Estocada a volapié,* when the matador throws his weight on to the standing animal, is indeed the more commonplace action in bull-fighting. How long the beating went on for I don't know. I think my mother may eventually have intervened between the two of us one time with a "That's enough now, Thomas," but I don't remember it clearly. When I was going through my own analysis, I asked her about the beatings, and she volunteered that my father was generally drunk when he beat me.

Fate waved the green kerchief, and I was resurrected in the kitchen. She was where I'd seen her, only kneeling before me now, wiping the tears from my face with an apron which smelled of cooking. She held me upright in her arms, clasping me to her shoulder until the sobbing, the *brón,* had subsided. But the irony of being comforted by this woman who hadn't intervened to save me was burningly apparent to me even then. And I've never forgotten that ambivalent question of exactly how much of a beating is enough, Thomas? And, Thomas, enough for whom?

The cover-up required that I sit up to the table as if nothing had happened. I was to quieten the shudder of my sobs, to dry my tears and hold my head erect. I wasn't to refer to what had happened, not to question it in any way, not to say anything whatsoever. I understood instinctively that I'd been beaten into silence: superb training for newscasting, for suffering malignant attacks as producer/director, transferential assassinations as psychoanalyst – not a flicker on my face, one foot out, but also one foot in. Always there's a commitment deep inside me to the story in hand.

The chair was tucked in, directly opposite this man who'd murdered me and to the right of this woman who'd agreed that I should be beaten to death. The three of us had our tea, plates of salad, "rabbit food" he called it. She gave me half a slice of ham off her plate: "I'm not going to eat all of this." It was a strange feeling looking at them from beyond the grave. There's a detachment that facilitates instant judgement, and at the same time feeling is closed down, quiet, and the securing effect can be quite isolating. They both seemed oblivious to the fact that the light had gone out. Afterwards, the man polished my shoes for baby room in the morning, while the woman did the wash-up, and they sang a duet: "I dreamt that I dwelt in marble halls." She girlishly opened up the lid of the piano which we kept at the end of the large kitchen, so that he sang his heart out in his excellent tenor voice to her joyful accompaniment until it was bedtime, and the two fruit gums were produced to bribe me up to bed. My favourites were red and green, the Mayo colours. I was tucked in, and the bedroom door was left ajar, so that I could see the light like the North Star shining just for me outside on the landing. "Infant Jesus meek and mild, look on me a little child, pity mine and pity me, and grant me grace to come to thee, Amen. God bless Mammy, God bless Daddy . . ."

At barely four years of age, I made the decision to move next door to my granny's. Terry and I have argued about this, because he believes it'd be impossible for such a small child to decide to move home without even the tacit agreement of its parents. My conviction from analysis with Helen Sheehan is that it was a survival mechanism: I didn't have a choice. And he also feels that Granny should have sent me straight back home if she'd had my best interests at heart, but then again, I hadn't explained to him in detail about the beatings of which my granny must have been aware. I did ask my mother what she remembered, and she confirmed that I'd wanted to go to live with my granny, so in a way I'd asked for permission, and that permission was granted. Certainly from a very early age I lived in the house next door.

Granny brought me upstairs and showed me the wide, comforting bed that was to be mine, and the washstand with the statue of the Child of Prague standing on it. Many years before, they'd bought this statue in Tullamore and they'd placed it on the back seat of the car for a journey home to Castlebar. She told me, "A wheel fell off the Model T Ford in Ballyhaunis, and nobody was injured thanks to the protection afforded by the Child." It was a concept that contradicted my certainties. There was a turf fire lighting in the grate of the bedroom, and the room was cosy and sweet-smelling. Granny had taken hot scones out of the oven, which we ate with melting butter and strawberry jam, and we drank tea out of two big china cups, Granny's everyday Crown Derby, just the two of us around the table in this new family, in this new house next door.

Terry was asked once by a brother of mine why I'm so different to the others. And he replied that as he understood it, my circumstances growing up were different, and that in effect I'd lived in a different family and had very different experiences. So this is my own story. It's the story of an only child, while at the same time being the eldest of five. The selected facts, especially the evil deeds, I know to be true, but the once upon a time of it isn't the truth. Certainly it's not the full truth of "The Murphys of the Mall", which would require the contributions of my brothers telling their story as well to construct a proper history. And yet, since the narrative is so lacking, that in itself tells its own story: it does aspire to truth.

Part Three: Secrets

I rolled up the right leg of my short trousers to pee behind the big door to Mellett's garage, when I was caught by Tom Aird in mid-stream, and he pulled me out by the collar of my T-shirt to the air pump. He held me with one hand, and with the other he grabbed the nozzle of the air tube and pushed it down the back of my shorts and tried to blow me up through my back passage like an over-extended tyre fit to burst. I had it in my mind that this had been accomplished in Scotland, a story I read about in the newspaper, and that the child had died as a result. He was guffawing about it with Paddy Mellett, and I managed to escape his clutches and run up home.

I was playing at building a hut in the back garden when I slipped on the damp grass into a bed of nettles over against the wall. My leg from the top of my ankle socks to the hem of my short trousers was scalded, on fire. I was rubbing it desperately up and down with dock leaves doused in spit when George Bingham vaulted across from the garage next door and asked me would I like to learn a wrestling move, how to wind an opponent, a protective move in case I was attacked. Any protection against the O'Malley gang from Mountain View would be welcome, so I said, "Yes," and he led me still limping behind the line of trees at the end of our garden into the darkness of the dense shrubbery. There in the shadows out of sight he backed me up against the stone wall of Bresnihan's orchard, and he pressed on to me, his arms outstretched upwards against the stones. I could smell the oil and grease off him as he moved his whole body up and down my abdomen like a bumble bee trying to sting.

"This is how you do it," he said, "how you wind an opponent" and his voice was hoarse. Up and down, up and down, crushing into me. Periodically he'd nuzzle into my ear, "Are you winded yet?" and I'd gently whisper back, "No." But I was calm, meditating on the leaf of an ash plant, which I grasped on to, holding the edge softly in my hand, concentrating on nothing but the leaf, on its yellow veins and its delicacy and, when at last I crumpled it, its odour. I knew that I'd never be able to use such a wrestling move. When it became too hard for me to breathe and I was suffocating under the urgent weight of his body, I'd reply "yes" to his questioning, and the lesson would stop for the day. I imagined that George was genial and my supportive, older friend.

He practised the move many times with me backed up against that wall, although in order to remain upright there, I'd to focus my attention minutely on the delicate beauty of a leaf and on the way that the sunlight slanted in through a gap in the foliage and caught it, because I knew that if I did that, then the lesson he wanted to give me would soon be over. But the imprint of his tutelage was to be without end. I soon came to recognise that after I felt something hard in his pocket against my tummy, the lesson would finish, and I didn't have to say anything. I recall that thrice magical moment of Easter, the church in darkness, "*Lignum Christi*" solemnly intoned by the celebrant during the Good Friday ceremonies, when the purple cloth covering the bulk of the processional cross is

slowly opened, corner by corner, to reveal when the lights finally blaze, a naked Christian saviour erect on a cross.

One afternoon, as I made my way down the garden path towards the house and George was climbing back over the yard wall into the garage, Mr Mellett saw, but it was me he called after: "Michael, what were you doing in there?" He was standing in his garden looking over the fence. The red-jowled face, a mark he'd received from a burning, was turned over in my direction, like the blazing red warning marks on the back of a Spanish black beetle. I was stabbed in the heart with fear, but I kept on going, shouting unconcernedly over my shoulder, "Nothing – he was only teaching me a wrestling move." He judges that I'm to blame for what's happened. What if he tells on me to my father again?

Mr Mellett continued to stand there looking after me, and I went on into the house feeling terrified I'd done something very wrong, that was a secret between me and George Bingham, and that I'd been exposed.

When I was a child, the ground-floor walls of the old hospital were still standing just beyond Mellett's garage. Our long sideboard press in the kitchen is actually the wooden operating table from that hospital salvaged by my grandfather, who built presses for saucepans into it underneath, in his workshop. We used to play hide-and-seek and cowboys and Indians in that ruined warren, clambering amongst the broken blocks and rubble. It was owned by the County Council. They've since built utilitarian modern offices there on the Mall, outstanding for the missed opportunity to create a cutting-edge design appropriate to civic offices for so blessed and republican a county as Mayo, where citizens should never again have to enter through a doorway off to the side. In my day, we referred to it as "the machinery yard." There were lorries kept there, and the enormous steam-rollers and huge tarring machines, piles of cables, red glass lamps that would be lit for a warning and large concrete pipes you could walk through, a haven for whiling away the time off from school. Because on the last morning of February in 1957, we heard on the wireless that the De La Salle National School in Castlebar had burned to the ground overnight and we had no school. That was the period before temporary accommodation was made available in the military barracks, and preparation classes for confirmation, the ersatz Catholic equivalent of the bar mitzvah, when a young man is initiated to become a son of the law, went on in the open air at the Lourdes Grotto under the church. Afterwards, we'd roll down the steep, grassy hill until Mrs Davis came out from the church and gave out to us for making noise.

There were also gypsy caravans there made from wood and tarpaulin, painted green, that the labourers used. I'd climb up the wooden steps to have a peep inside, and on one occasion, I was invited in to look by a man who saw me. There were two bunk beds at the rear, two big shelves with mattresses on them, and I can remember playing up on one of them, with the man sitting out on the outside. And then he said, "I want you to pretend that this is an ice-cream cone."

There was something wrong: we got ice-cream cones in Ducksy Mitchell's. He moved me on to the floor and pressed down on my shoulders until I was kneeling between his legs. I pulled away from what was in my face, crying, "I can't," but he held the back of my neck and brought me back in.

"Go on," he said, "lick it." He held on to my head, directing it as if I were undergoing a haircut, as the tears spilled down my cheeks. My spit was dry, and I had to keep thinking of lucky bags and the sherbet at the bottom to make the spit keep flowing, and I continued lapping at the pretend ice-cream cone, up and down, up and down.

"That's it," he breathed, "that's the boy."

I licked and I licked. And when the taste was purple, he let go of me and sank back on to the bed. I stumbled towards the door and down the steps and began to skip away with the relief, but he was calling after me. I turned around. He stood very tall in the shadows on the top step, fixing his belt. And looking down at me from a great height, he slowly put out his huge right hand, and his fist was as big as Desperate Dan's in the *Beano*, and he pointed at me with his finger. "Remember," he warned, "this is our secret."

"Sure," again over the shoulder, as I ran away wiping my mouth on the back of my corduroy sleeve, and I hid from his presence, crouching down among the ruins, the smashed walls, the crumbled red bricks and broken pieces of white plaster that I saved for chalk, for hopscotch on the path. It was to be like the Christmas day when I was twelve and I'd run away from my father's anger at me in the kitchen, with him following me out to the hall, yelling at me, "That's it, go on, and don't bother coming back, we don't want you here." A hiding away for hours in the ruined coldness of that same Council Yard's Christmas. A secret is a mystery, known only to initiates.

Part Four: The White Feather

I'd wanted to go away to boarding school in Newbridge College. Before I went, my mother received a letter
from Fr Louis McGauran, my granduncle and a brother of my
mum's mama, who was stationed there, which contained the
phrase, "I hope Michael won't show the white feather." The
single white feather has been a symbol of cowardice in countries associated with the British Empire since the eighteenth
century. I puzzled over the metaphor, never having heard of it
before. For the first time I understood that I was being given
intimations from my granduncle, who was recognising something about Newbridge, and who was also laying it on the line
to my mother, that an ambiguous thread was being drawn, so
that it crumpled the blank linen sheet sewn with my name tag
that was packed into the trunk, for dispatch to the open plains
of Kildare, levelled by the outspread cloak of St Brigid.

Fr "Coot" Flanagan, beaked nose, bald before it became a
fashion statement, gave me the gift of his time. On those after-
noons when I wasn't shivering on a rugby pitch, he sat beside
me on a stool in the eyrie of a dusty organ loft. With feet tap-
dancing heel and toe on the pedals, ten fingers alternating key-
boards and stops, he showed me how to play the organ with a
laying on of hands that derived its lineage and fingering from

Johann Sebastian Bach. With Coot, prostration in front of the altar wasn't necessary. We danced on air with upright composure, white habit swirling, fingers snapping, heel and toe stamping, tapping, a *bailaora* dance duet before the tabernacle.

I used to compose music at the organ, teasing out the various harmonics, elaborating musical ideas, creating sallies into new territories with panache. There was a shouting from below in the Newbridge College nave. I stopped playing and looked over the balcony at my granduncle, Fr Louis, gesticulating up at me.

"I'm trying to hear confessions, and with the noise that you're making it's impossible to hear." He was angry when he disappeared back into the confessional, slamming shut the door on me. But Fr Flanagan's blessing "In the name of the Father . . ." encouraged me to try out my revised version of "*Salve Regina,*" the final hymn to round-off evening devotions. The changes I made to the bass line, the advanced chord progressions, puzzled the boys and succeeded in rendering the chorus of the entire college tentatively mute. Afterwards, a sea of white faces gazed heavenwards at the organist, reproaching him for the innovation, as they filed out of church. I was able to hear how an audience is innately conservative, demanding that their familiar expectations be fulfilled, whereas I hadn't yet articulated that my experience of growing up under the heavy hand of my father had relieved me of that ligature. I'd slipped it, since I knew from very early on that the task it had set was impossible for me to fulfil, so I was doomed from the start to be different and to stand outside and to value distance.

I wear constantly an invisible helmet ornamented with a plume, which evokes antagonism in others when they imperceptibly catch even the barest reflection of it in the glass. It trails them provocatively, as the red *muleta,* the small cape of a matador nonchalantly held behind his back brushing the

sand evokes the primitive fury of the bull. It has to do with difference and the way that I openly bear that being set apart as
a standard which I plant on top of the highest hill for a rallying
point. The expectation is that I should walk with head bowed,
holding my banner tightly furled, and blend into the background, revealing the shameful weight of that difference as a
badge of dishonour. While I've been conflicted over it in the
past, that was never my truthful style of being.

From the cradle, I've had to take on board that there's a
radical difference between the layered way that I think and
other people's thinking processes: "Thus, gentle reader, myself
am the groundwork of my book." In addition, I've constantly
to keep reminding myself that there's always a juncture
between their perspective and my own, a horrifying gap from
the sudden shifting of two tectonic plates which can unexpectedly yawn open beneath my feet and into which I sink, scrabbling at cliff edge scraws before the inevitable downward
plunge into terror, unless someone riding shotgun for me can
sense what's happening and can point it out, give me a warning, or in some way act as a mediating bridge and interpret for
me a hostile reality which baffles. That's why working as a
psychoanalyst suits, because the rich world that I inhabit is
outside the arena of my analysand, under protection from the
blank screen of my silence. As a newscaster, my speech derives
from an agreed script, which again protects me as a blank
screen. Yet the challenge has always been to blatantly unwrap
these distinctive qualities and to let them breathe.

Fr Flanagan's empathy exacerbated the predicament I was
in. He deliberately took me out of the classroom and separated
me off from my peers, thereby increasing the tension I was
under. He taught me art in his private study, an extra-
curricular subject in which I easily excelled. I remember that
when I was seven or eight, I placed a sheet of cardboard from

the top of a large chocolate box on the shelf beneath the blue wall press at the end of the kitchen. I got Kie to sit on a chair in front of it and positioned a reading lamp with an extension lead so that his silhouette was thrown on to the paper. I traced his profile, and then coloured in with paints his eye, ear and his hair. The portrait that emerged of a snub-nosed child with chubby red cheeks and a big head was definitely a Murphy. Dad liked the image, and I was happy that I'd done well.

The play of words in Fr Flanagan's room made everything possible. He rolled back the wide sleeves of his white habit. "Paint with broad strokes, and boldly, Michael," he said on that first morning, as he challenged my indifferent Botticelli drawings into a painterly Braque pastiche by daubing the out-lines I had made with streaks of black and getting me to use slabs of pure colour.

"That's shocking."

"But it's the only direction to follow, isn't it?" And he explained the difference between Picasso and the isolated, intellectual master of colour, Matisse, who Picasso was always aware of and concerned with; and Matisse instantly became my hero.

His was also the correct advice for a young man tortured by scruples, a corrosive blistering from attempts at self-denial, of desperately trying to fit into whatever stereotype tradition seemed to require. I'd designed a Christmas card, a modern line drawing of a Mother and Child, essentially a woodcut, and Coot lifted from his desk a card he'd received from a past pupil, the artist Paul Funge, and he brought it over to my easel and placed the two of them side by side.

"Which is better?" he asked.

I appraised, and felt free to say, "I prefer mine."

To my astonishment, he buttressed what I had said, "I think your opinion is valid: compare the use of space. Look." And he showed me how to hold a pencil out in front of my eye and to use it as a measuring tool. Fr Flanagan was encouraging me to come forward and to take the place that had been prepared for me in the earliest language of my parents' expectations.

During those one-on-one tutorials, which went on during all of my years in Newbridge, we had lengthy, exuberantly open conversations about art and music, literature and religion, in that bare, saint's room which was pared down to the essentials – a desk, two chairs and an overflowing bookcase – so that our conversations ran ahead of our footsteps and continued on in my mind long afterwards, creating further dialogue, further pathways. I valued those times as a safe haven from the forbidding discourse of rugby, which had come to symbolise my disease, little realising I was serving an apprenticeship in *lebensart,* in a way of living well, to a renaissance master. Coot was giving me the permission to become an individual, and he taught me how to build a library to house the breadth of my spirit, even as I desperately kept refusing the keys to that kingdom, while despite myself the plate-glass walls of a futuristic structure were going up all around me. When I walked into the Fondation Maeght, built of concrete, Roman brick and glass in the south of France by the aristocratic Spanish architect José Sert, set on a hilltop amid the pines of the Provençal countryside, and saw the layout, the various levels, the open-air rooms, the planes of flowing water, the soft white light, I recognised it from my dreams. Fr Flanagan, that patrician who stands tall in my imagination, had fathered my soul into a dissenting, but wealthy eternity.

From an early age I'd read about the lives of the saints in the books that I borrowed on a Saturday morning from the Castlebar library. For me, they were the inspiring models who'd achieved the perfect life. Later, in Newbridge, during religious knowledge study time, I wrote out precepts I'd gleaned from that early reading that were designed to take me towards my idealistic goal. I'd great difficulty with breaking my will, of substituting the Father's will for my own, which seemed to be a key ingredient of sanctity. So that if I were out for a walk heading down beneath the trees towards the tennis courts, in response to a thought that would arrive I'd deliberately turn back, to frustrate myself. I was trapped in the torturous spiritual exercises of the obsessional that grew ever more complicated and compelling, so that my state was neither coming nor going. I inhabited a netherworld and brought myself to a liminal space of real suffering. This was my first encounter with obsessional neurosis that I experienced as coming from within and from which I'd no protection. The game of second-guessing was as invasive to my psyche as the expanding sore of cancer is to my body. It resembles the underground spread of scutch grass in a lawn: the final, unholy flowering more like the blue periwinkle, stems rooting out into the ground in an uncontainable spread, because I was becoming aware of the never-ending possibilities of sinning not only by deed, but by omission.

When I was jeered at because my uncle was the headmaster, or because my head was shaped like a rugby ball, or when I felt humiliated, isolated for being the non-rugby-playing fool, an egregious appearance in the all-male environment of secondary school that is identifiably worn like a dress, I steeled myself to turn the other cheek, to rise above it and to flash an open smile at my tormentors. Shakespeare: "The robbed that smiles steals something from the thief . . ." But as a member of the Junior House, I was frightened of having to run the gauntlet of this barracking from the door of the Senior House to the door of the arts and crafts room. Before study at a quarter to five, I'd obsessively do the rounds, kneeling on the cold marble step before each of the three altars in the church, and pray fervently to St Joseph, to the Blessed Sacrament and to Our Lady, imploring them to help me, that I'd be able to do the maths questions and wouldn't be beaten for my mistakes; for what I had done and for what I had failed to do, on the following day, or on the day following that, or in the despair of a boarding-school future without end, Amen.

At that time Fr Flanagan was also the biffer, and if on a Friday I wasn't on a teacher's list to be beaten – numerous possibilities daily – nor standing in the queue outside his door, I'd climb the stairs to his room voluntarily. We both had a private understanding, an unspoken acknowledgement of the equivocal nature of punishment, so that I could deposit in the bank the stinging lashes from the cane on the tips of my fingers, wringing them under my armpits to try to ease the pain. It meant that the unbearable weight of that mounting threat from outside wouldn't be thrust into my face for the whole weekend. I was trying desperately to gain a handle on my suffering, to somehow bring it under my control. But such beatings served as a proof of my inadequacy, which only increased my sense of failing. The quicksand of these memories has come alive in me again, because my defeat at the hands of cancer has so overwhelmed me, I feel I shall never again be able to walk with unbowed head on a supportive pathway which leads towards a future.

An absolute moment of terror occurred after the tea and raspberry jam sandwiches at twenty past three, when the scrum would look to the small rectangle of paper with typed names thumb-tacked to the green board outside the refectory, which sometimes imposed the ambiguous insult of letting the bull leave the ring alive. My name written there signified the humiliation that I had to tog out for Fr "Dux" Delaney's second year Ellers team, even when I was a fifth year. There were no classes in rugby; the others picked it up through osmosis. I never knew what I was supposed to be doing on the pitch, except that I learned not to pass the ball forward. I'd no choice about being dropped on to a visible arena of violence, which I wasn't equipped to deal with. Two teams played according to rules that were hidden from me, which makes for a lot of opponents, twenty-nine to one. And versions of that incomprehensible experience still repeat in my life today. There was also a sinking terror in being pursued by the ball. It's coming near me up the pitch, so I move forward to catch it. What's there to do when I'm holding it by the horns? Run, run towards the goal line, and choruses of "offside" ring in my ears, bringing my gallop to a halt. I feel shame as the ball is wrenched out of my grasp by the exasperated *peones*, my fellow foot soldiers.

The flakes of snow fell soft and melted against the heat of my skin. The sudden shower blotted out the edges of the pitch and transported us into the air so that we were weightless, moving like mathematical equations through flickering sheets of graph paper. What I did or did not do angered my fellow rugby players, which erupted in the jostling dampness of the steaming changing room afterwards, the stinging flicking with the togs and towels, the robbing and hiding of house-shoes: if you didn't wear them going into study and you were caught, you were beaten. Adolescence brought with it the painful knowledge of living life under a state of siege, of being granted life itself at the pleasure of an occupying foreign power. I felt constantly under attack, from within but also from without. In Newbridge, it was from the moment that I woke in the morning, until lights out at twenty past ten, and always I smiled. The maths teacher, Fr O'Halloran, a late vocation and an engineer from Cork, used to quote Shakespeare at me, "One can smile and smile and be a villain." The ferocity of the attacks, their incessant nature, was speaking to me over and over that I was a sinner who deserved my punishment. What I didn't realise at the time was that the sin of which I stood accused was presiding over an absence of being, like a photographic negative, a nascent being which was visible to others and which I inadequately protected behind the glass panel of my smile. The demand then, surely, was for a shattering breakthrough on to a visible and audible level, an arrogant shouldering through the scrum to score the touchdown, to print the photograph. But without two or three brawny team-mate protectors on the field, it wouldn't have been possible for me to have the freedom to play my beautiful game. Today it means posting that photograph on the web and sending it off into the immortality of cyberspace. Back then I was oh so fearful of being myself, of taking my place and jostling others and their words out of the way with my insistence on inhabiting that space of convinced self-belief, of inserting my own words into sentences which run on, of interrupting the incessant flow of the dominating discourse with the first person singular "I am": two omnipotent words which even today seem fraught with difficulty.

Study has always been an activity I enjoy, a refuge, a hut out the fields on my own, a tabernacle that I construct from the branches of trees and from the hay in Pelly's field. They kept the cows there, which Frank Pelly and I would drive home through a fog of midges on summer evenings for milking in the hotel stables across from us at the Mall. Apart from maths after the Inter Cert, I retained my place in the upper forms, alternating with Dunleavy and MacBride as one of the top three in the class. I particularly enjoyed sixth year and those balmy summer evenings doing the Leaving Cert to the roaring applause of the weir in Newbridge, when the rest of the college had gone home. We were given the adult freedom then to come and go as we pleased. And there was a vat of hot chocolate: we were served a ladleful each before we went to bed each evening, a privilege normally reserved for the junior and senior cup teams.

The only protection in a rugby-playing school is to be good on the pitch. The thought never occurred to me then. To protect myself, I made up a story about having been taught boxing in Castlebar. But it was my brother Kie who'd gone to the boxing club. And Fr "Esso" O'Shea quizzed me about it in the class, but I stuck to the lie, though it did sound fantastic even to me. I had to describe for him the medals I won. And I was ridiculed by a guy called David Nolan from Mountrath, who didn't like me and who persecuted me constantly from the desk behind with his compass and ruler. He needled that my dad spent his fortnight's holidays there in Laois each year drinking. It was an insult too far, and I challenged him to a boxing match.

The venue for the gladiatorial combat was set for the gym at twenty past eight before class. A student posted guard for the duration, while my classmates slipped in secretly to the building one after the other. They stood in silence, shoulder to shoulder in the centre of this gloomy arena forming a ring, until Nolan and I were surrounded. A prefect waved a handkerchief, and the fight began. We were in our stockinged feet so there was no sound, apart from the thudding blows which we rained down on each other and the laboured breathing from our exertions. Forward and back we fought, neither of us acknowledging the pain or the fright or the viciousness; we just continued on slugging it out until the bell rang for class at ten to nine, and the circle melted away as silently as it had formed. The entertainment was over.

I fought as best I could defending my father's honour, but I didn't know how to defend myself then, and I don't know how to defend myself now, especially since everything has been upended yet again, this time by the cancer. I guess I proved my untruthfulness in the eyes of my classmates that morning, and paradoxically, I told the truth despite myself: the red blood streaming from my nose was my cockade. But if ever it mattered to my granduncle, Fr Louis, had he chosen to hear the glorious, shining, creative spirit hidden within my music, I didn't show the white feather in Newbridge.

Part Five: Hounds of the Lord

After the formation experience of secondary school, I was supported in St Mary's Priory in Tallaght by the metaphysician, Fr McLoughlin. As a result of that one answer – "*Esse est supremus*" – I was given private tuition in scholastic philosophy from that enlightened Dominican every Saturday, while the others played rugby. He gave of his time, his patience, and he marked me out for Freiburg University in Switzerland and a career as a scholar of which I'd no conception and which didn't happen in the way that was envisaged.

When I departed the Dominican way of life, I was left alone in a small parlour. A suit of civilian clothes was laid out on a walnut table. For the final time I disrobed myself of the cincture with the big rosary beads given to St Dominic by Our Lady, and then the black and white habit of the Order of Preachers, and draped them sorrowfully over a chair. They looked like a cadaver imploding as they slid slowly to the polished floor, rattling the beads. When Fr Thoma Mac called me out for mispronouncing the word "ducats" while reading aloud during collation in the refectory, I had to kiss the scapula to beg forgiveness and then prostrate myself on the floor before the prior and assembled brethren. This time, there was to be no tap on the shoulder, nothing uplifting, no human touch. It was so sad: there was no wake, American or otherwise. When I was ready, I stepped out through a neo-Gothic doorway I'd never noticed before into the front garden bursting with spring crocuses, daffodils and flowering camellias, where my Uncle Huby was waiting to take me away. I cried bitterly in his car over that powerhouse of the contemplative way of life lost to me for ever: "Many are called, but few are chosen." I'd been expelled from Pelly's field for eating the forbidden fruit.

They'd sent me to a Scottish psychologist on Fitzwilliam Square to discuss my problem of occasional masturbation. By way of a referral letter, I'd been told, "This mutiny of the flesh cannot be permitted to continue, Br Dominic, because each time that this occurs, you are, in addition, breaking your vow of chastity, and so objectively it is viewed as the gravest of sins, on the double as it were. Are you consonant with me?"

By way of contrast, a wise, elderly man from Edinburgh looked at me kindly across his desk, and acknowledged, "What d'you expect? You're twenty years old."

I didn't understand. Did he not comprehend the enormity of what I was continuing to do? I was putting myself into the maw of a greedy hellfire, despite my best efforts, despite my life of prayer, and I seemed unable to control my sexuality: the normal, human impulse to touch was just too strong. Masturbation, however occasional, was incompatible with priesthood, so the problem had to go. Fr Luke Dempsey, whose fabulous, drawling use of language I had always revelled in, said, "We have to turn our minds to this issue at once, Br Dominic, before you sin again." I was gone the following morning.

I'd let that metaphysician down; his disappointment was palpable when I called in to steal a hurried goodbye. Fr McLoughlin was one of the many kind men, good father figures, who've taken a gratuitous interest in me, protected and guided me, and have used their influence to smooth the way at crossroads throughout my life and lead me forth. Another educator was Redmond O'Hanlon, who helped me win a scholarship to the University at Nancy in France after UCD, where I studied psychoanalysis for the first time and researched further the existentialist ideas of Albert Camus: "*Mais Sisyphe enseigne la fidélité supérieure qui nie les dieux et soulève les rochers. Lui aussi juge que tout est bien.*" But Sisyphus teaches the higher fidelity that negates the gods and raises rocks. He, too, concludes that all is well.

I was embarrassed for the family because the Dominicans are our family tradition: both my granduncle and uncle had been priors of communities on several occasions, my mother's brothers had been through Newbridge College in Kildare, and her sisters had been to the Dominican nuns in Taylor's Hill and Cabra. Kie was a student in Newbridge when I left, and my Uncle Charlie was still headmaster there.

I was also covered in a shame about Castlebar. I'd been home for one weekend between the novitiate year at Pope's Quay in Cork and taking first vows in Tallaght, wearing the black suit, white collar and Dr McQuaid-ordained hat of the priesteen, the *sagart*, around town, and now I'd to face the natives in civvies. How would I explain my fall from grace? I'd let all of them down; the gravest of sins. I'd failed in my career path, and I'd no idea what to do next.

"What d'you expect? You're twenty years old?"

I didn't even have a place to hang the fecking hat, even if I'd been granted permission to keep it. And now, forty years later, after the operation for removal of my prostate gland, another invasive assault on the fundamentals of my being, another expulsion resulting from sexuality, I seemed to have arrived at the same place, suffering the same anxious

uncertainties about the future. I was grateful for having survived the operation, but in the immediate aftermath, despairing questions flowed from that survival: how was I going to
pay for the operation, or more properly, for the weeks of recuperation that I was going to have to take off from work?
Would I be able to underwrite the rigours of dealing with
clients once again? How could I get back into broadcasting,
because technology is advancing at breakneck speed? And if I
could never work again, how would I support myself during
an early retirement?

On our first visit to Spain, with *un poco de español* and a
red Seat Ibiza SI 2002 Irl that drew amazed glances, Terry and
I made the pilgrimage back to Caleruega, the birthplace of St
Dominic. We drove through Bourgos on another day of clear
blue skies, marvelling that St Dominic would have had to
make his way on foot across this forbidding, mountainous ter-
rain to Toulouse in France, where we'd visited the altar housing the heart of Thomas Aquinas. There's a pillar in that first
church founded by the Jacobins carved in the shape of a palm
tree, whose twenty-two fronds uphold the roof. It symbolises
the strength to be found in a supportive community of equals,
but it also echoes the first mosque built in Medina, a conse-
crated talisman that Dominic placed at the heart of his new
church as a constant reminder of his beloved Moorish Spain.
We left in our luggage at the Parador in dusty, wind-blown
Santo Domingo de Silos, bundled back into the car and drove
the ten kilometres to Caleruega, which didn't feature in the
Michelin Guide, whereas the Jesuits' San Ignacio de Loyola
monastery does. We were climbing all the time upwards
through a gorge, steep green mountains on either side, on a
narrow, rutted road. When we finally turned a very large semi-
circle, it was five in the afternoon, and the huge rocks had a
rosy hue, set off against lengthening blue shadows. And there

opened up before us the plain of La Mancha, as golden as the olive oil, stretched out as far as the shimmering horizon, embraced by the circle of the mountains, ranging left and to the right. The smell was of wild rosemary, and the sound in the burnishing sunlight was the wind, playing notes of music through the royal oaks and the pine trees and tugging at Terry's blond hair. Blue eyes into mine: "The camera is with the luggage." Down below our feet was the little white village of Caleruega and the Guzman castle. I knew then from its commanding position that his powerful family had controlled the pass: Dominic had been an aristocrat.

> The flaring light of Spain
> Powders the air
> With a dusting of white gold
> Accumulating on the horizon
> Leaching blue from the sky
> A layering centuries old.
>
> The heightened light of Spain
> Brimmed at my eyes
> Like golden olive oil
> And overflowed into my soul
> Dripping unceasingly.

I knocked on the door of the castle, which had been modified into a Dominican priory, and eventually met a friar who understood my better French. When I explained that I'd been educated by the Dominicans in Ireland, we were welcomed like prodigal sons. He led us down steps to the cool whitewashed cellars and there showed us the circular glass tablet riven into the floor, marking the exact spot where St Dominic had been born, one thousand years ago. The vast area was simple and austere. I'd come home to pay my respects to my hero, out of gratitude for all of the supportive teachers in New-bridge College, who gave me that unstinting, liberal Dominican education, an energy let loose upon the red earth of Spain by the birth of this valiant Spaniard, Domingo de Guzman, who founded the Order of Preachers. He required his friars to work with their minds in preaching and teaching, and to shine the light of divine knowledge on the world. They became known as *domini canes:* hounds of the Lord. In season, out of season, these friars set up universities, walking two by two the length and breadth of Europe. They cultivated untrammelled minds: St Albert the Great and his pupil St Thomas, and that great German mystic, Meister Eckhart, precursors of the Renais-sance. Their unmerciful shadow was Savonarola in Italy, who burned books, and Torquemada, the first inquisitor general of Spain, who burned nearly two thousand people, fanatically fearful dogmatists both, who died in the same year of 1498. The darkness within their souls spouted screaming into the waning, medieval light like grotesque gargoyles. They projected outwards the rage of their annihilating attack on to difference and freedom and God's own creation.

Across in the cellars was the extraordinary tomb of Fr Fernandez, who had been master-provincial of the order when I was a Dominican student, a token figure to me, whom I'd met during his *ad limina* visit to Tallaght. The monument consisted of six life-size figures dressed in the black and white Domini-can habit, hoods up, capuces empty, bent over with sorrow, carrying a bier. Taking into account the Spanish love of gesture and those "big hair" statues of the Virgin, this seemed osten-tatiously out of place.

Afterwards, the Dominican brought us across the street to the local *venta,* where he stood us a welcome beer shaded from the blinding heat under the rush roof and introduced us to an ageless man, José, who promptly invited *los touristas* to his *bodega* in the caves above the town. On our way, Terry remarked on the warmth of this priest, who knelt before and clasped with both hands the faces of his female parishioners, cradling them, as they knitted and crocheted seated on the tiled steps of their houses, warming themselves in the embers of the evening sunshine and calling to one another like the swooping swallows.

A young woman, dark curls flying in the breeze, skidded her bicycle to a halt, and Terry saw that she suffered from polio. Soon they were comparing notes: Terry contracted his paralysis in 1955; she contracted the virus twenty years later, but his leg was more withered from it. She was studying medicine in Vallodolid, and Terry told her that he also had done nursing. As we climbed up the mountainside on the edge of the village, with natural feeling the priest placed his arm firmly under Terry's and carried him all the way, brothers in arms.

José's cave was halfway up the mountain. He opened the gate, lit an oil lamp and shone the golden glow on to many aged barrels, of which he was so proud. In a centuries-old ritual, José drew off his wine into a goatskin, and then on the terrace at the edge of the plateau, he held it aloft against the setting sun, squeezing a shower of glittering rubies into his mouth, then cast it down, before sharing his wealth with all of us. Down below a tiny figure dressed in black was walking steadily through the streets of the village, carrying what turned out to be a basket with bread and a bowl of squid ink, covered by a folded tablecloth. It was José's wife Pepa. When this graceful, hospitable woman reached us, she brought out a trestle from inside the cave and some folding chairs, and laid a table. We held a paschal supper that evening, rich with laughter and with song which tumbled out into the darkness of the plain and the star-strewn sky to be heard by God, and we broke bread dipped in black ink and drank wine the colour of the sun, in Caleruega with Santo Domingo. And we all belonged.

Part Six: Childhood Retrospective

Around the time that I was waiting to be born in 1947 in the big bed at home, that baroque musician Richard Strauss was nearing the end of his life. He was eighty-four years old, living in exile in Switzerland, and was composing his final major musical work, the "Four Last Songs" for soprano and orchestra. They were a summation of his life's wisdom, and at the same time a tender leave-taking. On what was originally St Dominic's feast day, August the fourth, Strauss sketched in the final notes for one of his most inspired settings of a Hermann Hesse poem, "*Beim Schlafengehen,*" which, as I recover from the prostate operation, has overwhelming resonances for me. Following a letting-go in the first two verses, the master turns us towards a moment of stillness in an orchestral interlude where the violins carry the melodic line, setting the scene for the contented leave-taking to come, which also marks a new beginning. The soprano returns to gather her resources, and as her cultivated voice soars out over the orchestra and up towards the heavens, she triumphantly declaims in song that the soul will fly unfettered in the dark, to live life a thousand-fold in the magic circle of the night, profoundly:

> *Und die Seele, unbewacht,*
> *Will in freien Flügen schweben,*

Um im Zauberkreis der Nacht
Tief und tausendfach zu leben.

The relevance of Strauss's music for me today, embracing as it seems to do the conception of my spirit with the eternity of its being, captured for ever in the moment of its dying, sustains me with the spark of hope that I can hear Strauss discover in the terrible blackness of the night that surrounds.

I introduced that song-cycle to Uncle Charlie, the Newbridge headmaster, in my first house in Knocklyon, shortly before he died suddenly of a heart attack in the Newbridge sacristy after saying the evening mass. That afternoon, legs stretched out together, he'd received the final sacrament from me, as music thumbed a cross on his forehead and recited prayers to strengthen him, before his soul began its final journey into the night sky. When the chaplain anointed me with holy oil before the prostatectomy operation, Terry, who was in the room, and I were both moved to hear the ancient Latin words of succour, and when I felt the warm touch of his skin brush my own, tears spilled over at the kindness of a God who bent down to carry me. We both heard what it meant to be free of an earthly inheritance, and my uncle marvelled at the sheer beauty of the voice and the music which beckoned to him. I met Gene, his step-brother and Grandpapa's son, in the porch of the church at the removal of his remains. Gene is the only one to carry on Grandpapa's surname through his son Charles, although the Rice O'Beirne family no longer lives in Ballinamore, nor in County Leitrim, where their name and their struggle against authoritarianism are now almost forgotten.

When I was a child, Uncle Charlie used to buy the *Radio Times* from Nelly in Hanley's corner shop on his way back across the Mall from saying the morning mass that I served proudly as an altar boy in the Convent Chapel. I'd follow him and try to walk in his large footsteps, imprinted on the dew-sodden grass. After perusing the paper, he'd tune in to BBC 3 for the first classical music concerts that I heard with him, the Proms, and also for that sporting meditation, cricket, on our wireless in the sitting room at home. He also enjoyed listening to the dry humour of my father over dinner. Dad made him feel welcome in the only family home that he knew. Uncle Charlie listened to Dad, just as I did, talking about the Castlebar characters that he loved, and in whom my father took such huge delight. Stories about old Mrs Leamy, who was trying to matchmake for her daughter: "Our Eileen has shkin on 'er like brown welwet, an' she uses the palm an' olive soap."

About Pat Lavelle, the blacksmith, who was speaking of a well-upholstered bride to be, "All the calico in Balla wouldn't go round that wan."

And about Padraic Flynn's irreverent father refusing a bra to a countrywoman in his wife's shop: "Shure your diddys is too big."

About Nellie Tansey's riposte over her shoulder to my granduncle Fr Louis's delicate, "Oh I see you have a statue of Blessed Martin de Porres."

"Arrah, blasht you, are you blind? Haven't I a sweep ticket shtuck to his arse for the past year, an' feck all miracles has he worked for me." Turning around, "Oh beg your pardon, Father."

Even Rita Quinn's reply to a drinker at the bar who boasted once too often of his manhood: "If I'd your apparatus, Seánie, I'd piss in your eye!" showing that she took for granted the male control over the direction and flow of urine. But it's a skill which I learned as a child through writing my steaming initials in the snow and which I've now to relearn after the prostatectomy, because muscles also lose their memory.

My father's humour had to do with the pride he took in the richness of the pronunciation and the idiom of the language in which we were reared, always with a compassionate eye for the human nature expressed in it, a perspective that was heightened by the slightest, off-centre squint. He passed on that legacy to me. And he was certainly bright enough to be also serving up a lesson in irony for the contemplation of all those who were Dominican trained, on the best china from the dining board, laid upon the laundered linen tablecloth.

It was Charlie's brother, Uncle Huby, who surprised me by saying he too had left the Dominicans, and at that time, in the thirties, he had to take the mail boat to England, where he sold *The Communist Worker* to survive. He offered to pay for me at University College in Dublin, if I'd care to do study there, and he offered to put me up in his home in Serpentine Avenue, Ballsbridge. When he died early in his fifties, I inherited his bookcase and the legacy of authors that had informed him: Siegfried Sassoon, Wilfred Owen, Graham Greene, Aldous Huxley, George Orwell, *et al*. English tolerance and fair-play at its best. He was a true Fabian. As a going-away present from Tallaght, I'd asked the prior for, and was allowed keep, the five volumes of St Thomas's *Summa Theologica,* with the unusual caveat "that they don't end up among the second-hand books in Eason's basement". All of the books accumulated over the years grace my library's bookshelves still, both here and in Spain, and St Thomas's definition of truth in the *Prima Pars* is well-thumbed: ". . . *adaequatio rei et intellectus.*" In the baleful light of the most recent explosion from cancer, I wonder whether the construct of an equation between the thing and the intellect still holds true, because the darkest melancholy, the vacancy I feel inside from the months of suffering after the operation, from the incontinence, is a bile so much at odds with the brightness of the Spanish light outside.

I can marvel at the Mediterranean pines, which glow with such a green luminosity against the blue sky that they appear inspired by God's spirit. I reproach myself for the apparent abandonment to self-indulgence, but there are days that strike unexpectedly with the raw fierceness of the Spanish sun at mid-summer, when my thoughts and feelings flay me alive, and I am consumed by the flames, flanked by two serpents and the extended wings of a vulture which nobody else can see. They leave me solitary.

Certainly, the definition of truth has become less black and white for me over the years. I like Schopenhauer's valid truth that "The world is my representation . . .", which was published in 1819, some five hundred years after Aquinas. In the same tradition, the doctor of a secular church, Sigmund Freud, proposed psychical reality a century later, that phantasy and reality are equivalent; in other words, include the movie and the soundtrack as well. These days it's Bach and Richard Strauss and all of the memories crowding back into the house of the gathering, constantly being reworked. Of old Miss Thornton from next door, for whom I used to collect library books as well, thrillers that she'd mark with a pencil on the rear cover once she'd read them. She had 78 records of the Dublin comedian Jimmy O'Dea, which she let me play on the gramophone, perched on the arm of her sofa in a sitting room smelling of daffodils, laughing together at "Biddy Mulligan the Pride of the Coombe". I raised the bottom sash of her window from the street, and made off with the daffodils from a vase on her windowsill and gave the bunch to Mum, not realising that Miss Thornton was in the sitting room and saw me do it. She told on me. Afterwards, I filled her bloomers on the washing line with nettles.

Fr Shannon, the new curate fresh from Maynooth who had a bicycle with its own stand, introduced me to Beethoven down in the presbytery. On icy winter evenings after national school, lit by the strong firelight in his room, he'd play for me the symphonies and rippling concertos, which we listened to in the warmth of a companionable silence, so that I could dream in the flames and the spitting sparks as the music thundered about us from the massive speakers. Our shadows danced upon the walls with the chuckling streams of water, peasants pounding out their dance, a storm increasing in force, expanding the parameters of altar serving, choir and carol singing, all of the gorgeous panoply of a gold and silver church liturgy into a secular arena of sentiment, grown-up perfection, of breaking musical rules in order to advance, where God spoke through the senses of hearing and of reverberating touch up through the soles of my feet, so that I was as full to overflowing with feeling as the can of warm milk in the scullery upended to my mouth. Skating home on the staves of violins, blown by the brass and the woodwind through Market Square, swinging out of the chains of the massive tied-up weighing scales, cold like my nose and my cheeks, to the harassed preparation for tea in the kitchen, an equivocal letdown was like being shoved into the bright foyer of the cinema after the thrilling Sunday matinee horror "The Creature from the Black Lagoon." Knacker Gannon broke the toilet bowl in the cinema, and he was hauled up before the judge: "Have you anything to say for yourself?"

"It was a dear shite, Your Honour."

Part Seven: Withholding

Towards the end of my first year in college at Earls-fort Terrace in Dublin, I guessed there must be previous exam papers somewhere that'd give me an idea of the type of questions that could be asked in the upcoming exams. Nuala O'Faoláin was a lecturer who'd inspired me, talking to us about Walter Pater burning with a hard, gem-like flame. She said the greatest novels at the moment were *Dr. Zhivago* by Boris Pasternak, *The Tin Drum* by Günter Grass, and *Herzog* by Saul Bellow. I bought all three of them in Eason's out of the money I'd saved in the States during the summer, working at New York's La Guardia airport, polishing with enormous pads soaked in Aluminum-Nu polish, the silver outer covering of American Airlines planes. I developed a lifelong love of that wonderful Jewish writer, Saul Bellow, thanks to Nuala's introduction. I determined to seek her out. I knocked at the windowed door of the office she was using and entered.

"Are you busy?"

"I am," she said. She was standing.

I persisted nevertheless, "I just want to know about the type of questions that come up in the exams . . ."

"Are you asking me to give you the exam questions?"

I was taken aback and started to stammer a gauche protest,

but she began to elongate off the ground until her tiny head was just a mouth almost hitting off the ceiling. She looked down at me, and lashing with her voice she rode roughshod over what I was trying to explain, her clothes descending and widening, folding noiselessly into every corner of the room, leaching the light until I was squeezed outside the frame of a Picasso painting. From the top of this bizarre triangle, she lectured me furiously. So articulate and vigorous a dressing down I'd never experienced before. And she rounded it off by demanding my name.

"Michael Murphy."

"Well, Michael Murphy, I will remember your name when I come to correct your exam papers. Goodbye!"

I was still holding on to the doorknob, and I pulled the door gently shut behind me. I was shattered, wondering what I'd drawn down upon my head, and what were the implications for my future that she'd left me with, as I walked through the students thronging the building, down the steps in front and crossed the road to the bus stop at the Sugar Company. It was a dark evening and drizzling with rain. As I was waiting for the 15A Terenure bus, who should come along but Nuala O'Faoláin, wearing her beige coat and a red, woollen scarf. She spotted me as she was crossing the road, and she nodded her head at me as she passed me by, as much as to say, I've got your number, boyo, and I'm satisfied that your university career is now over because I'll make sure that you fail. As I stood waiting for a bus which never came, I felt that my life was over. I've encountered a succession of people like her since – mercifully, I can count them on the fingers of one hand – who are initially seductive, but who change for me, and whose intractable disposition I'm unable to deal with head on. Jung's advice was to get a female to engage with them, animus to animus; or better still, employ the tactics that worked with

Medusa, and work through the reflection on your shield with these particular people.

When my supervisor, Mairéad Hanrahan, was made professor of French in London, I needed a supervisor here in Dublin to complete my PhD thesis on Jean Genet. So I wrote to Cormac Gallagher and asked whether there'd be a home for me in the PhD programme at St Vincent's University Hospital where I'd done my clinical training. The PhD programme didn't exist when I began my studies in what was then the French Department at UCD. Cormac replied that he was retiring from the position as director of the school, and to my disappointment, in a neat but lateral arabesque, he suggested that I apply to his successor. I guessed that Patricia McCarthy would get the position, because she'd proved herself through many years of devoted service, but my heart sank when the news was confirmed, because I knew that I'd have difficulty moving forward with her. She was still finding her feet in a difficult job, but after several unanswered communications from me, she rang to say that the course had been changed and that the thesis had to be a medical one, and pre-emptively for a psychiatrist, she said that I'd probably never speak to them in St Vincent's again.

I did speak in St Vincent's Hospital at the 11th Annual Congress of the Association for Psychoanalysis and Psychotherapy in Ireland in November 2004, and it's the only occasion I can recall that the correct course of action to follow would have been to withdraw and not to have had my say. I submitted a paper on Jean Genet's *Our Lady of the Flowers* which was accepted on behalf of the organising committee: "Genet's masterpiece, *Our Lady of the Flowers*, was written in prison, which becomes – in this timely introduction – a metaphor for language." When the schedule for the day arrived, I saw that I was to be the final speaker of the morning session. During coffee break, as Terry and I mingled with the busy crowd in the lobby of the Research Centre, Patricia Stewart, a friend of mine from the Vincent's class of '94, came up to us and said something to the effect that this congress wasn't designed to showcase a personal platform. I didn't comprehend the remark, wasn't quick enough to ask what she was saying, and because it hung uneasily in the air, it struck me as odd. When the coffee break was over, the speaker who was preceding me crossed the length of the room to tell me that his PowerPoint presentation wouldn't work in the lecture hall. It was when he had gone away that Terry said to me, "They're not going to let you speak."

"This is the annual congress of psychoanalysts: don't be ridiculous."

"I'm telling you, Michael, a decision has been taken not to let you speak."

I've accepted over the years that where my safety is concerned I don't see danger because the normal protective walls were breached when I was a child. However, I know that Terry is an accurate diagnostician. His intelligence is razor sharp, honed over a lifetime of psychotherapeutic work, where he's made a name for himself dealing with the most extreme of human situations. So in an attempt to ward off whatever was planned, I went over to the chairman of the colloquium, who was standing in front of the door to the lecture hall. I asked him to monitor the time closely and suggested that we recommence by five to twelve.

The speaker before me eventually began his presentation about Nadia, a television personality – the irony was not lost on me – at twelve fifteen, about the time that I was scheduled to have been speaking. He finished at twelve forty-six exactly, the time by which I was scheduled to have been finished. So we were out of time. A full hour, the time allotted for both sessions, had been taken up with his problems. As Patricia McCarthy was lauding his presentation from the floor, it was now lunchtime, and the clatter of crockery was audible through the doors. When the chairman suggested we move on to the second speaker, I stood up and I asked him directly, "Is there any time available for my presentation?"

"I intend to press on anyway," he deflected. And then he challenged the people in the lecture theatre, "Can I ask the audience whether they want to hear Michael's presentation?"

Some voices behind me clearly said that they did. So my instinctive response was to get up and approach the table. However, the previous speaker had sat down in the only available chair at the table, so there was now no room for me to speak from that position. I turned away and placed my jacket and attaché case on an unoccupied chair off to the side. The chairman was saying, "As there's no time, I won't give the introduction I had prepared, but everybody knows him anyway."

I shouldn't have spoken, because both time and space had been withdrawn from me. I was floored, not by the unforeseen nature of what was taking place, because I'd been given a warning, but by the effect that the absent, unseen nature of the attack was having on me: I found it difficult to breathe, and the words wouldn't come out. The onslaught of the assault when it was actually happening was so shockingly unexpected, and I was so thoroughly affected by the rejection it implied, that I'd to keep taking sips of water in order not to disintegrate and just to continue speaking.

A version of that battle is the one that keeps repeating in my life: being cast aside, being overlooked, being silenced, discounted, disinherited, disowned. For years I smiled to cover my reticence and tried to plough on regardless; as a result I've been criticised for being autocratic. On occasion, my shyness and natural distrust of other people has appeared rude and unrefined. Those defences of mine were always heaps of rubble; the ruins never held. But the assault from cancer has knocked me down, and as I try to stand upright again with great difficulty, I'm asking myself what's the valid way out of this predicament for a man? The word is a rose that opens slowly for me, hiding at the heart of its corolla the Latin *praedicare,* to assert or proclaim publicly. This book is a predicate, that which is said of the subject. The way forward I've chosen is to predicate upon that earlier noun and base my actions on whatever I shall say, be it wild or barbarous, before the blown petals shall fall.

I'm speaking truthfully about the impact that pain has had on my life, during this period of increased sensitivity following the prostatectomy operation. I'm assured by the doctors that these distressing feelings are normal. And still I can be accused of whinging, peevish speech, even petulance. The good thieves, defeat and failure, are the shadow which raises me into relief where I find myself at five in the afternoon, though they disappear in the blinding optimism of midday, where once I tried to live. There's also a part of my indomitable Mayo spirit, an inverted arrogance if you like, that could never accept a beating from any cabal exercising power: one foot in, but also one foot out. When Matisse discovered in 1936 that he was the only major French artist who wasn't offered a commission by the State, he donated his most precious possession, Cézanne's *Bathers*, which he had minded for over forty years, to the city of Paris, in order to teach the State a lesson. The correct decision for me on that day of the psychoanalytic congress in St Vincent's hospital, and paradoxically the one that would've had the greater impact, would have been to have minded myself, to have put what I had to say first and to have taken control of the situation by withdrawing, so that my dissent would've shone a spotlight on the ungenerous nature of the injustice that was being perpetrated, instead of having it pass by unnoticed. I should've placed a higher value on me than on others and have respected the hard work that I'd put into my presentation by not speaking to a constituency who'd withheld, for whatever inexplicable reason.

A lesser absence occurred for me last summer, when I was slowly getting back on my feet after the prostatectomy. I was invited to open an art gallery in Castle Street owned by David Douglas, a media marketing entrepreneur in his early thirties. David is a lean, impassioned young man, very strong in his voice. He fought for many years to reclaim his father after a difficult parental divorce, even to the extent of posting a *"J'accuse"* statement on his internet blog, where others would have walked away. His open work space was alive with activity: rock-music blaring, staffers serving wine, guests mingling in the new gallery, with pop art from New York on the walls and iconic photographs of sixties' music idols for sale. There's also a cut-out in the plasterboard wall of the gallery's conference room, which shows off the old Viking walls of Dublin, a visible square of crumbling wood and brick, of which David is so proud, history which he insisted on incorporating into his up-to-the-minute venue. The programme gave a blurb on the various personalities involved in the venture, listing the art work which was available, the musician who was going to sing some songs, but made no mention of the fact that I was there to do the official opening. I wasn't named. And when I spoke to the young woman engaged to do the publicity, it was obvious that she knew nothing at all about me. As nobody was prepared to do the introductions, I began the few words I'd prepared by prefacing, "I want to compliment David on his bravery in inviting a psychoanalyst to open his gallery."

David, watching from the sidelines of his beautiful gallery, called out, "There's nothing wrong with my head!" as his brother Donny, almost a twin, heckled to uproar, "I'm not too sure about that."

Today I seem to have lost heart, or rather my heart has been repeatedly stolen from me over the years by people who've withheld. And then again, I've had the broken pieces of my heart restored to me by the magnanimity of the many souls who are well-wishing. At university, I barely passed all of my first year exams, and got 40 per cent in my best subject, English, even though I'd avoided the questions set by Nuala O'Faoláin. I appealed the result to Professor Denis Donohue, who suggested that I should repeat the year. Instead, I transferred to evening lectures, and Uncle Huby again helped by getting me a day job as a creditors' ledger clerk through his Newbridge College connections in Hanlon's fish shop in Moore Street, where I tabulated chickens and made the money to pay for my fees. I did so well in my final results with the on-going encouragement of the French lecturer, Redmond O'Hanlon, that I won a scholarship to France. I still have the medal awarded by the French government: it has on it the profile of a Jacobin wearing the Phrygian cap of liberty. I had to come back early from the States to sit an examination at the French Embassy and to undergo a month-long induction course in the elegantly baroque, cultural capital of Lorraine before my studies proper began at the Centre Européen Universitaire de Nancy, which is allied to the Freudian Institute at Frankfurt. There I studied psychoanalysis for the first time, and in a windfall from the gods, I found my *métier*. No courses of such breadth were given in Ireland. In university, I'd studied practical criticism, which amputated the author from the work, whereas the author now became central to the understanding of his creation. For the first time, I could study human nature, which even today, some forty years later, I find a bewitching study.

The realisation of being an analyst has clarified over the years. There are days when I share Freud's pessimistic view of the human condition. Then again, I've been warmed too often by the sunlight of the human spirit which I've seen triumph against the odds, and I've grown under the loving openness of those who've shared with me the sorrow of its generous rain.

My first masters thesis was written in Lorraine in French, on obsessionality in the novels of Albert Camus. That first line in his novel, *L'Étranger* (*The Outsider*, 1942) has still the power to shock me because of the implications of the dual nature of Camus's speech in both what he says and what he doesn't say: "*Aujourd'hui, maman est morte. Ou peut-être hier, je ne sais pas . . .*" Mother died today. Or, maybe, yesterday; I can't be sure.

Part Eight: A Broadcast Life

Maybe the cancer growing inside – not consciously recognised, there were no symptoms at first – was the reason I came back on air after a long absence, to inhabit the voice one last time and to experience the intoxicating liveliness of presence once again. Terry Prone, a public relations consultant for whom I'd worked briefly after I'd left the national broadcaster, RTÉ, sent me a kindly letter:

> Dear Michael
> Nearly drove off the road last Friday at dawn when I heard your lovely voice on the first bulletin. When I got to the Radio Centre, the receptionist flapped a "wait a second" hand at me. When she got off the line she explained she was swamped in calls rejoicing in your return. People in the reception area – total strangers to each other – joined in a conversation, each telling where they were and how they'd reacted when they heard you. It was extraordinary.
> With love and continuing regret,
> Terry (Prone)

The voice is something that doesn't belong to me, but it's something to which I've been graced with access, a

Gottesgabe, a gift of God into which I enter when I go on air. Intention, understanding, pronunciation, phrasing, glottal stops, pace, emotion . . . It's still a supple instrument with which I make music, playing on the words of the script with the attention that Glenn Gould gave to playing the notes of the piano, stroking or striking or barely touching them with the tips of his fingers. I believe that for both of us, sound issues from a *cosa mentale:* it's an intellectual exercise. The microphone is a hand's length from my nose, enhancing the bass notes, transmitting the intimacy of my vocal caress so that I don't have to project like an actor on stage, flattening out the voice into the narrowest of ranges: I can make use of the fullest spectrum of colour effortlessly. I hold the whole architecture of the news bulletin in my mind as Gould would a score, so that I can differentiate appropriately between the stories and pace the bulletin, holding the listener's attention to prevent channel hopping. His rehearsal always consisted of studying the score: he rarely went to play music on the piano until he arrived in the recording studio, so sure was he of his technique. Then he'd experiment with various approaches, which either worked or didn't. My approach is the same, except that I don't have the luxury of several takes, so I don't experiment in studio. All I have is the now.

I vocalise in the newsroom to make sure that the written word isn't in the jargon of journalese, gobstoppers, like ones I was given the freedom and the time to choose with deliberation in May Leonard's sweetshop, which are now relics from a past time when jobs in the new world of broadcasting were filled by newspaper journalists. My technique has been built up over forty years of telling it like it is in a conversation with a silent listener. I read the scripts over and over, constantly hearing new possibilities in them, using a question and answer session with the listener so that I thoroughly understand what

I'm talking about and can respond to a questioning ear with the answers that are written down in the text, or rewritten in a double inscription with scribbled notes into my own speech patterns. A listener picks up on the authority that the working through of those subtleties gives to speech. He feels included in the attitude set up by the process of questioning, without even noticing. But it's my job as a broadcaster to deliver the fullest communication without the interference of drawing attention to the technique. I tell my own communication students: "Reading news is akin to the musical score that accompanies a film. If at the end of the bulletin you can't remember who read the bulletin, but you can remember what was said, then the newscaster has done a good job."

I was one of the youngest newsreaders in Ireland, barely twenty-three years old when I began in RTÉ. The others had been there for some time: Maurice O'Doherty, Andy O'Mahony, David Timlin, Jim Sherwin and Don Cockburn, all trained newsreaders who'd been chosen for their exceptionally beautiful and resonant voices. They knew how to read and present scripts fluently, which they'd the ability to deliver with a clear and accurate Hiberno-English pronunciation. A new newsreader was so much of a novelty in those early days of television that Charles Mitchel, the senior newsreader, was interviewed about the public competition by Gay Byrne on the *Late Late Show*. And in the audience that night was a young man in a wheelchair, who'd a beard somewhat like mine, and who'd also applied for the job. Gay Byrne talked to him on the show, and Charles gave him great praise. Some weeks after taking up the position, I was told by a floor manager, Alan Gibson, that he'd been drinking in a pub in Wicklow when he overheard the following conversation:

"You see yer man on the telly there with the beard?"

"I do."

"D' you know that he's in a wheelchair?"

"Is that a fact?"

There was a long silence, during which pints were supped, while the recipient of the information digested it. Then after closely examining the image on screen, he added: "An' d'you see that wire sticking out of his ear?"

"I do."

"The poor hoor must be deaf as well."

I was accosted one evening in the canteen by an indignant woman, who gave out to me because I wasn't in a wheelchair. I explained the origin of the misunderstanding, but she was having none of it: "Sure didn't my sister nurse you in the Rehabilitation Institute," and she left me standing there, open-mouthed. The audience still likes to hear things its way.

If educated users of speech don't hear on the radio the pronunciation they expect, an invitation has been given for pedantic phone calls to the newsroom, the malicious glee of a *schadenfreude* which the former newscaster, Emer O'Kelly, used to deal with by asking for the holder's television licence number. I was filling the tank with petrol at a garage in Milltown when a woman approached me and said the country is pronounced "Beldjum" and not "Bel–gee–um", which echoes the pronunciation brought back by soldiers from a war that was never spoken about but that surrounded my youth in Castlebar: Mons Terrace, mons pubis – both desecrated, with scars left over in memory of the invasion. The aim always is to eliminate the responses to those irrelevant challenges, not to have to answer, to be self-employed, to live in a building that I own and not to be at the mercy of another: a broadcaster in front of a silent microphone and camera, a silent psychoanalyst in front of an analysand who does the talking.

Patrick Kinsella, who used to be a chief sub-editor on television, has the distinction of having had a blazing row with the majestic Emer O'Kelly immediately before the nine o'clock television news, not that you'd notice her discomfiture on air due to her professionalism. She swept back into the newsroom and continued the battle with a devastating criticism, delivered to him in a crystal bowl: "Reading a bulletin on air is at the best of times, Patrick, like walking on a tightrope. But when you are sent into studio without the bloody rope, it is not possible to do the impossible!" The nature of wanting, of always wanting the unattainable, flitting like a butterfly from flower to flower, is structurally impossible, but as a broadcaster, you have the opportunity not to die on air in the attempt to achieve it. Not to die, never to die on air, despite the temptation. For me as a broadcaster, it's been writ large: I must not die.

Patrick is now a member of the academic staff in the Communications Department of Dublin City University. He stood by my desk in the newsroom recently, and I could see by him that he was mystified as to why I was back in the newsroom, doing a job which the students he taught were doing on the pop station, 2FM. He didn't rate my job, but he missed the point completely. To broadcast is a right granted to few individuals. Blessed with a voice that's instantly recognisable, when the red light goes on in the studio, I enter into that voice as you'd step into a rowing boat, with skilful delicacy and care, and skim over the waves to the one listener who's listening to the radio. I respond to the invitation the person extends to join them in the intimacy of their bedroom or kitchen, or to accompany them on a journey in their car. There are no clothes or facial characteristics to distract in any way from the voice, which is naked. It's the purest sound, making a special connection because of those conditions which are rarely granted to anybody else. Not everyone is allowed to be a ghost. The voice is the way that the ghost can be present, because the news is the one programme that's never recorded: it is pure being in the present moment, the exuberance of a Mayo child at play on the Mall, ring-fenced from external attack in the radio studio. Michael Good, the Director of Radio News, came up to me on my first morning back on air to welcome me home, and said, "When you read the news, it's reassuring; I know the bulletin is in good hands." He turned back smiling, "And the world sounds a safer place."

I used to take volume one of Schopenhauer's *The World as Will and Representation* to work with me and devoured it at the radio desk between bulletins during my first few years as a broadcaster in the seventies, when big Jim Flanagan from Roscommon was the radio chief sub. He'd cut down the whins from any reporter trying to sell him a story: "How many bodies?" The Head of News at the time, Jim McGuinness, a staunch republican, passed by the desk one morning on the way to his office. He paused diffidently, caught the chief sub's attention: "I heard our story at seven, Jim. I see the BBC got it wrong again." For a moment he was occupied repositioning the clump of newspapers under his elbow before he continued on his way. It was always difficult for RTÉ being up against the greatest broadcasting station in the world, but a protective civility that we didn't mean had kept us on our toes down through eight centuries of occupation, so maybe the freedom from being subjects of the Crown had gone to our heads at last. The pendulum always swings back.

It was five minutes to one on a Saturday night, and I was weary when I picked up the last bulletin of the evening shift which had been left on my desk in the newsroom. As I turned to go down to the studio, the overnight man, Conor Nolan, said, "There's a story coming through on the wires about Princess Diana being involved in a car accident in Paris, and I've stuck it on to the end." I glanced at the script as I walked along the corridor and eventually reached the final story before the weather. There was a rush of adrenalin, and I knew this was news and not just a story. When I pushed open the studio door, it was two minutes to air. "Michael Murphy here," and the red light flickered on and off, signalling the voice check had been received across in the Radio Centre, as I read the lines over and over, mentally preparing: "There's something that I have to tell you . . ." The minute hand clicked the final seconds: three, two, one. I pushed up the fader, the red light showed live on air and flashed red outside the studio door as a warning not to enter, the crashing news signature tune was playing: "RTÉ News on Radio One at one o'clock with Michael Murphy. Good morning. Princess Diana has been in a car accident in Paris. . ." Like the newsflash at a quarter past ten one morning in late August of '94 when the IRA declared a ceasefire. Or the morning of the Good Friday Agreement. Or in those early days when I was reading the Six O'Clock Television News the night of the Dublin bombings, and we flew by the seat of our pants reacting to the horror as it happened. These bulletins were never made up of stories or headlines: they affected mothers and fathers, sons and daughters, brothers and sisters, husbands and wives who had their lives changed for ever by the truth of what I was telling.

I was broadcasting during Mary Robinson's joyful years as president, when her representation reflected back to us a pride in being Irish. Whenever I had to speak of her on air, I smiled. She gave voice to our story, calling to us to come dance with her in Ireland, that she would be our witness. I understand that better now. Those women who have graced my life, in particular the cancer survivors Anna, Helen and Ursula, have nourished me with their life stories so that I could survive. It was a transfusion of words which lifted me when I had been depressed into silence, so that when my voice began to return I could draw from their storehouse, and also speak from within a company of good-hearted women. Along the beach at Tarifa, we danced hand in hand through the surf under the hot summer sun, and I grew stronger because of that connection. Mary Robinson hails from Ballina, and I come from down the road in Castlebar: we are both Mayo people. To the world she was the seventh president of Ireland, but I thought of her more as Mayo's second citizen president, following on John Moore's short-lived presidency in 1798; her pioneering work both here and in Europe as advocate for the rights of those who are marginalised had continued that heritage. I was reading the RTÉ Six O'Clock Television News the afternoon she resigned the presidency at the United Nations in New York to become High Commissioner for Human Rights, and we went live to the Chief News Correspondent, Charlie Bird, across the Atlantic, and the words that had been set dancing, soaring and pirouetting, shape shifting, rejoicing, stopped short, then seemed to bleed out into the cold sea-mist over Clew Bay. I still remember how bereft I felt through the rest of that bulletin. The dance was over.

I'm passionate about what I read, believing in what I've to say with every fibre of my being. The voice is one of the means by which I go out beyond myself and extend into the eternal space of childhood: there's neither past nor future, only the pure play of the now. I embrace my listener all over with my voice and capture them. It's a seduction, licensed to only the chosen few who're able to sustain it. And that privilege of the Order of Preachers, broadcasting the good news, is something I've had to fight for in external, public competitions, and continually since then with every broadcast that I make on air. Fifty per cent is that licence to broadcast which is granted by the Head of News. But the other 50 per cent is what I bring of my own personality to my reading, a Mayo warmth and compassion that marks me off, makes me different from my colleagues. My abilities have increased with age: recklessly confident, I throw myself on air, assured that this is the best there can be at this particular moment. The trumpets sound, and I feel like a matador, whose deft work with the *muleta* has opened the final act of the drama. I've thrown aside my hat (inevitably it falls closed) and I've faced my adversary. I'm supremely confident in what I do and play the *bicho*, literally play the bull, with the grace, originality and the boldness of my passes. And if there are dissatisfactions with the truth of what's been achieved in any one broadcast – and nothing in this life has any business being perfect – there'll always be another bulletin in which to rectify it. The back-up of that second chance has been an unconscious support and protection, an unthinking part of my life, until now. Prostate cancer has just announced that I'm moribund, and Death has brought down a barrier across the road. I can see it ahead: I'm going to crash into it because the brakes no longer work.

I've often been asked what the presenters talk about while the opening credits are running. Anne Doyle and I were presenting the *Nine O'Clock News* on television, and during the preparation in the newsroom, we came across a story about "mad cow" disease. It was the first time that either of us had heard the phrase. As we were working through the scripts, we bantered about who, in our opinion, was the maddest cow in the newsroom, and we came up with a few candidates, backing up the title with reasons; we were very bold, *dána*. So we arrived in studio at ten minutes to nine for rehearsal, and Anne was to read the mad cow item. Suddenly, through the earpiece, we heard that another story was to be dropped, so the mad cow piece came to me. And there was great fun between the two of us, and relief on Anne's part that she didn't have to read the story, particularly in light of the unofficial Oscars list that we'd concocted earlier. The floor manager began the countdown "Ten seconds, nine, eight . . ."

Anne was describing a dress she bought for a wedding: ". . . a little black number slashed to the waist, which I'll wear with a pale rose and a big picture hat . . ."

". . . three, two. . ."

"Eyes, teeth and tits, Anne," I said.

"You're live on air," warned the floor manager, as the signature tune blared for the headlines.

"Good evening, and welcome to the *Nine O'Clock News* . . ."

Five minutes into the bulletin, we heard that a package was held up in editing, so the mad cow story reverted to Anne. I cheered and teased her during the playing of a VTR insert, and she took the joshing. Before long, back it came to me. Renewed hilarity. And at the last minute, it finally came to her. As she read, the hint of a smile showing that she was struggling to hold it together, eyes pleading desperately, I slowly slid off the chair and sank underneath the desk, shaking with laughter from "mad cow in the studio" syndrome. Anne was mad at my behaviour, certainly, and as we were coming off air she berated me volubly for it, but with the merest hint of affection: after all, we were brothers-in-arms.

One night in the middle of a television news bulletin, a group of shouting Irish language protesters burst into the studio waving banners, and, with great presence of mind, Luke Smith, the director out in the control room, immediately pulled the plug on the transmission. They were desperate to be heard, but I continued speaking into the narrow direction band of the microphone above the shouting that I presumed only I could hear, without registering on air that anything was amiss, until the five or six men and women were fighting with the floor manager in front of the cameras trying to have their banners be seen, and I heard through the earpiece that we'd been taken off air. Inside I was frightened. The breach of security and the invasion, the failure to protect, emphasised for me the vulnerability of the presenter who's carrying the can for the production and who's open to attack by placing himself in that position of responsibility where he's both seen and heard. On that occasion the fabric of reality was rent with a violent force, which mocked the vulnerability of the adult choice to entrust my soul to another in the team. The conflicting voices, and the questions they ask about whose words should override and be heard, rode roughshod over the individual, who was lost in the hubbub. Back then, there never was a debriefing; I just got on with it as though nothing had happened.

A maxim which has stood me well in my broadcasting career is: nothing is ever as good as you think it is. The converse is also true: nothing is as bad as you think it is either. Although one of my worst was a radio link I came up with early on, maybe even it was my first morning on air, when I very nearly aborted. It was a Sunday morning in the Henry Street studios. I'd to fire an advertising cart – the first ad was for the supermarket chain, Quinnsworth – after the mass. I flicked down the microphone switch and said, "Now, from the sublime, to the ridiculous," and fired the cart with the ads. I felt it was literally true. Within ten minutes, a variety of people – Una Sheehy, one of the first female newsreaders who'd trained me, and the comptroller of radio, Michael Carroll – were milling around in the presentation studio, involved in the subsequent post-mortem.

A similar "disaster" occurred during my first year as a television producer/director for the new station, RTÉ Two, based at the old Johnston, Mooney and O'Brien site, in Ballsbridge. I'd made an experimental film, a documentary on the making of a video. It starred the film actor Gabriel Byrne, a personable guy with a great sense of humour, and the beautiful Mai Pang, who lived with John Lennon for over a year and a half and who was in constant communication with him up to the time that he died. In order to gain maximum publicity for this film, I invited in a critic from one of the newspapers, Tom O'Dea, a Mayo man from Claremorris, to view the film before the broadcast. And I showed it to him on the editor's cutting bench, so that he'd be familiar with what I was attempting to achieve, and to that extent I could direct his response. He gave my programme a rave review, comparing some of the photographic sequences to Antonioni's *Blow-Up*. But the assistant controller, Ted Dolan, was horrified – I think I'd boasted to him about my coup – and he made a very big incident out of my revelation, with the result that my probation period as a television producer/director was extended for a further year, and I was docked the standard increase in salary. In Ted's eyes, and in RTÉ Two's eyes, it was wrong to show a programme to anybody before it aired, but I don't see any merit in that perspective. What matters is the programme, and anything that can be done to achieve maximum favourable viewership for it has to be done as well; it is still self-evident to me.

One of the programmes I produced for RTÉ Two television was *Donnacha's Travelling Roadshow*. It was recorded in Kiltormer, County Galway, and Donnacha O'Dulaing, who used to work for Ford in Cork, borrowed the pope mobile to arrive in style at the start of the programme. I was to have a new production assistant, and one day a woman from Northern Ireland, wearing an ankle bracelet over the daintiest shoes, introduced herself to me on the stairs.

"Hello, Michael, I'm Ray Lindsay."

I told her that our first outing together would be the Donnacha programme, an outside broadcast to be recorded in Galway.

"Oh Michael," she said, "I've never worked in an outside broadcast unit."

"Not to worry," says I. "And it's going to be in Irish . . ."

"I went to school in Northern Ireland, and we didn't do any Irish."

"Ah, sure we'll get around it," I said. "By the way, we'll also be recording a station mass during the programme, and the new bishop, Dr Cassidy, is the celebrant."

"Michael," she said, totally deflated, "I'm a Protestant, and I've never been to mass celebrated by either priest or bishop."

We survived, and we'd great fun on the road together because of Rae's unwitting sense of humour.

I was recording an awards show in the old Stardust in Dublin, and the headliner was Cliff Richard. He arrived on time for rehearsal, and we put him through his paces three or four times, because I wanted to make sure that the cameramen knew their moves on the night and that the soundmen were happy. Cliff was patient with everybody and generous with his time: he knew that the extra rehearsals we were taking would be to his advantage. As we were breaking for tea at five-thirty, Denis Byrne, the floor manager, let me know that The Fureys had now arrived and wanted to be rehearsed. So I had to tell their angry manager that since they'd missed their allocated rehearsal time earlier in the afternoon, about which Rae had informed them well in advance, I'd no choice but to pull them off the show. That night, there was a noisy build-up of excitement among the audience when Cliff Richard took to the stage and launched into his opening number. We were winning. But there was a sudden silence from Rae Lindsay, even though she'd two stopwatches in hand. I took over counting the zooms for the cameramen – "three of eight, four of eight, camera four standby, six of eight . . ." –

and nudged Rae. "Rae, what's the matter? Eight of eight and take camera four . . ."

Without taking her eyes off the screen, she sighed, "Oh God, he's a wild fine thing!"

We went on a recce to Birr, where we planned to film a performance by the Irish Ballet Company. We were invited to lunch by the Earl of Rosse, and when we arrived at the castle, we were shown into a drawing room. Rae sat down in an armchair and delicately positioned herself towards the edge. The earl arrived, "Please don't get up," and he pointed out that the suite was genuine Chippendale, although quite fragile. We discussed what we hoped to achieve in the programme, and the only point of tension appeared to be the filming of the supper in the castle after the performance. "I'm concerned that it might be an invitation for thieves," he said.

There was a knock on the door, and we turned. A butler in full livery stepped into the room: "Luncheon is served, milord." By way of response, Rae's ankle bracelet and the Chippendale armchair somersaulted backwards across the room in a slow-motion dance, full of grace and wonder. She wasn't hurt, and we rushed to help her off the floor. The fragile Chippendale chair was undamaged, luckily, as we surreptitiously checked it out, placing it back on four legs gingerly. We dusted ourselves down and staggered on towards lunch. The long table was set beautifully with a floor-length tablecloth in front of an enormous Gothic window, and the first course was a green object in the centre of a large dinner plate.

"What is it?" I mouthed to Rae, but she did not know either. The butler did the rounds with a bowl of golden liquid, which I refused.

"It's clarified butter, sir," said the butler helpfully, "for your artichoke." When I was growing up in Castlebar, there were carrots and parsnips, onions and turnips, fresh peas in summer and Brussels sprouts at Christmas, but no artichokes. Following the example of the earl, I managed to strip some of the leaves with my teeth, and I dipped them in the clarified butter, sometimes before, and sometimes after. Dessert was a reassuring apple pie and cream, served picnic style in a summerhouse by the lake, surrounded by the exuberant vegetation of the exotic gardens, which are now open to the public. It was an idyllic, hot summer's afternoon, and the earl and countess had gone out of their way to make our visit memorable, as had we, albeit inadvertently. When we drove back down the avenue at five-thirty, howling with hysterical laughter, we'd achieved a compromise in the negotiations which didn't take from the film, and we headed straight across for Dooley's Hotel and ordered big steaks and chips: we were behaving like starving peasants after a visit to the Big House.

When we arrived to film on the day, the countess was already up a ladder decorating the sides of the proscenium arch with armfuls of foliage and flowers. At dusk that evening, the Rosse party emerged in full evening dress from a little door in the high stone wall surrounding the castle. The dowager wheeled across the road in her wide gown as if on roller skates, her low-cut bodice showing off the Rosse emeralds. Oliver Messel, the famous designer, was her brother, whose costume sketches we'd seen in the castle. There was a respectful silence from the audience (some of the women were wearing head scarves), as the Rosses and their guests took their places in the reserved stacking chairs at the front of the local Marian Hall. The highlight of the ballet company's performance was a trio, which was danced in slow motion to the third part of *Mahler's Symphony No. 5*, the idyllic world of the *Adagietto*. We'd filmed it from alternative angles during the afternoon rehearsal, shots which we edited in on the cutting bench. Afterwards, we filmed the supper party in the castle, and we didn't, as requested, film the large, silver centrepiece on the table, a stately swan whose back was overflowing with flowers, in case it would invite thieves. I remember I'd a layered conversation with Marina Guinness in the early hours of the morning about a train set which was so large and intricate that it extended throughout the cellars of the Big House, and which became an allegory for the production-making process. Rae was more than happy that we'd achieved our objectives without causing further diplomatic incidents for the ascendancy.

I was chosen to film a drama for the European Broadcasting Union in Kilkenny city, and during the shoot, a family arrived back at their car which they'd parked in the High Street. They put their shopping into the boot and revved up the car to pull out into the traffic. But I'd set up a sequence of shots that we were in the middle of taking, which used their particular car as a pivot in the frame. I was suddenly hammering on the roof of the car and yelling at them: "Can't you see that we're trying to make a film here, and you're unbalancing the shot?"

The stage manager, Maggie Smith, came up to me and said, "If you don't behave yourself, Michael, I'll walk off the set."

"It's not a set, it's a fucking street, Maggie, and that's the problem." I said, and I held up my arms in surrender to the helpless, out-of-control situation I was experiencing. We looked at each other, and we both laughed at the ridiculous nature of the business we were in: important to do a good job, yes, but ultimately unimportant when compared to the soul-work of real life events, such as a family doing the weekly shop. And yet, our endeavour would eventually bring into existence a television programme, which would create a world of colour out of light. I was brought to my senses, and I apologised to her and to the crew, and primarily to the startled occupants of the car. And yes, they generously pulled the car back in, and yes, I did get those final shots. But I'd hope to be more cognisant and continent of myself today, wiser perhaps. There were times when I wore a *marbhfháisc*, a deathly "cling-film" look, from the pressure to deliver and from the anxiety, streaming up from things going wrong, equipment breaking down, from the unpredictable events which will occur when there's no time left and which are magnified through the lens of a camera, like a car which would magically disappear from shot when two pieces of film were spliced together, or the roaring sound of a jet plane drowning out speech via the wind shield covering a microphone and which would make a sound edit impossible.

I was walking through the Personnel Department in the RTÉ Admin. Block when I caught sight of the then controller, Muiris MacConghail, who is a son of the artist. I ran after him and said "I've this crazy idea for a programme which would take an outside broadcast unit all over the country, and we'd move it from place to place and let community groups make their own programmes by using RTÉ personnel."

"Do it," came the reply over his shoulder, without a slackening of pace.

I asked him years later, when he rang me to grant an interview about *Access* to a student of his who was writing a thesis on community television, why he had agreed so readily, and he replied that he needed something groundbreaking for his schedule. The series also won the *Prix Jeunesse International* in Munich for a cross-community programme we made in Derry at the height of the Troubles, beating off competition from the BBC and programme-makers from the rest of the world. The series also netted a further Jacobs' Award for my presenter, Ciana Campbell.

It was while I was making one of those *Access* programmes, on addiction, that I first met Terry. He was then a senior counsellor in the Rutland Centre, Ireland's premier addiction centre, and he was a member of the programme team who took part, so I'd met him face to face on a number of occasions during the planning stages. But from the distance of the outside broadcast unit control room, I was able to observe him in action over the three twelve-hour days that it took to make the programme.

A camera lens and a microphone are like an X-ray: they have the ability to penetrate under a person's skin to reveal the truth of their personality. From the director's seat through which a stream of snap decisions is constantly flowing in answer to questions – is this the camera shot, do you want the lamps positioned here, how are you going to mic this, shall I dress the set? – the eyes and the voice reveal a person's soul in such clinical detail that instantly an accurate judgement can be made about a person, and the picture they present is then built up in layers like a gestalt, always animated by the life-giving soul. That picture is normally just another decision and part of a producer/director's daily work, an ability which I've carried over into my therapeutic work as a psychoanalyst. By the time that Terry and I sat side by side at a celebratory dinner when the programme was in the can, I already appreciated his intellect, his generosity of spirit and the rigorous steadfastness of his integrity. Over the years of admiring companionship, of table fellowship with Terry, I've come to know that his qualities derive in part from the painful experience of his polio, when he was terrifyingly wrenched from his parents' arms at the age of five to spend two years in hospital, a trauma which bedded him early into the tradition of the wounded healer. At the end of the dinner that evening, I offered to meet him again, and he accepted that offer of trust.

In a two-week cycle, the outside broadcast vans rolled out of the Montrose studios on a Monday morning early. We taped those *Access* programmes on Tuesday, Wednesday and Thursday: an intense whirlwind of work at the farthest end of the country which barely harnessed the impulses multiplying from the collective unconscious. There was a dazed re-entry back in Dublin on the Friday afternoon late. About thirty people were in the crew, all with essential contributions to make. Mick Troy, head rigger, a tough guy, took me aside once when I was an artistic novice and striving too hard. He sat beside me after a particularly difficult day and he gave me the most important lesson of my career, upon which I've meditated many times since.

"Look Michael," he said, "if you want to film a man drinking a pint, you don't shoot through the arse end of the glass. His hand goes out; he takes the glass, brings it up to his mouth, he drinks, and puts the glass back down on the counter. That's how you film a man drinking a pint."

His "keep it simple" advice has stood me in good stead, and I've stepped back and renewed my trust in the abilities of others to deliver their best for me.

There was never an occasion on the road where anybody gave less than their best. Well, maybe once in Donegal where the hotel owner produced a bottle of *poitín* late at night, and there weren't many spectacular camera moves on the following day, which would have required some blood to be visible in the pallid faces. And I recall an occasion when a stranger was at the receiving end of somebody from the crew's urgent efforts. I was wakened by a frantic knocking on a hotel door in Killarney very early before it was light and overheard a Kerry voice calling out, "Bridie . . . Bridie . . . He's from RTÉ, Bridie. He'll be gone in the morning, and you're on early breakfasts!"

The second week was spent in the editing suite. When I walked in at eight o'clock on the Monday morning, the VTR editor would turn to me and ask, "What's the first shot, Michael, and where is it?" Because from the various tapes of sequences that had been filmed the previous week, a finished programme had now to be built up in sequence, shot by shot. It was the time of truth. There really was no room for error, because if I were to change my mind fifteen minutes into the completed programme, which would have involved abandoning one or two days of detailed work, we'd have had to begin the programme all over again, if editing time were to be made available for such a luxurious eventuality.

"We'll begin with the wide shot of the car in the main street, which is on tape three, about four and a half minutes in, and then we'll move to tape four, where there's an opening interview of about two minutes' duration in the same street taken from different angles; that's about thirty-four minutes into that tape . . ." And the painstaking work of editing would get underway and go on late into the evening until exhaustion set in. I loved editing. The beginning, middle and ending of a programme would've surfaced into consciousness for me over the weekend, when I was engaged at home with other activities. I'd the ability to see and to hear in my mind's eye what the finished programme would be like and to pace the storytelling accordingly. While the various sequences shimmered off each other, held with an evenly suspended attention, tremulously they were reflecting the free play, the indeterminacy of the meanings. But all the while the emotional narrative would be building, sequence upon sequence, ever building towards a culmination of expression, which would have the effect of retroactively reordering the programme in the mind of the viewer. As the full stop of death does, to a life which is thrown into the highest relief by the spotlight of that limit, ". . . how valiant his life its shape now almost completed . . ." as Desmond Egan, the poet, wrote about the death of his father.

I'd invited submissions from amateur drama groups around the country to participate in a fourth series of *Access Community Television*. The programmes in the three previous series resolved themselves when edited into dramas, so as producer/director, I determined to ask these drama groups, who thrive throughout Ireland, to compose short plays dealing with aspects of contemporary Irish life, and I told them we'd film these stories on location, using a more flexible, smaller crew than the more unwieldy outside broadcast unit. Irish Actor's Equity, which was then my union, wrote me a letter, saying there'd been a meeting about this project, and they were against a drama series in which their members weren't involved. Although a paid-up member of Equity, I hadn't been invited to that meeting, so I wasn't represented, and my ideas for the programme didn't receive a hearing; this letter was the first I'd heard of opposition. Gerry Gregg, responsible for the massive documentary on the Limerick politician Dessie O'Malley, who'd trained with me on the RTÉ producer/director course, sat down unexpectedly at my table in the canteen one evening. Gerry was very active politically, high up in the unions, and he has a clever mind. During the meal, he dropped the broadest of hints that while I appeared to have independence as the series producer of *Access*, I was in fact very exposed and wide open to attack. We bantered over his assertion, but generously he was alerting me to the fact that there was opposition afoot and that I should mind myself and take care.

The news that the series wasn't going to happen was broken to me that autumn by Bob Collins, who explained that he was one of a new triumvirate of television controllers, and that he'd overstepped his authority in giving me the green light before the summer holidays. From now on I had to deal with Joe Mulholland. When eventually I met him, he offered me a new environment programme. I'd be the series' senior producer, and a novice television producer, Adrian Moynes, was already working to that brief. Adrian, a tall, lean man from the North of Ireland, who'd grown up with the Troubles, was having a coffee in the canteen. Joe had just seen him there, and he suggested that I go over and introduce myself.

I felt robbed by the loss of *Access*, because this new series that had already completed the planning stage was going to be the culmination of all the work that had been put into it and all of the knowledge that had been gained about this type of community television during the course of the previous three years. It had also become part of my identity as an RTÉ producer/director. I'd written a manual about how to make these programmes, which was lodged in the library. That was the track I was on, and the final series would have been the crowning achievement of my production life in RTÉ. Perhaps it would even have led to the setting up of a permanent Community Television Unit under the aegis of RTÉ, and I'd have enjoyed heading up that and opening out the television process to others, driving it even farther than I'd dreamed. But my train was derailed by Mulholland's decision.

I went over to the canteen and introduced myself to Adrian Moynes. I could see by the look of shock on his face that he hadn't been told of my arrival, much less that he was to be my assistant on the programme. Mulholland had landed me in it. I didn't see it then, as Gerry Gregg had already perceived it, but those initial encounters with Mulholland and Moynes were the beginning of the end of my career as a producer/director in RTÉ.

Some weeks into the environment programme, there was a showdown between Moynes and myself. We were sitting in the office; there was nobody else there. I was behind my desk, and Moynes leaned forward until he was about a foot from my face, and he said vehemently, "I think you're a fool."

Without blinking, I replied, "You're entitled to your opinion, Adrian."

I can imagine in my mind's eye a street fighter from the Kingdom in my consulting room, a very physical man, say a *bádóir,* warm as wool, bouncing up and down with excitement in the leather armchair opposite. "See here, you cunt," he'd roar, whacking his right fist into his left. "An' I'd shlam a head-butt on him, and the fucker would drop like a shtone. Then I'd calmly walk away." And grinning with delight, he'd recall previous battles: "There's a code of honour: you never leave a buddy behind."

I did know that "There's a great deal of energy wrapped up in those feelings that you seem to have lopped off."

"Sure the law would have me, like," he'd say. "But I want to tell that cunt to fuck off," deadly serious, screwing up his face, his eyes blazing. "D'you know what you can do, you cunt?" and he roaring. "You can take your fucking fancy remark, and you can ram it up your arse," bending double with the laughter, which could turn into deep, throaty, delighted peals, again and again rolling over the room, as he bends up and down. "Oh, I feel good," he'd say, sitting upright in the chair, shaking his head from side to side, and his blue eyes glittering with tears. "Nobody is ever gonta come in there an' fuck with me again." And the power in his words would draw a barrier around him which silences opposition. I could hold the silence, but I would find holding his gaze more difficult, since automatically it'd be scanning my soul and the purity of my integrity.

Incredible as it sounds for someone who's devoted his life to channelling everything into speech, I should have, in words of brotherly advice such a client could offer me, "clocked" Moynes, "an' decked' im." There's no other way for a man to deal with so undermining an affront, where you're judged to lack sense and made to appear ridiculous.

That altercation with Moynes was the first act of a drama dealing with my demise as an RTÉ producer/director. I should have confronted it physically, but instead I made a complaint to my line manager, Clare Duignan, about the situation. I knew at once by her reaction, "Look, I'm very busy," that I didn't have her support. When she eventually conceded a meeting with the two of us, I explained again what had occurred, and she seemed to treat the "I think you're a fool" statement as an irrelevance, whereas to me it was a personalised attack on a colleague, which went to the heart of the matter. In this, the second act, I was wrong-footed by Moynes, who'd kept detailed notes, chapter and verse, of the times he felt that as senior producer I hadn't listened to him at programme meetings. It was evident that he'd begun a thorough preparation for this particular meeting a long time ago. I looked on in amazement at the growing alliance between the two of them, as the Moynes version superseded my own. I considered his treacherous action to be murder, not manslaughter. Duignan's interim solution was that we go for a pint to sort out our differences. But the signs are there that I've had to plough my own furrow to survive, and I don't drink pints. I can remember spending a Thursday locked away editing a film about the amount of valuable tropical hardwoods arriving by the shipload at Dublin docks, a wasteful exercise because it was never aired. Late in the evening I was summoned to Duignan's office to be told that I was being moved off the programme, although Moynes wouldn't succeed me as senior producer: he was to remain in the same position as assistant. The third and final act was over. The tragedy was now complete.

Con Bushe, the former Head of Young People's Programmes, who'd let me thrive when I worked for him and who'd supported and encouraged my talent as a fledgling producer/director, was very helpful in talking me through the difficulties I was experiencing on that environment pro-gramme, and I was grateful for his insights. The feelings which flooded up from the *tobair*, the spring wells of my soul, were actually ones of carefree relief, of being released from the oppression of a prison, of regaining control of my independence and of finally being able to move on.

Almost twenty-five years on, I can see what those feelings could have told me: that I was in the depths of mourning for the loss of the *Access* series. Freud designated mourning an illness, and the working through that it involved – the sudden raising from the depths of the memories and those frozen feelings from the past so that they can thaw, then slowly allowing them to sink back down to take their more appropriate places – as the killing of death. I was the novice there. As luck would have it, I ran into Moynes in the car park, and I told him I was gone. I was emotional about the situation. A senior cameraman came up to me in the canteen, Fergal Collins, full of concern and delighted to see me back after a brief holiday.

"I heard you had a bit of a breakdown, Michael."

I smiled. "I'm fine, Fergal, really, but thank you for that."

With a thousand other applicants, I applied for the newly advertised post of newscaster in the republic of the newsroom, an independent nation which has always been so kind to me, and after undergoing yet another RTÉ interview and day-long audition in open, public competition, I was ushered in by the senior newscaster, Anne Doyle, who had brokered my re-admission. I was welcomed back into the fold by Rory O'Connor, the Deputy Head of News, a warm-hearted, bluff man from the Kingdom, who had once been chieftain of the O'Connor clan. He made a point of telling me that he valued my ten-year stint as a multi-award-winning senior producer/

director. It was a reassurance that helped me, and for which I'm still grateful.

During the time that I hadn't been in front of the cameras, I'd done a voice-over for a television advertisement for Andrex toilet tissue, which was just then being aired. Rory got wind of it, and he called me into his office.

"Tell me, what's this I hear about you doing an advertisement?"

"Oh yes, Rory, it's for Andrex."

"And what's involved with this advertisement?"

"Well, a little puppy goes yap, yap, yap, and I say, 'It's long and smooth . . .' "

"A little puppy goes yap, yap yap . . ."

"And then I say, 'It comes in a range of colours . . .' "

"A range of colours . . ."

"And then the puppy goes yap, yap, yap again."

"Oh, worse and worse."

"And then I say that Andrex is the best toilet tissue money can buy."

He looked at me aghast: "I can't have one of my nooscasters doing an advertisement for arse-paper!" And with a straight face, without skipping a beat, he looked me in the eye and said, " 'Ou'd need a period of cleansing after that." So I was off air for a period of about six months.

As luck would have it, I was followed into the newsroom by Mulholland, who puffed on very large cigars when he was appointed the new Head of News, but I kept upwind of the smoke. Some years later, when he was given a few moments to clear out his desk and his legal team negotiated a large severance package, there was a sense of *déja vu* about how political business was done. I was given a Jacobs' Award by the critics for my work on the three series of *Access Community Television*, and although that acknowledgement of my abilities as producer/director gave the lie publicly to my being a fool, it felt bitter-sweet, since my career as a producer/director was over, and I was unable to settle back into the permanent and pensionable job in the newsroom. I still have the programme for that Friday night, 5 June, Jacobs' Radio and Television Awards in 1986. My citation reads: "For his imaginative and painstaking work in assisting amateur drama, and his encouragement of writers, producers, directors and actors all new to Television in the uniquely successful venture known as Access Community Drama."

After a number of years as a programme-scheduler working for Bob Collins, Adrian Moynes was made director of RTÉ Radio, and Bob Collins became the director-general of the entire station. By that stage I'd left the RTÉ dream factory behind and had opted for dealing with the reality of dreams out in the world encouraged by Terry, where I began work as an independent psychoanalyst. Terry was the first to take the plunge, when he left the Rutland Centre, which he'd helped consolidate as Ireland's premier addiction treatment centre. He went on to found the St John of God's Granada Institute for abuser priests, and for the victims of abuse, with Pat Walsh and Marie Keenan, where he hoped to abolish for ever that so-called "mystical place" in which trusting children are abused by the businesslike theft of their power and the deliberate strangulation of their spirit.

Political manoeuvering occurs everywhere. For another of us who simply has had his career derailed by other people, the God within asks that I give myself completely to words in order to forgive those who trespass against us, or at least try to love my neighbour as myself. With hindsight, there must have been a dangerously powerful shadow part of myself which was in sympathy with the train crash, because while I recall that working year with Moynes as being stressful and barren, ultimately it proved to be a pivotal period which forced a change upon me. It promoted unforeseen growth and a renewal of life.

Part Nine: Psychoanalysis

I was forty when I first entered analysis with Richard Green in the Monkstown house of the poet Rupert Strong, the founder of psychoanalysis in Ireland. The atmosphere created by the world of words that Rupert had inhabited encouraged a shape-changing fluidity, which over time could coalesce and rise up like a guardian angel to look me steadily in the eyes in the open way that the Spaniards do. The authority in his blazing gaze transferred to me the massive truth of being the fool, a shadow identity that I'd striven all my life to suppress. But following the RTÉ battle with Moynes, it was painfully exposed, like a suppurating wound burst open to the air, so that I'd no choice but to own it. However, through the successive years of analytic work that I'd just embarked on, I believed the time was ripe for the buttressing difficulties inherent in being called a fool, and of somehow allowing others treat me as a fool, to collapse and fall away like the few white feathers which moult from wafting wings.

Terry had preceded me to that venerable place; the same leather tongue was still keeping the hall door open, where he'd met Rupert on a biweekly basis for five years. Twice a week I too would make the forty-minute trek over to Belgrave Square. On the journey, I listened to Bach in my car, playing *Art of*

Fugue and the *Brandenburg Concertos* over and over to soothe the pain in my soul, because I understood that the fundamental order and beauty of Bach's music could put the deep structures of my mind in order, rather like a meditation on a musical mandala. It could facilitate the psychoanalytic work, that realignment of the railway tracks, switching back the points so that where I found myself now, isolated, raw and way off target, could be undone junction by junction as my tongue was loosened and the past was rolled back, opening the way to memories that had been mislaid, misfiled, which had set me up as, what I took to be, a misfit. I knew that one day I could return as redeemer on the clouds of heaven, to take ownership of myself once again. Only then would I be able to live with the proclamation that sealed my fate: live as an outsider from the time that I was born. While I walked away with the normal expectations which still continued to gnaw at me from the exile of the house next door, come the day when the healing waters of my gratitude would spill over uninterruptedly, because simultaneously there's been room for me to flourish in that singular inn. Then I shall cry out in return, "I'm at my granny's," as I raise a glass of vintage wine.

I'd never been in analysis before, and I was very puzzled by Richard Green's behaviour. Like Rupert, in the description which had been handed on to me, Richard was also a tall man, who'd suddenly appear at the door of the waiting room, arms by his side, and gesture slightly with his right hand. I was given to understand that it was now my time for analysis, and would I lead the way to take up my position lying on the couch in the room across the hall, looking out through the big window into the square. The awkwardness of his stance, like a child unfamiliar with being held, should have told him that in attempting to sever the personal encounter from the analytic session, he was doing untold violence to himself. He was throwing up a barrier against me, instead of opening himself up to being fully present.

I would free-associate, moving easily from topic to topic as the words sparked thoughts and feelings, telling the truth as I believed it to be, but I was telling lies on the couch. Like the remnants of those Irish castles blown apart by Cromwell's soldiers, the defences that I'd built up over years to cope with humiliation had been manifestly breached, but the remaining walls were still in position for a good reason, and they'd only be dismantled laboriously stone by stone. At the time, I felt I wanted Richard to help repair and strengthen those walls, even though they left me little room. Richard sat in an armchair behind me, out of my line of sight so that I couldn't navigate by his reactions, and he scribbled notes to himself in a notebook. Unlike Rupert, he never spoke, apart from explaining to me one day that we were going to have to bring the analysis to an end because he was emigrating to New Zealand. I read about him climbing Mount Everest some years later. Richard was the first explorer of the mind that I met on my own quest, and he took being the silent, blank screen to such extremes that I thought he was a follower of the French school of psychoanalysis, founded by Jacques Lacan, which can be coldly unnerving, because the analyst is always listening to something elsewhere in your speech, paying attention to the want which animates it. The jargon word is "desire", but the Irish don't use that word as the French do. Cormac Gallagher, who ran the School of Psychotherapy where I later did my clinical training in St Vincent's University Hospital, surmised to me that Richard was a follower of Freud, the writer who created a new language for psychoanalysis. Today there are indeed many psychoanalytic churches. Cormac himself ended up in court being sued by some client who felt he wasn't getting his money's worth because Cormac was so silent. It demands courage and vigilance to shoulder absolute freedom, to eventually acknowledge that "I know" myself better than my analyst, particularly when the continual tendency is to constrain that freedom by yoking it to a purpose.

What I began to articulate in those sessions is that one of the unconscious hooks I have in my soul is the archetype of the abandoned child. I scan other people and seek it out in them to turn their trauma into triumph. Another hook, which as I spoke in analysis was in the process of becoming more conscious, would be that of the scapegoat. I have attracted negative attention and named it over time in analysis as humiliation: humiliation by beating, humiliation by abuse, bullying and expulsion. A memory came back of being placed up high on top of a large wooden crate outside Clerys in O'Connell Street by my father and told not to move until he came back. There was a clown dressed in yellows and blues, with a white face, red nose and orange curls, who was relentlessly making his way up the crowded path towards me, and my father was gone. I couldn't get away from this tall, terrifying stranger, who didn't look like anyone I'd ever seen before, because I was on top of this tall crate. He was filling me with dread by beginning to shout up at me as he approached and gesticulate wildly with his arms. By the time my father returned, I was screaming in terror, standing on my island, beaten back to the other edge of a crate in O'Connell Street, being mugged by a presumptuous clown. For me it's the archetypal image of being the vulnerable child, ostensibly valued by being placed on high out of harm's way, but ultimately neglected through a father's careless dereliction, plangent reverberations which re-echo noisily in my ears, down through the deep well of the years and back up into the present.

I've always found clowns and the violent humour they generate sinister. One of the first films I saw starred Laurel and Hardy. I didn't know it was a film: I thought I was looking through a window. Hardy put his head through a hole in the wall, and somebody slid an open toilet seat down over his neck, so that he couldn't get his head back out. And dogs began to snap at his behind. It was horrible. I empathised with him, I was frightened with him, but the audience in the Castlebar Cinema were shrieking with laughter, and I turned around towards them and started shouting at them all to stop. I remember the cruelty in their faces lit by the flickering light as they laughed and laughed. My dad dragged me out by the arm, still protesting the horror of what I'd seen, dazed by the lack of empathy it had evoked.

My second analyst was Jasbinder Garnermann. She was a charismatic woman from the Punjab, steeped in a knowledge of Jung's analytical psychology. When I asked Terry to remind me where she was from, he said flippantly, "She used to wear a dog collar: what country is that?" He was referring to a party the Garnermanns gave in honour of Jasbinder's mother, who was visiting Ireland for the first time. She was a sedate woman, who'd dressed elegantly in a beautiful red sari for the occasion. But by way of juxtaposition, Jasbinder wore a costume she used to wear while waiting on tables in London: it was a bunny girl outfit, with fishnet tights, topped off with a very large leather dog collar around her neck.

Those years of working with Jasbinder studying Jung have particularly informed my work with dreams. Jung's idea that we are visually literate and can understand the imagery of dreams applies more than ever in today's world of the imagination, created and shaped by media. Analysis with Jasbinder was as far from Richard's anally retentive approach as could be. She and William kept a large apartment on Fitzwilliam Street in Dublin. They had two big cats which constantly prowled around the apartment, and also an enormous hairy retriever called Max. During my session, one of the cats kept retching and getting sick, so Jasbinder would get up out of her chair and delicately drop a newspaper over the vomit. By the end of the session, there were little paper tepees dotted all around the carpet. During another session, the dog's tail brushed against a Superser gas heater and went on fire. We were alerted by a smell of burning in the room, and Max's big bushy tail was flaming like a torch. So in true Jungian fashion, the open realities of the analyst's life as they were lived in the moment became part of the analytic process, and what those feminine and masculine aspects were communicating had to be taken on board as well. When Jasbinder had her first child, Sophia, she used to breastfeed the baby while discussing my dreams and shush her to stop her crying. It was a wisdom metaphor that was a step too far for me.

I moved to another Jungian analyst, Fr Jack Finnegan, shortly after that experience, and we worked well on a basis of equality while my brother Kie's exhausting battle with cancer was in its last few months, slowly eating him up so that he looked ravaged. I experienced it as an agonising time of helplessness. His suffering was frightful, but he wanted to live as long as possible for his children. It was his ultimate act of love. I dreamed of Kie being perfumed before he died, so I brought him some eau de toilette that he could use in the hospital. He was a skeleton, barely able to move in the bed, and that was the last time that I was allowed to see him alive, ten days before he breathed his last. I made a resolution that if ever I was to contract cancer, I wouldn't try to fight it to prolong my life; I'd let the cancer take its course. And yet when the consultant gave me the news about my tumours, instantly I said to him, "Take them out." I was so terrified by it that I didn't want to wait the three months until the next consultation in order to have considered other options, whereas he was assuring me that prostate cancer is slow growing.

The final sequence of my analysis was accomplished with a Lacanian, Helen Sheehan. We met three times a week for nigh on seven or eight years. When I was paying her one day early on, I had my wallet in my hand as I handed her the notes.

"And you also owe me for last week."

"But I'd given you notice that I'd be away in Spain for the week."

"But I was here, Michael. You know what analysis entails: there are no excuses."

And it's as if her right hand reached into my wallet and took out the notes to cover the three days that I missed, leaving in my hand the empty wallet. Such a metaphor for an abusive relationship, rifling my wallet, choking my creativity, removing my prostate, is something I came back to again and again in analysis with Helen Sheehan, and it was something that I never succeeded in putting to bed with her. We went through the farce of buying my freedom every eight to ten weeks when, as in Jung's practice, I took a short break from my own work and the analysands I was working with were thrown back upon their own resources. I don't ask my clients to pay for sessions they miss through taking short breaks, unless they're masters students who expect the traditional rules in their training analysis, as in my own analysis with Helen Sheehan. The basis of my practice has always been the dignity and equality of my clients, who know themselves better than I could ever hope to, whether they choose to abuse the adult freedom they inalienably have or not. I wouldn't tolerate for them a throwback to Freud's Viennese practice from the last century that clients had to take their holidays when the analyst took his six-week break during July and August, and I regret that I never said so in my own analysis, until now.

There were at least two occasions when the unremitting pressure of my analysis with Helen Sheehan became too much and I bolted from the room. I was in Germany and needed to cross the border from Freiburg into France, just to have a coffee in Colmar, to relax for a short time before facing again into the unspoken, impossibly high standard of living properly that strikes you across the face in Germany. From Helen Sheehan's perspective, steeped in Lacanian dogma, I had come up against the law: "When you're in analysis, there are no excuses." Neither were there any explanations. Sometimes when I arrived at her house, there'd be a note stuck to the door saying simply that there'd be no analysis on that day. Deal with it; get on with it: there is no mystical place. Ultimately, I'm responsible to myself, so I take that accountability on board and choose how I want to live, lest I be chosen by something that's not of my own choosing. This is an impossibly high standard of living, something worthwhile to strive for, which yields a freedom beyond even my wildest dreams.

The French psychoanalyst and theoretician Jacques Lacan developed the variable session – it could be three minutes, it could be twenty – to inflict castration through enforcing the limit and commanding analysands to keep to the point, directing them towards embracing absence and loss. Samuel Beckett, that spare Irishman who lived within the narrow precision of the French language, understood too well the psychological consequences of this: "Fail better" was what he wrote. Intellectually, the paradox does provide some consolation, because physically I've failed as a man. Viewed through the prism of prostate cancer, this is the analysis of an avowed failure, an absence that began to build as a boy and that has shadowed my presence: I've been preparing all my life for this latest castration by cancer and for the ultimate battle with death.

When I talked to Helen Sheehan, I traced my lineage back through my Castlebar grandmother, as though she were a Sephardic Jewish mother carrying that all-important gene which validated my Mayo legitimacy. Her round face with the little chin confronts me whenever I look in the mirror: Leachim Yhprum. *Le'Chaim!* I was circumcised as the first-born, an attack and consecration both, and I've lived the introverted life of a rabbi, one of lifelong learning. My dad didn't recite the prayers of *brit milah* for me, accepting the physical manifestation of God's covenant with Abraham that every male shall be circumcised. The patriarch was prepared to sacrifice his son Isaac, but God intervened and stayed his hand, so that Abraham sacrificed a ram instead. My father didn't honour that principle. He didn't participate in an emotionally binding connection with his newborn son, nor align himself with relationships which stretch back over the millennia. And yet, I'd been set apart by that symbolic inscription in cultural patrilinearity, as opposed to the imaginary order of nature, primed to prosper within a rich social and intellectual heritage.

The significant removal of my prostate, this latest loss and mutilation, feels like God the Father, the very archetype of life itself, has now reneged on that solemn consecration of my manhood, savagely exposing the vacuousness of the special relationship with the father that it implied and that was gifted to me but never activated, some sixty years before, so that a large hole has been torn in the webbing of my existence. I've been relegated by the radical prostatectomy, doomed to wander alone in the wilderness because my penis will no longer work as it was meant to do. Among men, I feel that I could be an object of opprobrium, an ineffective man, a eunuch whose future function in the bedchamber has shrunk to being an attendant.

I found this profound absence of connection in analysis. I relate to my brothers not through a shared *pater familias* experience, nor through debating questions of sport, which hold no interest for me. I regret not having saved a letter in my dad's handwriting offering me tickets to an all-Ireland final; the kindness of his misplaced recognition should've been framed. Neither can I talk with them about women: Jean Genet, the *poète maudit* who was homosexual pointed out that for him half of the population simply didn't exist. I've mostly approached women within the circumscribed *temenos* of an analysis, and yet they've reached out to me in my recent illness. Always there are those valorous women whose strength is that of the true warrior, who take arms against the odds stacked against them and who fight to the death only as a very last resort, and whom I do so much admire.

My mother is the ambivalent paradigm for my relationship with women, whereas the experience I had of my grandmother was universally positive. It must have been difficult for my mother, having lost a competent mother of her own, to have had so competent a mother-in-law living right next door with her eldest son. The morning after their honeymoon, my cousin Aidan came around the back way carrying a turnip from Granny for Dad's dinner, and it was Aidan who showed my mother how to prepare and cook it. Mum still jokes that in her innocence she believed there'd always be a "Parkes" to do the cooking. She was thrown headlong into a sharp learning curve that she accepted. Her brown soda bread was as good as Granny's in the end: a pinch of this and a pinch of that, and both tapped the base to see that the cake was baked through. When Granny died, Pat Flannelly said that it was a real Castlebar funeral, because "there were no blow-ins in attendance." My mother had earned the freedom of Castlebar.

Around this cancerous time, I've felt supported by the *meitheal* of my brothers' care and kindness, their banding together with solicitude for Terry and for me, by their phone calls: "And how're you now?" My cancer has shadowed the three of them: we share the same genes. I wonder at the endless stream of cards and gifts from analysands, and from people who don't know me but who know or work with Terry and who've responded to his concern by sending me prayers of understanding and fellow feeling. Katherine Zappone: "We miss you both and hope we can have a glorious reunion in the fall. Michael, we will be storming the heavens for good results." And Ann Louise: "Hearing your voice on the radio a few weekends ago raised my spirits – I ran and told Katherine, 'He's back.'" But this is a new time for me, an untried way of relating directly to the spokes of the wheel, because I miss not being able to tell my mother the horror of what is happening for me, her second son to have cancer. Her second son, or the second of her sons? To tell her of how despondent I feel, so that she could mediate me in her words to the others. I'm sorrowful that she has now turned into a pixie, a *luthargán* sitting at the end of the rainbow, waving goodbye, "*Slán agat,*" as she imperceptibly fades away into the lost distance of dementia, taking with her the past, which she carefully packed in her suit-case, layered in tissue paper. She leaves behind on the kitchen table a vase of yellow *feileastraim,* the wild iris which she'd gather on her Mayo walks through Elysian fields and around which her sons shall gather in commemoration, having received her message of trust in the goodness of God, which has been built up over years of offering the gift of softened edges through her proximity. It'd be unfair to burden yet another person with a responsibility I know that's mine and at twilight time expose her to the obscenity of my zippered scar to kiss it better, an injury done to the flesh of her flesh, where the two flaps of my abdomen overlap, stapled together with eighteen iron staples, like those stuck pigs I saw in the Castlebar Bacon Factory, trotters clasped into a steel cuff so that they were whirled squealing off the ground and raised on high by a conveyor belt. The butchers in blood-stained white aprons sliced them open alive with deft strokes of a scalpel, one after the other, as they screamed for mercy, spilling sausages of steaming guts on to the bloodied floor, tearing out the remainder of slippery innards that were trampled on in rubber wellingtons that gave no protection against the stench, or the vision of hell, or what could one day happen to a child the size of a pig. Conrad's Kurtz: "The horror! The horror!"

Part Ten: Death

A defensive sang-froid has served me well through-out my career, both as a broadcaster and as a psychoanalyst. My ability to never show anxiety was tested beyond endurance the afternoon that my brother died. I got the call from my brother John, his voice tight with sorrow, to say that he was with Mum in the Blackrock Clinic. I didn't want to go there, because I guessed that the encounter with her daughter-in-law wouldn't be easy. Mar's immediate reaction to an exhausted Mr Quinlan's telling the two of us that Kie's initial operation had failed, that he wasn't able to get all of the cancer, that it was too extensive, was to turn to me and say, "Keep your mother and your aunt off my back." She must have been as unimaginably shocked and terrorised by the news as I was, but the harshness in her tone, as well as the sentiment expressed, was as unexpected to me as the devastating diagnosis, although when I'd called to his room earlier before he came back from theatre and begun to push open the door, Mar had called out to me, "Go home, Michael." But I was his eldest brother, so I waited in the hospital foyer.

The roster on what we refer to in the newsroom as "the wailing wall" slated me to read the main *Nuacht* bulletin that evening, so I proceeded to RTÉ as usual, leaving a terrified

Terry behind, and began the preparation of the scripts at the far end of the newsroom. Because Irish is my second language, it demands a great deal of concentration on my part to understand exactly what it is that I'm saying, to pronounce the words correctly in the *idirchanuaint,* the special between-dialects that I'd been trained in, and also to reread the scripts sufficiently so that I could deliver the nasal tone and flatter rhythm of the language as if I were a fluent Irish speaker, completely at home and in control of the flow. Periodically, I'd look up and think that nobody sitting at these desks knows that my brother has died. Mairéad Ní Éithir was working on the *Nuacht* desk that evening, and she was one of the many people – former colleagues, but also friends that know me through the music of my voice – who took the trouble to ring up and leave many messages that it was wonderful to hear me on air again when I resurrected from the dead after a long absence from the newsroom. Had she and they known that evening about Kie's death, I suppose they'd immediately have found a substitute, but I needed the straitjacket of what I was about to do to keep me sane.

I faced my adversary and went live on air two hours after my brother was dead, and in the supreme effort of will, I dedicated every syllable of that Irish bulletin to him. Each was a bead of the *paidrín,* the rosary, which we recited as a family after tea, kneeling in the kitchen or in the sitting room, a lasso that had held us all together. The flickering blue kerchief of the television screen saluted Kie's prowess, and like a mule I carried the body of my dead brother on my back and did a lap of honour for him around the arena.

Being boxed into the image on screen, everything serving the performance, gave me the focal point that the show must go on somehow. It was the best bulletin I've ever read, flawless. Reacting appropriately to the stories, moving correctly from camera to camera, looking down at the script to find my place for names and numbers I couldn't possibly be expected to remember, I even managed to smile a *slán leat*, that good-bye at the end of it all. And whenever the panic would start to rise in me, I concentrated on the reality that I was speaking to two or three people in their kitchen or their sitting room, and my training held: they deserved to hear what the chief sub-editor had written without detraction. The all-engulfing panic was about me feeling that the whole world ought to suspend normal living, and hear in the cronauning background what I was really announcing: "My brother Kie died this evening at five in the afternoon after a long illness which was horrible. He was far too young to die so cruelly: it goes against the natural order of things. I loved my younger brother with all of my heart, and the four Murphy brothers who are left shall never be able to talk about Kie again among ourselves beyond this awful evening, because the searing pain of his loss has laid us waste. At every gathering in the future where the four of us are present, we'll crash into those Mayo stone walls, that there's one further Murphy of the Mall who's destined to be for ever present by his absence."

As I wiped off the make-up and came face to face with my unprotected reflection in the mirror for the first time, still holding it together from inside, I could see that underneath the mask I'd received an almighty battering, a *leadairing* from which there was to be no recovery. The mirror had slipped through my fingers and crashed to the floor, shattering into lethal shards and seven years bad luck. There could be no going back. I never read a *Nuacht* bulletin again.

I arrived at the Blackrock Clinic. When Mum visited Kie early in the morning, Mar had her removed from the room by the nurses because she was crying, and Mar didn't want her to upset Kie. So we found out later that our seventy-five-year-old mother had spent the entire day on her own, praying either outside the door of Kie's room or in the chapel. She was having a cup of tea in the canteen when a nurse left the queue, came over to her table and said, "Oh, Mrs Murphy, I want you to know how sorry I am that your son Kieran passed away."

My mother was delivered a blow. "What about Mar and the children?" she enquired.

"They've already left."

"And Kieran?"

"We've moved him to . . ."

She stood up. "I want to see my son."

In half an hour, they'd brought back Kie's body and rearranged the room so that his mother could see for the last time the dead son that she'd borne, needlessly saying goodbye to him after he was dead. I could never bring myself to ask her about the terrible loneliness of her experiences that day, because no greater pain for an adult exists than the loss of a child. It was a sacred space into which nobody had a right to trespass. A photograph of Kie and Mar taken at Tom's wedding appeared standing up at her place on the kitchen table recently. Mum must have rooted it out from some drawer. She tapped it with her finger, and I knew that she'd forgotten the names. "A terrible tragedy" was all she said.

Over the bleakness of those funeral days, the phone would ring at my aunt's house in the morning with requests: all of the Murphys were not to carry his coffin; all of the Murphys were not to be in the front seats of the church. My mother and my aunt paid a courtesy call on Mar the day after the burial, and although her sister-in-law Daphne was staying with her, visible through the sitting room window, Mar answered the door herself, by all accounts understandably wild with grief. They attempted to calm the situation by backing away down the garden path, saying, "It's all right, Mar," and they went back home to my aunt's, shaken by what had occurred. We subsequently learned that all the Murphys of the Mall had been banned from what was now Mar's home.

Mum wrote out word for word on a sheet of paper what Mar had said to her that day on the doorstep, and she kept it closed in her handbag in an envelope, but she puzzled over it and parsed it down through the years. My mother had lost her second child, and she'd now also lost three of her grandchildren. She rang up the house once, impatient with the nonsense of the situation, to say that she wanted to see her grandchildren. She explained that she was staying up in Dublin on one of her regular visits, and could she take them to tea in the Radisson? Mar said that she'd ask them, and after a moment she came back to the telephone and said that they didn't want to see her. So Mum rang Mar about four times each year to find out how she was and how the children were, and Mar entertained those phone calls from her former mother-in-law. And, until her memory started to slip, Mum posted into the silence three birthday cards with money she saved from her pension on each of her grandchildren's birthdays, and she also sent the same at Christmas. But she no longer informed any part of their lives.

Now more than ever since I too have been marked with a palpable hit from cancer's rapier, I can comprehend terrible anger and despair at being cheated of a future by death. Kie had just been appointed the Europe divisional director of Masterfoods, based in Milan, when he was diagnosed with cancer, and he returned from Italy directly to the Blackrock Clinic. I can understand those underground springs of emotion that rise to the surface and take all of us by surprise; mostly, eventually, they run dry.

There was one incipient incident which was telling. I'd finished giving the best man's speech at Kie's wedding in the

Killiney Court Hotel by welcoming Mar into the family. And Kie took me aside afterwards, and he was very annoyed at what I'd said: "Mar is marrying me," he reprimanded; "she's not marrying the family." There was no evidence that Mar had prevailed upon Kie, whose mind was immediately derailed by morphine, to lay the cause of his death at his mother's womb. But that was the effect of yet another premature death of the father. Kie's spirit was set free on the 22nd of August, the date of his parents' wedding day. It was a pot of purple forget-me-nots with a congratulations card that nobody wanted to receive.

Part Eleven: Expulsion

My story is writing itself in answer to a question. And my sense is that the questioning will turn out to be more important than the answer, as all questions do since they keep querying the wanting that leads me on. This complex work of art absorbs me, and keeps my mind off my present symptoms, while I deal with the underlying structure of sufferings from the past that have been laid bare by the cancer and try to reorder them. It's an alchemy of roots and sap, the fruit and branches of a living, cosmic tree of the word over which I'm in control. How like the yellow, blue, green and red pieces of ceramic tile, outlined in black, are these words that have chosen themselves to find their rightful place, *alicatados* in the complicated geometric patterns which decorated erstwhile palaces in Spain, and that now adorn this book.

There's a photograph in existence of the five Murphy boys like steps of stairs in short trousers and Fair Isle jumpers. There's me, and then there are the four others from next door, and I'm inclined in towards them. It looks benevolent. Perhaps the golden mean juncture in positioning was due additionally to the three year age gap between me and Kie; the others are closer in age. There's another photograph which I hold of just the two of us. It was taken by Dr Mongey out on the path in front of our house on the Mall. Kie was playing with a ball, and I knew that the only way to get him to be still was to clasp his hand in mine and to hold him firmly around the waist. Both brothers stand side by side, facing the camera with happy smiles. If only that frozen photograph which captured the life of his spirit could have moved forward, keeping time with me. Then I would have held on to him for ever, protecting him as I should have done from the utter abandonment of being given away to a hospital, which left him wide open to invasion by the doctors.

Yet I always felt that Kie was the eldest son of the family that was living in the house next door to me; hardly the classic case of an intrusion complex where an older child feels displaced. I often wonder whether that burden of being the eldest, an abandonment that I placed on his shoulders by taking his ball with me to the far end of the garden and out of play, contributed to killing him, another second son who had to shoulder an unlooked for responsibility. Kie's capitalism, his ambitious skill with business and with marketing and money, his devilish charm with the women, his charisma with the lads and his interest in sport, his being a family man with a wife and three children: these were the extroverted qualities that I've never possessed, and they qualified Kie for the role of leading the others into a more useful, practicable world than ever I could aspire to do. He acknowledged to Mum in the hospital, on one of those rare days when Mar didn't keep vigil, that it was the experience he gained from working with her in the Wool Boutique, the first dedicated wool shop in the west of Ireland that my mother had opened in our dining room on the Mall for cash-flow support, which gave him his educational start in business. That was the day he also told her that of his brothers, I was the best of them. And so were you, Kie! I know that your independent spirit feels at home in this book, and that you stand four-square beside me, as always.

The familial honeycomb that held us locked into position realigned itself yet again after Kie's death. Was it ever possible, or even desirable, to retake my rightful place *primus inter pares* and move back somehow into the leader's position, that Norman custom of primogeniture, which fitted well with the family's Fine Gael allegiance on both sides? Following the invitation from the priest, I was the first up to give Kie a gentle kiss to his cold forehead and emaciated, wax-like face, pausing to wish him Godspeed. And at his funeral mass, in a great amen, I reclaimed his body for his family of origin by saying aloud into the microphone for all to hear what I'd wanted to say: "I am Kie's eldest brother, and all five Murphy brothers are gathered here together today for the last time." It was the first time that I'd explicitly acknowledged my role as firstborn, because there was an obvious space in the front seat, only now it was being occupied by death.

The act of expulsion, of driving out with force and treating the living as though they were dead, is a mechanism that's been used by the body politic in Spain to rid itself of what was incompatible: the Jews, the Moors, all those who were different were scapegoated and disinherited. I've personal experience of the condition of being expelled, which is perhaps another reason to be affiliated with Spain: the mindset there is familiar to me. When Kie my brother underwent expulsion, this time from boarding school at Newbridge College, it was my mother who took the train to Dublin and then down to the college, where she appealed on Kie's behalf to Fr Valkenburg, a Mayo man from Ballinrobe, to give Kie a second chance and not to expel him. But his action was too audacious, and too many people were involved. Kie had imported contraceptives from England and had given the address of a day boy, whose father had opened the package. It seemed as if the whole country had heard of the scandal. She never said what that diplomatic mission had meant to her, nor how she felt at having to deal with her brother's newly installed successor as headmaster. That day, in sixties Ireland, my mother had to speak about the subject of contraceptives with a stranger priest in the Newbridge College parlour. But Kie and several other boys were expelled. She did say that when she dressed up and put on her coat and walked down to the monastery in Castlebar to see Br George to beg him to take Kieran into the secondary school, she'd found that situation difficult. He asked her why Kieran hadn't gone to secondary school there in the first place, and in a last, desperate effort, she'd reminded him of the close connection between the De La Salle Order and her husband's family: Granda Murphy had been schooled in the De La Salle motherhouse in Castletown in Laois. Burleigh House, indeed our own house, was always open to the brothers, who visited and drank whiskey with my father and his father before him. My mother fought bravely and tenaciously for her second son, and she'd saved his future. But both of them were robbed of it by a premature death, which was repeating now in the family endlessly, as if on a loop.

It was Dad who used to say, "Educate the eldest, and the others will follow on behind." I can hear an acknowledgement of sorts in that statement. So now I sit silently in a consulting room, the wall papered with degrees, making death present through my stillness and through psychoanalytic interpretations: "I think we'll leave it on that question for the moment." Most recently, I incarnated death when I used the phrase "I have cancer," thinking of Kie and how he had cancer. I could read death back in the horrified reflection from the eyes of my analysands when I told them I'd be taking a break. Manolete, the matador from Córdoba who was lured out of retirement, was universally admired for his moments of dramatic stillness in the bullring, and for his clear-cut gestures against death. He excelled at *suerte de matar:* the kill. He didn't sidestep his responsibility, and after sinking his steel, he was killed in his turn by the right horn of the black bull at Linares, in the year that I was born.

Kie's class in national school was taught by a religious brute, Br Denis. He was a violent man, who battered the children entrusted to his care *in loco parentis,* and his deranged behaviour engendered a sense of loyalty to each other among the classmates that was distinctive. Their code of honour in the face of this tyrant required that you never leave a buddy behind. Br Denis' class hired a bus to drive from Castlebar to Dublin to attend Kie's funeral mass and burial. Over the length of that evening, one by one, each of his classmates came over to sit by my mother and tell her stories of Kie's exploits. It was raucous, full of fun and fond memories thanks to their solidarity, and my mother learned things about Kie that of course she knew, but had never before heard expressed.

When Kie was sent up to bed at night, his St Gerald's classmates would carry a ladder round from back of the Green Bay Café, and he would escape out the window to assignations up the lake. After my sojourn in St Mary's in Tallaght, I introduced Joan Baez to the Mall, and she immediately became one of our torch singers. "Sweet Sir Galahad came in through the window in the night when the moon was in the yard . . ." could have been written for Kie, and captured his rebellious spirit. I'd be woken from sleep by a tapping on the window: Kie would've crawled along the top of Mellett's wall and wanted to get in. So I'd raise the sash, and he'd sleep in the other bed until morning. Then he'd sneak out without Granny seeing him, by which time the latch would be off the hall door next door, and he would appear in the kitchen as though he'd got dressed upstairs, in time for a dish of Dad's lumpy porridge, which had been simmering overnight in the steamer on the range.

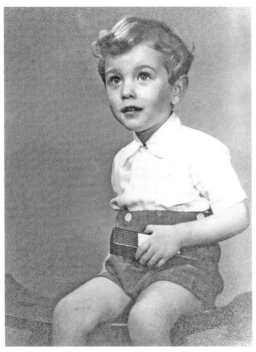

Michael Murphy at the age of three

Michael and his mother walking the Mall in Castlebar (Keith Heneghan)

Anna Timmerman, in her house in Elviria in Spain (Conor Ó Mearáin)

Helen Dring, on Tarifa Beach in Spain 2007 (Conor Ó Mearáin)

Onward towards life – Helen, Anna and Michael, Tarifa Beach, Spain 2007
(Conor Ó Mearáin)

The Cancer Survivors – Michael, Anna and Helen, Tarifa Beach, Spain 2007
(Conor Ó Mearáin)

Michael in studio (Ken Hammond)

*Michael and Ursula at the opening of Ursula's photographic exhibition
(Conor Ó Mearáin)*

Anna and Helen at the Hurricane Hotel in Tarifa, Spain (Conor Ó Mearáin)

Michael working on the book in La Mairena (Conor Ó Mearáin)

Michael in Anna Timmerman's house in Elviria, Spain 2007 (Conor Ó Mearáin)

Michael standing by the pool in La Mairena, early evening (Conor Ó Mearáin)

Terry (Conor Ó Mearáin)

*Michael, Anna and Terry dining in a restaurant in La Linea in Spain
(Conor Ó Mearáin)*

The view from Yunquera, in the Sierra de Ronda, Spain (Conor Ó Mearáin)

Walking along a dirt road, near El Burgo, in the Sierra de Ronda, Spain.
(Conor Ó Mearáin)

The summer that Granny Murphy died, Kie was working on the Long Island railroad, and I was working at La Guardia airport, polishing aeroplanes. We were both staying with Auntie Má and Uncle Joe in Queens, New York. The two of us had got tickets for a Joan Baez concert in Madison Square Gardens, and we went to see her on the day that Granny died. Our reasoning was we might as well be there as anywhere else, seeing as we weren't going home to Ireland, when the cold reality of Granny not sitting contemplatively in the shadows, lit by the flickering firelight in the cosy dining room saying her rosary would become painfully apparent. I used to sit opposite her in that silence, prodding the turf to sparks, sometimes sharing thoughts with her, unconcerned. When we returned at the end of that summer, Granny's house had been sold, so Mum brought me up to the guest room with my suitcase and showed me where I was to sleep in the spare bed. Years later Joan Baez came to Ireland, and I booked three tickets in the National Concert Hall for Kie, Mar and myself. When I called by Mount Anville to collect them, Kie answered the door, and he looked dishevelled, hair uncombed, wearing a striped, woollen pullover. Baez was still in great voice, and when she sang "Brasiliera" a capella, I led the ovation, but Mar seemed reluctant to join in. She said in my ear over the applause, "Ask him about the doctor!" I suggested a quick drink across in the Conrad Hotel. I knew Kie had been plagued by an undiagnosed pain in his back for a couple of months, not able to carry his suitcases through airports – he'd admitted to me he even tried acupuncture – so that when I asked him how things were, he rolled up the leg of his trousers and showed me a yellow bruise on his leg. He said, "That's cancer, Mike." I was horrified for him, and we scanned each other's eyes. I read, "Oh, Jesus, Mike . . ."

And helplessly in the face of this violence, all I could muster back at the time was, "Oh, Kie . . ."

I am remembering the evening that Dad found out about Kie's nightly escapades up the lake. This was on top of the Newbridge College scandal, about which he'd said, "I'll forgive, but I'll never forget." There was a scene in the sitting room when my father was beside himself with rage. He came in with a poker in his hand and brandished it in the air in front of Kie's face, and he was shouting, "I'll take this poker to you – you won't behave like this under my roof!" Kie was worked up as well, but after the experience of Br Denis and the hurt of the Newbridge expulsion, he was insistent he wouldn't be coerced by Dad.

That night I could see for the first time, in the mummers' folk play enacted between the two of them in front of a blazing turf fire, that the imaginary, uni-dimensional father I'd built up out of childhood terrors was no longer an omnipotent monster. He wasn't a titan, a Cronos who devoured his children, but a man of below average height, who worked long hours in the Medical Hall on the Main Street struggling to raise his family, and who didn't intend to use his poker. My father was impotent. And that night I was filled with a sense of unease and embarrassment, distasteful feelings that have just burst over my head again with the thought that I'm like him: I too am impotent from the cancer. Was it he who'd beaten me into that impotent state, a one-time silent surrogate for himself which he'd lacerated with self-hatred? Or was he more like Kie was that night, vigorously refuting this fate, so that neither of them ended up beaten? It yielded a stalemate, as opposed to the king is dead. I question my relevance in never having been a father like my dad and examine the selfish nature of my life, which has been a pointless one from the perspective of that dominant discourse. The temptation inherent in "it were better if I hadn't been born" permits the hooded figure to grasp hold of my foot and drag me remorselessly towards the cliff edge, and the final, desolate slide into an oedipal abyss and the falling for ever.

Dad had suffered a heart attack in 1956, when I was nine and Kie was six. I can remember him telling Jessie Kelly from Tanseys' in a voice slurred with medication that he wanted to be buried in a glass coffin so that people could kiss his arse. Kie was sent into exile. He stayed with Mum's friend Mrs O'Dwyer, in Station Road, and he was kept from calling to the house for the weeks that it took for Dad to recover, each day having to pass by on the far side of the Mall, walking the long trek to and from school. During that period of quarantine, it was my responsibility to call in to the relieving officer in a house beside the monastery every Friday afternoon after school, to collect a weekly cheque, so that we could survive. I walked down the corridor and stood waiting beside his big desk.

"And how is your dad?" he'd ask, as he opened up a ledger.

If I say that he's well, will this man refuse to give me the money? "He's still in bed, Mr Durcan."

"And is he getting better?" as he began to write on the cheque.

I think that he's getting better, but what if I were to tell?

"I think he's about the same as last week."

I see him examining me. "Well, be sure to tell him that I was asking for him," as he tears the cheque out of the big book.

"I will, Mr Durcan," as he hands over the cheque into my shaking hand, looking at me quizzically over his glasses. I gallop down the corridor, turn the knob on the door, and run out into Chapel Street with my schoolbag bouncing up and down on my shoulders as I run all the way home, still holding in my hand the cheque. I stumble and fall outside Burke's garage in Ellison Street, scraping my knees and my wrist, sore trickles of blood from the grazes, sick in my stomach, but I manage to keep the cheque out of a puddle.

Years later, when I chose to leave full-time employment in RTÉ, there was a period when I too had to go on the dole. Each Tuesday afternoon, to collect my stamp money, I'd hurry past Locks restaurant on the canal in case I'd know some of the diners, who could wave at me and ask, "How're things?" and I'd be put under pressure to come up with an answer which spoke of success. I furtively joined the long queues before the counters in the Labour in Victoria Street, shuffling our way slowly towards the front. "Hello – I'm Michael Murphy, and I've had two days' casual work in RTÉ this week."

"How many hours?"

"Sixteen."

The man behind the counter used his calculator "OK, Michael – this is what you're due – bring that over to the cashier. Any chance of permanent work?"

There was an afternoon when two gardaí arrived, and they began the process of arresting the young man standing in the queue in front of me. He looked pinched and defeated. Brutally: "Did you steal this shirt out of Dunne's Stores in Rathmines?" as they examined the contents of his plastic bag. That was the last day I collected dole, stamps or no stamps, which were to go towards a pension. I'd been given too many educational advantages not to immediately find another means of earning my living. My expectations of myself had been lowered to such a degree by the absence of employment that so little served to satisfy, which was unworthy of me.

There was an invitation on the table for a sixth class reunion in Castlebar, but things at the time were very tight, and I'd no cash for petrol, nor for the train fare down. Overnight, the pillow of middle-class certainties had been whipped out from under me. An advertisement was being carried on hoardings to do with the prison service. The louvred blinds would switch over, and another advertisement would take its place. It emphasised for me how quickly fortune can change, and I reflected how easy it was to end up in a prison of unemployment, homelessness, of being alone, a prison where you languish away through sickness. All it took was the shock of the unexpected knock on your door. Kie said to me, as he led the way out through his hall in Mount Anville, "Michael, I've more money than I know what to do with." It was his way of offering help, but I couldn't bring myself to beg from him. Granda Murphy had a saying, "Will-ya is a bad man."

Kie brought me out to dinner in a restaurant at this time, and the conversation took an odd turn. He said, "What we need in this family, Mike, is a star."

He was a marketing manager, and I was on radio and television. "What d'you mean, Kie?"

"A real star," he emphasised. Looking across at me "Something worldwide."

With hindsight, I think that he was beginning to set his sights on the managing director position in Masterfoods, a job to which no Irishman had been appointed and which would lead on to an offer of the international job in south-east Asia, which he then had to refuse because Mar wouldn't live in Japan for family reasons. That hurt him. Maybe his was a challenge, a reminder to me that we'd been brought up by our mother to reach for the stars and never to accept second best: if it's not working for you, just move on because life is short. I didn't grasp the allusion, and the conversational thread petered out there as quickly as it had begun, resolving itself inevitably into talk about Dad. Pouring wine into his glass, he continued the theme by saying contemptuously, "Dad lacked ambition."

"Didn't you know that Dad had wanted to be a surgeon, but Granny and Granda stopped him going to college in

Dublin and apprenticed him instead to a chemist in Laois, Dickie Roarke."

He looked at me with that raised eyebrow, bottle in hand suspended over the glass, and a lop-sided grin. Another conversation completed with illustrative body language.

Dad helped me to buy my first car, a Fiat 127, from Mellett's garage next door: it cost eleven hundred pounds then. He paid for an enormous carpet in the living/dining room of my first house in Knocklyon, and in later life he was always there to contribute financially whenever I needed a hand-out. Over the years, my father did what he could to help me. Not a bad epitaph, that. When Dad was dying, I brought Terry down to Castlebar because I wanted to show him that I was going to be all right. And they chatted amiably in the bedroom about Laois, where the both of them spent many happy summers as children running about on the farms in that placid, leafy, planted countryside. Terry's mum was an O'Carroll from Rathdowney – a Catholic O'Carroll had married a Protestant Mansfield – where life was as easy as the midlands' accent, in which consonants are elided.

Dad was dead a week later. I cried about him, tears that took me by surprise, supported in my mother's arms, shocked, when I arrived down to Castlebar for his funeral. They flowed from a broken heart; the guilty grief issued like pus from a fracture that freezes unendingly in death. "Bless me, Father, for I have sinned." I'm full of remorse, conflicted between the father I remember as the only child and the dad that my brothers came to know. They are altogether different people. I feel compunction, because I've been waving in the wind the long brown jacket he wore back in the fifties, frayed from the rub of the years. It retains a medical smell from his hard work as a chemist, but he has slipped away.

I know that my dad loved me, though he never explicitly

said so, and that he loves me unconditionally in the present moment, because I learned as a child that when the Archangel Michael had fought with the fallen angels, he banished all the evil spirits from heaven. Or perhaps the situation in that kingdom is that positive and negative impulses are identical when they are winnowed by truth, as in the unconscious.

My mother got into Tom's car recently after her sojourn at the Alzheimer's Care Society, and said easily, "I've been thinking it's about time that you got married, Thomas." He said he nearly crashed the car. Could she have been repeating a conversation that she'd overheard with another Thomas, from another time, when my father was forty years old, and she was twenty-six? In her confusion, did she feel free to speak about it now, revealing yet another colourful weft fibre about my father, adding it to the tangled mass of the tapestry's fixed warp, which has become unravelled as I write, so that it doesn't do justice to his fading picture?

Part Twelve: Noeleen

The summer that Terry and I arrived in the south of Spain for the first time, we stayed at Media Luna, a small house on the Mijas road outside of Fuengirola. We were late arriving to collect the keys. Noeleen, the owner, guessed that only a *feygeleh,* a gay man, would stop at the supermarket on his way to a holiday let. This had a grand piano in the lounge, lace-fringed linen and a large terrace which gave on to the pool. That evening we ate an abundant salad with yeast bread dipped in green olive oil, baking in the heat from a blazing pink sunset. There was a procession down the steps from the villa above: Noeleen preceded by her two daughters, Sarina, who had dealt with us over the booking, and Deborah, who did publicity for a flamenco troupe in Sevilla. It was to be the start of a tangled love affair, with Spain, with a new way of being in the world and with Noeleen.

When the trio had departed, Terry and I sat talking into that velvet, star-strewn night on the steps by the pool, putting off the inevitability of having to unpack. Out of the darkness, padding up towards us loomed a massive head, with glittering eyes and large, upright ears. It was an enormous Alsatian. We felt fear coursing as he sniffed and licked the salt off our cheeks. Then he sat upright between the two of us, his head level with our own within biting distance, red tongue lolling out. Mickey was happy to see us in Media Luna, and we were smitten.

Noeleen is a glamorous woman who has a great sense of style. She's also a huckster who buys and sells, and she has a stall on the Saturday morning *rastro* in Marbella, where she sells at a best price silver items to her wealthy clients. She told Terry, "Michael will never make it here on the Costa Del Sol because he doesn't have it." Paradoxically, for the first time outside of my relationship with Terry, Noeleen was someone who favoured me. When Terry took the plane home to Dublin for a flying visit with his mother, who was in hospital, Noeleen suggested I come up to the villa and she'd cook dinner. We talked freely, openly, late into the night. When the evening was over and I sauntered down the steps to the pool at Media Luna drunk with Spain, Mickey came along to keep me company. We sat in our accustomed places, but I was feeling as Noeleen had all of those years ago, sitting on that beach in Fuengirola under a blue sky, listening to the song of the sand blown about by the wind coming off the ancient Mediterranean, which was washing in the surf pieces of pottery last handled by a Phoenician, a Carthaginian or Roman, by a Moor, which held the tangible answer to ways of living a different life.

Noeleen married a Jew in fifties Ireland, and her mother promptly said goodbye with one wave of a tassel from the end of her fur wrap, "her skunk" as Noeleen derisively called it. Ian Henry was the leader of a jazz quartet, which appeared regularly on the fledgling RTÉ television station, and Noeleen enjoyed the *vie bohème* of being involved with the programme-planning and rehearsals in their small flat. That's how they met: Noeleen went to Ian for jazz piano lessons; he told her to go off and study the little-explored sonorities of Debussy as a basis for harmonics. But Ian and Noeleen were also suffering from a *feribel,* a shunning by Ian's relatives in Dublin, which seemed to be orchestrated by Aunt Lottie. Came the day that Noeleen took the bus to the South Circular Road and knocked on the door of Aunt Lottie's house. It was answered by Uncle Fred.

"I am Ian's *shiksa,*" she said.

"Who is it?" a husky voice shouted from inside.

"It's Ian's *shiksa.*"

Aunt Lottie loved Noeleen's effrontery immediately, and she was welcomed like a long-lost relative. But the exotic couple eventually had to go into exile in London's melting pot, and Ian got a doctor's job in the East End. Noeleen prowled the second-hand furniture and antique shops and nurtured the talent for buying and selling on that she was to learn from her husband's father. Like a good Christian, he brought his stall from parish to parish all over Ireland, selling rosary beads and statues during the missions: one week for the women and one week for the men.

It was Noeleen's Spain that we were introduced to, a world of contrasting textures and colourful materials in terracotta and pastel blue from *el mundo de las telas,* a wonderland of second-hand stores from San Pedro to Estepona; to garden plants, their perfumes and scents, mimosa, jasmine, and the heady *dama de noche,* in which you drown. At the doorstep of Media Luna, we'd find a basket of free-range eggs and the rough, country bread that Noeleen had left, to reacquaint us with the taste of fresh produce. In her presence we discovered a legacy of the New World: *salmorejo,* the thicker version of *gazpacho* served with bits of *jamon* and chopped egg, which we first tasted outside the Mezquita on an induction visit to Cordoba. Noeleen's *rustico* taste in tiles and furnishings was impeccable. And always she'd strike a bargain, standing right up close in people's space, Spanish-style, which we later discovered was partly due to her atrocious eyesight and her vanity in not wearing spectacles. She translated Spain into an Ireland that had once belonged to all of us.

We eventually bought a villa in Vista Verde, and we called it Casa Alquimia, the House of Alchemy. It seemed to embody Barragan's architectural precepts of beauty, inspiration, magic, sorcery, enchantment, and also serenity, mystery, silence, privacy, astonishment. It looked and smelled like an old monastery, with big, studded entrance doors, wooden beams inside and large reddish-brown floor tiles that had been burnished to reflect the light. The only drawback was the number of steps up through the garden levels to the hall door: thirty-six of them, which posed a problem for Terry with his polio.

On the torturous road above the clouds, on our way back down from a visit to Ronda late one night, where we'd purchased a blue tiled pilaster, moulded with a white Bacchus complete with yellow pomegranate, Noeleen was being mysterious in the back seat, something about the tall, empty wall that supported the typical cathedral ceiling in our lounge. It emerged that she'd acquired a large oil-painting of an American ambassador to Spain in the Eisenhower era, who'd also been a film star. And the man that she christened "Daddy" went up in a golden frame on the borrowed wall of the sunken lounge. The elongated shape of that canvas linked in harmoniously the balconied terrace of the library above. He was a handsome man in his naval dress uniform, and he added a touch of resplendence, looking down on the two oversized table lamps and long, cream sofas, plumped with terracotta cushions. It was Noeleen's eye that carried it off, but in that gesture, she was gifting to us a piece of herself that remained hidden to others and initiating us into an intimacy that made her known.

We inherited José, Noeleen's gardener and handyman, and she even organised us to pay an additional contribution towards his pension. During the winter months, he'd constructed a tank for water under the front lawn and raised the level of that lawn so that, for the first time, it had become a flat, usable space, where he planted yellow flowering rose bushes, in keeping with our *"Inglés"* sensibilities, since we'd become the proud owners of a ha-ha. José was a courteous gentleman, who understood Noeleen and protected her. He put up the pilaster by the pool for us, so that in our eyes Bacchus became José. It gave us enormous pleasure to catch sight of him peeping out from behind the huge terracotta pot of well-watered plumbago, the heads of light, pastel blue flowers twining through the deeper blue, glittering window grille. And when our best friend Barbara's daughter Carla visited us when she was four, she caught sight of José's reflection in the shimmer of the pool and was afraid to jump in because she thought that José was alive and moving in the water. To celebrate her birthday that year, I surrounded the pool with scores of little candles shaped like flowers in colours of red, green, blue and yellow. At dusk, a time of enchantment in Spain, Terry and I helped Carla light each one of them in a moment of magic, under the proud eyes of her loving parents and of a benign but blind José. By that stage, the pool was occupied by a sailing Shamu, who moved about noiselessly with the wind.

Terry says, "You wrote Noeleen a poem." Yes I did. And I read it aloud in St Vincent's, at the end of a paper on Phantasy and the Psychoanalytic Act I gave at the 1999 APPI Annual Congress, because it made far better sense about the hysterical relationship between consciousness and the unconscious than the five theoretical abstractions about the end of analysis enunciated in the paper, and it also illustrated what I'd wanted to say about "the redeemer becoming the redeemed." The chairman of the discussion on that day, Martin Daly, tinkled his little bell and appreciated the truth of it and what it said about the unconscious, personifying as it did one of its effects. But I got a phone call later from Helena Texier, the editor of *The Letter*, to say that she'd run out of space, so she had to cut the Lacanian poem from the published paper. Dan O'Shea, television chief sub, sticking his head around the editing room door before the *Six O'Clock News*: "I don't want art, Michael, I want it now."

What do you do
When a woman gives you the gift of herself?
How do you repay that?

When she enfolds your hand in hers
And looks through your eyes
In an instant entrusting herself to what she sees there
What can you say in return?

I know a woman in Spain
Born at the time of the Christ child
Who takes the weft of God

And tries unendingly
To weave the threads of man through it
So that now you are always at the centre
And never at life's edge.

How do I make amends
Or do I do you a disservice
By not responding in a new way?

Do you see that little boy
And know the meaning of the joy
That each new day's dawning brings for him?
You cut him free from the prism of ice that skews his light
By calling up the man,
"Relax – it'll be all right – you're at your granny's."

Now that I am here in focus
What do you want of me

Nothing
Utter indifference
I be me in my way
You be you in yours
And from the tension of the opposites
We create together the Godhead
A new word yet to be spoken on earth
So that I can continue
To weave my thread through.
Haven't you heard it yet?

I need you for this
That is why I never stand in any man's light.
She gently polished my forehead with a kiss,
"Shine," she whispered.

"Shine," I said
And I switched on
The universe.

When first they moved to Spain, Noeleen lived beside
Maria and Pepe, a younger couple with a family of five girls
and one boy, and the two families became firm friends. When
she built her house, as well as being her mentor, Maria
cleaned for her in the thoroughly energetic way that Spaniards
do, perspiring in the heat – "¡*Qué calor*!" – although she
grumbled at not being permitted to use bleach because of the
smell. When we bought our villa, there were three outsized,
naked ladies at the end of the pool in Alquimia, who stood
on top of a very large fountain, lit alternately by red, green
and blue spotlights, giving neither charm nor beauty. Noeleen
promptly arranged for the *triúr striapaigh,* those three ladies

of the night, to be chased to the street in front of Maria's *finca*. So Pepe cooked a barbeque one evening, to which were invited his extended family and his mother and father from across the courtyard. Terry and I were the guests of honour, to be thanked. The three were centre stage, a cause for celebration when we arrived, displaying themselves in the paved space in front of the house. We were being welcomed into a Spanish family gathering, for which the women had prepared a banquet as if for a wedding. Terry and I sat to the table together and held a deep, psychoanalytic discussion in the night air with Maria and Pepe over the *pinchitos* and the *pollo asado* (in rapid-fire translations by Sarina), about Maria's son and the motives, *"un nido de víboras"* – "a nest of vipers" – of his latest unsuitable girlfriend, who wouldn't be welcomed into the house, at least by an indignant Maria. Pepe's mother, now in her eighties, who earlier had shown us the vegetable garden, her wrinkled face animated, graced by the warmth of the sun's dying glow, sat listening at the top of the long trestle table, breaking bread like beads through her hands. She looked bemused in the yellow light which spilled out from both houses, surrounded by conversation, ruminating on her memories, looking at her daughter-in-law as my own grandmother would have done.

We got an urgent phone call from Spain. José had gone up to tend the trees and shrubs around the house and seen water pouring out from under the antique doors. It was washing everything away like a baptism down the garden steps. He went inside and found a swimming pool in the sunken lounge: both sofas and the coffee table were afloat. The cistern at the back of the toilet in the guest bathroom had split in two, and the newly installed water pump from the tank in the lawn pressured the water out into the house with powerful force. José reckoned it could have been like that for at least four days, because the water stains were a third of the way up the plaster walls. No, there was no need for us to go down especially, because José's wife and Maria and her family, who had arrived with buckets and mops and towels, had cleaned up the mess over several hours. The sofas were drying out in the sun on the front lawn, and José was putting in the new cistern. Noeleen had already rung the lawyer to whom she'd introduced us, Juan Vincente, about the insurance claim, and it was in hand. I was impressed with his obligating, personal sense of history and the implications he felt it had for us as newly arrived immigrants into Spain, when he sent me an *emilio* about that contract: "The Romans left it very clear: *pacta sunt servanda*: contracts are to be honoured." Terry and I are now able to claim another heritage and draw on another tradition of integrity to strengthen us. It brings us back to first principles and can shore up the beam of Catholic morality which split under the weight of abuses.

We finally got down on a Thursday morning. We climbed the steps, Terry clinging on to the newly installed balustrade. The yellow roses were in bloom, and José had planted colourful carnations. We deliberately left our cases down in the wagon, and we turned the door key with trepidation. The first thing to strike us was the fact that the floor tiles had leached salt and lost their lustre. The area inside was sombre, and you could smell the mustiness. That holiday we kept the windows open as much as possible, to dry out the wardrobes particularly, and when our friends Barbara and Tiernan arrived on the following day, Barbara filled the house with scented flowers, lilies, so that when you opened the doors, their heavy fragrance was what you smelled. And with Carla running about the place, in and out of the pool, her lively voice questioning, "Why are you always here?" as I sat beside her once again on the journey back from Granada, clarifying my place in the pecking order, soon the house became lived in, and it took possession of us slowly, and we grew committed once more.

We suffer fatigue from the unending weeks of work, of paying the closest attention to the literal meaning of what each analysand says and to what they are not saying, holding in our minds their stories, moving them inexorably towards the end of analysis. We'd got up at three o'clock on the day that we arrived, so we opted for the luxury of a siesta, stripes of warm sunlight streaming through the slatted shutters of the French doors to the balcony muffled by panels of white muslin. Bliss. The phone ringing woke us up. It was Noeleen: "Where are you?"

"We're here in the house, Noeleen. We were exhausted when we arrived so we went to bed."

"But I was expecting you here for dinner."

My heart turned over. "I'm sorry. I thought that was a loose arrangement, and that we were free to go or not to as we pleased."

"If I go to the trouble of preparing a meal for somebody, it's not a loose arrangement. So I'll expect to see you in ten minutes."

Noeleen lived by the gates of Vista Verde. We had to pass her house each time that we came or went. It had proved difficult to escape her notice in the past, particularly since José brought her up all the news of our doings from his days working in our garden; she gave him a breakfast on the days that he worked for her.

"We've had a new occasional chair delivered from Benitez."

"Oh you have, have you?"

"Yes, Noeleen, we have: I know you'll like the shape. It will go with the table you chose for the telephone alcove."

We'd a quick shower and drove up for dinner. We brought Noeleen presents of Irish brown bread and smoked salmon, rashers and sausages, jams from home and the newspapers, which she loved to read in bed, and we renewed acquaintance with Mickey. Noeleen's other dog, Sheba, who was older and infirm but who kept Mickey in check, had passed on since our last visit, and Mickey, now top dog, lay sprawled across one of the sofas. At one stage during the evening, I got up to examine a photograph on the mantelpiece, and without warning Mickey was above me, his paws digging into my shoulders, standing high on his hind legs with his huge head with the very long muzzle looking directly into my eyes. Noeleen was across this, and she raised a branch from the *ciseán* of logs beside the grate to threaten him. He dropped to the ground and loped out the side window, glancing at her over his shoulder. "Did you see that?" Noeleen explained that she was the subject of a *denuncia* at the Town Hall in Mijas because Mickey was tearing the rubber strips off the side of cars, and somebody in the vicinity had complained about him. She felt his behaviour was due to a grief reaction following Sheba's death. Although he was a big dog, Mickey was still a pup that Noeleen had found wandering in the *campo,* so maybe he was still feral. But it taught me a lesson about how protective he was of Noeleen.

We'd great fun that weekend after the arrival of Barbara, Tiernan and Carla, visiting new building developments with them and planning how they'd furnish their dream home in Spain. We passed on to them how the Spanish build their houses in the shade, to look out at the sun. On the Tuesday morning, Terry and Barbara came home from a visit to Lidl and reported that they'd met Noeleen doing her shopping there.

Barbara said, "Noeleen pushed a shopping-trolley at us in the car park."

"She did not," said Terry. "Noeleen gave it to us as a gift – there was a euro in it."

"Terry, I saw her, and I know what I'm talking about. She flung the shopping trolley at us."

After a wonderful week's holiday, with visits to the Alhambra and Tivoli World, an amusement park where Barbara and Terry were catapulted heavenwards – "Oh my God!" – and hilarious tipsy barbecues by the pool, we went for a meal on the final night to Benahavis. It was a flamenco evening, and Carla and Tiernan were invited up on stage. They did a Riverdance with the Jen Kelly "flying shirt" to the rhythms of Spain, a resonance that was natural, albeit new, and it confirmed that we were somehow home. It was a *seanchas* of the blood, a folk knowledge. As Tiernan said, in his exaggerated Dundalk accent which he has borrowed from Barbara, "When we're out we're out, and when we're out we're big!" A journalist, I think it was Tom Savage who hails from the Cooley Peninsula, described that way of speaking to me once as "rolling shite around your tongue". On the meander back to the car, we called into an art gallery and met the owner, Drahoslav Solta from Bratislava. His paintings are big and bold. Barbara and Tiernan bought the two of us a gift: a large canvas in blue and terracotta for the stairwell in Alquimia, a still life bursting with oranges and lemons, with behind the platter a stick of bamboo supporting a white magnolia in full bloom. It was vivid, and Fr Flanagan would have given his imprimatur to the technique. I carried that tangible expression of generosity like a trophy through the village that night, and we were united in supporting it over our heads on the car journey full of laughter back towards Fuengirola. We were so sorry to see them all go home on the Friday and felt great *uaigneas,* a loneliness, after them.

It may be Guidera
That forebear of my great-grandmother
Set sail aboard a galleon
From Galicia.

My father's sister Aunt Isabella remembered visiting
Two Guidera women
In the twenties
In Borris-on-Ossary
And my father always said his father
Had a sallow complexion like a Spaniard.
We have the photograph to prove it
A Laois *campesino*
Rich with Guidera blood.

Tradition in the family says Guidera was a guide
Who survived the Spanish Armada
Like St James Matamoros.

Cast ashore and cut adrift
What did he feel
When first he saw the coast of Ireland?
To misapprehend the green like Galicia under the sun
For what was cold and unwelcoming as winter.
What sort of map did Guidera have
That he could negotiate a shipwreck
In of all places Borris-on-Ossary?

Was he inured to harshness?
Did he experience tenderness
Charging the loins fuelling Irish lust
Some seventeen-year-old
With sallow skin and agile body
Exotic as Spanish olive oil?

Did they share a faith in common–this is my body–
Was their pleasure all the sweeter for Catholic guilt?
He traded her a name against another son for Spain
His children exiles in their own land
But she gave him place.

Nevertheless the mystery remains:
What compass guided Guidera
And did he return to Spain
To reclaim his heritage
Or did his son become the pilgrim
Or was I the one to undertake
The Camino de Santiago
And bring his relics home?

Terry and I were up in Mijas on the Saturday at around one o'clock visiting Palomino properties, when I got a call from Noeleen. She was crying on the phone.

"What's up?" said Terry.

I put my hand over the speaker. "It's Noeleen, and she's very upset."

The upshot was that she felt we were neglecting her in Barbara's favour. That call laid a cold hand on my heart, because I was beginning to feel surrounded by her anyway. Dad had always said that Detective Sergeant Mullins was the only person in Castlebar who could surround a house single-handedly, and as a child I solemnly believed him, so I knew that it was possible. Noeleen enjoyed scouring the second-hand shops on the Costa, and when she saw an item of furniture that would suit Alquimia, she bought it, and we paid her whatever she asked. But almost imperceptibly, an understanding overtook us that we couldn't buy anything for the house without gaining Noeleen's approval first: that we'd lost our privacy. More than that, I now felt that our freedom was in danger of being taken from us. Terry took a much more robust and sociable view, and he told Noeleen on the phone, "Barbara and Tiernan were only here for a week, and they're our best friends in Dublin, Noeleen, and we can spend all of next week with you." But she rang again that evening and wanted to come down to the house to have it out with us. Terry had recently buried his sister Eileen, the last remaining member of his family, and he was tired, so he took the phone from me and explained this to her, but Noeleen was tenacious.

She arrived dressed in white, with a white wrap, looking as beautiful as Gena Rowlands in a Woody Allen movie, and like a true Capricorn with cardinal qualities, Noeleen took centre stage. There was awkwardness until we suggested a cup of tea out on the terrace to continue the conversation. As far as I was concerned, the rules of the game had been broken, and I spoke truthfully of the difficulties that I was experiencing. Noeleen had wanted nothing from us; at least, that was what we'd understood, and the rules of engagement were written down in that poem I'd composed for her. It was my pre-emptive strike, but she'd known I wouldn't make it in Spain. I had tried to imprison her in those words, but she negotiated her way through those steps to the inversion, instead of embracing the equality which is endemic in the lines: "I be me in my way, and you be you in yours." When I'd played snakes and ladders as a child with Mum, she always won, even though it was a game of chance. There was never any winning with her. So finally I upset the board, and I never played that game again. If an analysand were to tell me at the end of a psychoanalytic session that she was refusing to leave the room, I'd leave the room instead. It's three in the morning, and everyone has gone home, shut up shop. As the bull rakes the stones on the far side of the fountain, I am an amateur without the suit of lights, without a sword. And this is a *capea* in the silent village square.

The next time we came down to Spain and opened the door into the lounge, Daddy was gone. José must have come in, opened up the ladder and lifted the painting off the wall. Terry was unsure whether we'd been robbed. "Shall I ring Noeleen and find out?" His eyes were twinkling at me as he stroked my cheek with his finger. I could see what had happened, and I knew our serenity had been taken.

> Dear Noeleen,
>
> I phoned you on Sunday morning for a chat, and I was very sorry to have missed you . . . One of the main things I wanted to tell you is that Casa Alquimia is on the market. Because of post-polio syndrome, Terry has been finding it increasingly difficult to manage all the steps, so reluctantly we decided to dispose of the house now, before he finds the steps impossible to negotiate. Out of respect for your involvement in the house, it was a cause for concern that we didn't have the right opportunity to discuss our decision with you . . . Even so, we miss the light of Spain. We avidly plot the latest air fare deals to Malaga over the internet, so you never know . . .
>
> Regards to Debbie, to Sarina, and to yourself.
>
> Love, Michael and Terry

La Dama de Noche, her perfume,
Visited me in my room.
She suffused me with scent,
Tried to seduce me with blandishments.
"You know," she said, "that Spain has set a place at table
Just for you under the sun."
It was natural not to yield, to question "Why? Why me?"
While this simple extravagance of *La Dama's* gift required
    the response "Why not?"

She was insistent that place-setting was mine.
"It's in your name," she said. "If you don't fill it, then who
    will?"
The initial choice, it seems, was made by Spain.

In the ninth month of ninety-nine, I was born a child of
    light.
Dare I disturb the universe and make that choice my own?
If I refuse, it will be as if I never had been,
Withering without taking root.
If I assent, then all that I had been I will lose.
I desire to take my place
To flower in daylight
Scenting the air with my presence.
I desire to espouse *La Dama de Noche*
And become a powerful man at the bounteous banquet of
    life
Under the nurturing sun of Spain,
So that I, in my turn, can give light
And become, in my turn,
A courageous son
Of Spain.

Part Thirteen: Helen

We drove through Marbella down to Sotogrande to meet our friend Helen, who has the same Christian name as my Lacanian analyst. She's true to that prototype of female beauty. As we pulled up beside the calm blue waters in the marina, I could see her seated alone at a table, her blonde hair framing a face that is startlingly beautiful. She stood to greet us, and as she leaned forward to kiss on both cheeks, her dancer's body was still petite and full of grace.

"Michael, Terry – how wonderful to see you both."

Helen is one of the Huggards of Glenellen, near Tralee, and she has an impeccable Anglo-Irish voice, a cut-glass accent, inherently careful of the words that she pronounces. Her father had worked for the British colonial service, and she tells the story of one hot afternoon up country in Kenya, when she was playing happily with the native children in her tree house. This was the natural habitat in which she grew up, a place of safety to which she could withdraw and peer out at the vastness of the uncertain world beneath. She clambered down and ran through the lawn, up the steps of the veranda, across the polished wooden floor and burst into the drawing room. To her surprise, tea was being served in the Limoges, and Mwongi, dressed in his white kanzu with the red fez, was holding the silver tray. Seated in the middle of the sofa like a film star was a woman she instantly recognised from the cuttings in her scrapbook. Mum was wearing her afternoon dress.

"Helen, I want you to make a curtsy, because this woman is the Queen!"

It was the Queen Mother. She thought to pull up her white stockings as Mwongi led her from the room, with the promise of a plateful of sliced tomatoes and fried bacon sprinkled with sugar.

It was the time of the Mau Mau, and Helen hardly slept for fear of something coming out of the dark. Sometimes she'd feel her bedclothes being pulled down off her as silently as a snake, and she knew that an African standing outside in the pitch-black night had poked a bamboo shoot through the bars of the bedroom window with a hook on the end and was attempting to steal her blanket. She was exposed, but she dared not move, nor whimper, nor grasp the bamboo rod which was studded with razor blades. She lay rigid with fear.

"The Africans are silent: you never hear them coming until they're at your shoulder."

She knew from adults talking that pressure would be brought to bear on the houseboys to turn against their European employers and slaughter the family. Her father was chief medical officer for British East Africa, and they'd been made aware that he and his family wouldn't be touched: "But where was the certainty, Michael?" So when her father was away, Helen slept on the floor of her mother's room, with a wardrobe pushed up against the door. It was a pathetic gesture at safety, because there was no protection from the blackness of the African night.

When Terry went off to do some shopping, Helen told me that she'd been on a trip to Bulgaria with a friend of hers, and that the opportunity arose to have a brain scan in a hospital there at a fraction of what it would have cost in Ireland. It had shown up a tumour on her brain. My stomach sank with shock, but I remained impassive. She'd noticed that her memory wasn't as it should be, which was a first symptom that something was wrong, and also that it was painful for her to do a backstroke in the pool. Helen has something of the breath of God about her, such a beautiful soul, that it would be unimaginable to conceive of the world without her presence. She found our conversation emotional. She'd never liked "the messy stuff," and reprimanded herself in Swahili, "Bass, bass!" This was the first time that she'd put what was happening for her into speech. And she too was hearing now what she was saying. She could see, laid out before her on the table, the surgical precision of the words she was using, with the implications of what she was talking about. Helen had made practical arrangements with a consultant in Dublin and would be travelling back there to sort it out. I was devastated.

Originally, Helen had been a faithful analysand for the best part of a decade, and it was my suggestion that she move to Spain, as opposed to Cyprus or Crete – ironically, "White cardigans and sandals, Michael?" But she'd chosen to live out in the Spanish countryside, to be nuzzled by the animals for company, an echo of her childhood freedom in the Kenyan bush. Her new home was to be up beyond the barrier of modern windmills, up beyond Tarifa, on the top of a hill from where she could see her beloved Africa across the strait. It was a happy coincidence that her daughter Tanya and her two grandchildren, who are so loved, had followed her to Spain and were within driving distance. She relished the opportunity to reforge family links, which had been constrained by Tania's husband Jeremy, whose crude aggressiveness reminded Helen too much of her own former husband, Tania's father. Now she was attacked by a cancerous tumour on her brain.

When Terry returned, he told me later that I was white as a ghost. He knew something devastating had happened. And as Helen began to speak to him, I had the premonition that what she was describing was also going to happen to me, because from years of psychoanalytic work, our unconscious had become so attuned to each other's. Death sat at the table, having a *café americano* with the three of us, and making a perfect foursome of our little family through his absence. He was wearing the black outer covering of what I took to be the Dominican habit, but which was the standard medieval dress of the pilgrim in Spain. The hood was up, shielding his face, and the sleeves fell back on his arms, revealing long, thin hands of ivory, as he matter-of-factly suspended the bowl, sipping at it quietly. Pity is the correct word, because it expresses something that causes regret, as well as feeling sympathy or sorrow for the sufferings of another, and it reaches out to touch, to show mercy. When I'd arrived at my fifteenth year working as a psychoanalyst, I knew that God isn't concerned about the messes we get into. He has an overarching rainbow of love that bathes the person in colour so that they glisten with light and expand on themselves to fill the room. There is recompense. Death, however, was unmoving. "It's an unfortunate chance," he said drily, "and that's all." Helen later had dreams of a ravening black sheep dog, bounding with ferocious energy through a series of pens. And someone had left the gates open.

When it was time to go, Helen saluted goodbye out through the driver's window of Bella, her enormous old Mercedes that had no air-conditioning, "Shhh – don't say anything bad in her presence, she has feelings" – and she disappeared over the hill in a cloud of dust, which blew about in the wind and the sudden silence. As we turned back on the road and began the climb over the mountain towards Marbella, Terry was playing a song by

Diana Navarro, called *"Sola,"* and it was unbearably poignant: alone with my pain, she sang, alone with my sorrow. Navarro's plaintive, flamenco voice arched with the sadness, reverberating Arabic-style as if she'd thrown *un lazo,* a lasso, into the night air, whipping it around in a *plaza mayor*, chasing the dust off balconied windows through the purity of her *cante hondo,* her deep song. Helen's life had always been solitary, facing mounting odds that she'd no choice but to overcome. She returned to Ireland to nurse her father with love and respect in his final illness. And when he died, she disposed of family belongings from his colonial days, the chests, the carpets, the keepsakes, and consigned them to memory. Divested of possessions, Helen stamps her heels on the red earth *zapateado* which she sweeps with her dress to the left, to the right. She noisily claps her hands in a *toque de palmas* against the dark, then holding the back of her right hand to the forehead doctors will splay open like the fan of a scallop, she sets her face steadfastly towards the west and al-Andalus, once more a pilgrim, with further lives to be lived *con pasión.* The ghosts of the Moors call out *olé* from the minarets of the surrounding sierras.

Cancer encroached upon the enclave of heartfelt freedom she'd established for herself in legendary Tartessos, and like a contemporary Don Quixote, her only remaining option was to tilt at the windmills. When the time came for Helen to return to Ireland, it was her son-in-law Jeremy who drove her to Malaga airport. He found her a trolley and piled up her suitcases for her. He embraced Helen warmly and wished her Godspeed. Just before she went through the sliding doors, she turned around to wave goodbye, but Jeremy was slumped over the steering wheel, sobbing. He was recovering from testicular cancer, so he knew at first hand the vulnerability that a serious operation opens up, which can scarcely be masked, but against which there's no defence.

Autumn arrived early this morning
So unexpectedly in Elviria.
I surfaced from a dreamless sleep shrouded in sweat
And blundered to the bathroom to piss and wet the floor
    tiles.
The leaves of the palmeras barked in a sudden levante.
Souls that got lost in their solitude out past Tarifa
Saw me inside and rattled their bones
Begging for the love of Allah.
I had to close the open window on their terror.

When I awoke the whole area was being painted
With wraiths of cold mist which dimmed the lustre,
Savaging the sunlight, writing shape-shifting cuneiform
Characters telling me that autumn has arrived
In a shiver of circling black and white storks,
Hundreds of them turning around overhead
Streaming south in the thermals,
Drawing the ghosts in their wake.
I thought I heard or read a despairing scream in autumn's
    echo
Just before the fog burnt up the tale of the damned
In the blazing searing heat of the Costa del Sol summer.

Part Fourteen: Prejudice

In the final week of January 2007, I was watching daytime television in my hospital room. Jade Goody was evicted from the *Big Brother* house for perceived racial comments, and Cardinal Cormac Murphy O'Connor blithely wrote to Tony Blair demanding an exemption for the Catholic Church from anti-discrimination legislation. He wanted legal permission to continue to discriminate against gay sinners, and he was supported in this by the Anglicans and by the Muslims. Nobody has called this discrimination homophobia, with the honourable exception of an editorial and opinion in the British *Independent*, which Terry brought in for me to read: *Now the Cardinal accuses ministers of trying to impose a "new morality" in Britain. If this new morality means it will henceforth be impossible for religious groups to discriminate against people simply because they happen to be homosexual, we fail to see the problem with that.* (31 January 2007)

The one-thousand-year-old city of Weimar on the edge of the Thuringian forest is the spiritual heart of Germany. It's a beautiful university city of baroque buildings, set in green parkland beside the Ilm River, that lends itself to pottering about in the creamy sunlight of its atmospheric streets. Terry and I take a short break there from psychoanalytic work each spring, to coincide with the Thuringian Bach festival. Johann Sebastian Bach lived in the house next door to the Hotel Elephant on the old Market Place, which was founded in 1696, fourteen years before Bach had arrived in Weimar. He too must have received the waiter's cheery "*Der erste Hunger gestillt*," the first hunger pangs allayed. The black and cream art deco style and masculine restraint of the Elephant, becomes an elegant home base for excursions to the many towns and cities round about associated with Bach, which host concerts and recitals of his music, given by the local orchestras, choirs and musicians. But not in this spring, nor in this year.

Last year, we were driving home along the autobahn from Eisenach's *Georgenkirche,* the triple-aisle sixteenth-century hall-church in which Johann Sebastian Bach had been baptised, where we'd heard a heart-stopping performance of his *St Matthew Passion*, cramped into the ancient wooden seats on the first balcony. I understood that Bach considered this "Great Passion" to be his most significant work, vocal-instrumental music, new steps which advanced out of *The Well-Tempered Klavier*. The lovingly preserved manuscript carefully written out in his hand in two colours of ink, red and brown, attests to this. The performance had commenced German-style at the eminently civilised hour of exactly five in the afternoon. There was no applause afterwards; the music of this wondrous Good Friday vespers had charged the air and bled softly into the silence. It was an overwhelming preparation for the resurrection trumpets of the Easter Sunday cantata. And as we sped along the three-lane *autobahn* towards Weimar, drawing our attention in the darkness over to our left was an enormous, floodlit monument. It is the *Mahnmal der Gedenkstätte Buchenwald,* a memorial, but also a warning, constructed over graves in the Ettersberg beech forests, honouring victims from thirty-five countries who lost their lives in one of the biggest concentration camps of the Hitler regime in Germany. Three hundred thousand human beings were interned there: Germans opposed to the Nazis, Jews, Gypsies and the largest number of homosexual people to be incarcerated in any concentration camp. Fifty-six thousand of them were murdered, under the slogan in bold, black lettering on the entrance gate, "*Jedem das Seine*": to each his own, or in the context of the work camp, you get what you deserve. Each night that beacon floods light out into the darkness, lest we forget. The brutality practised there was hidden just four miles northwest of this cradle of humanism.

Terry and I have visited this camp. We saw the outlines of the accommodation huts, dead black rocks filling in the foundations, as if each were a soul for whom nobody cared. We viewed the operating slabs for the gruesome medical experiments, the crematoriums where the disinherited of that regime were burned and the quarries for forced labour, which hastened death. We were both ill afterwards. I found it a chastening experience to be brought face to face with the ravening Shadow which lives in my heart.

The Americans liberated the camp in 1945 and commanded the Weimar folk to walk from the town to see for themselves the rotting piles of naked, dead bodies, the starving and diseased inmates bereft of hope, to recognise what had been perpetrated in their name and on their doorstep. I am solemnly indebted to those who suffered vicious cruelty and horror in Buchenwald, or who were sent on from there to other death camps, so that a covenant now exists with the soul of each one of them, never to allow any form of discrimination to begin to flourish in my heart; and to shelter from harm in my attic a person who isn't considered to be anybody, but who is in fact a somebody because the individual is loved so profoundly by God.

As a child of the Mall, I used to call in on the Farleys, the Methodist minister and his wife, who lived in the house adjoining the church founded by John Wesley on the Mall in May of 1785. He'd toured the West on horseback, evangelising the non-conformists. Mrs Farley was an industrious woman. She made tray loads of plaster-cast models of Irish thatched cottages, which she kept in her sitting room. She painted these by hand and sold them to shops like Wynne's of the Main Street, who sold them on to American tourists as souvenirs. Sometimes she was too busy to let me in to visit her, but one summer afternoon, I was sitting up on her kitchen table as she was making scones, framed by the window which gave on to the green swathe of the Mall, and she taught me a hymn:

> Jesus loves the little children,
> All the children of the world.
> Red and yellow, black and white,
> All are precious in his sight,
> Jesus loves the little children of the world.

We sang those words joyfully over and over in her kitchen on the Mall, in an Ireland where religion was once a visible furrow on the land, highlighting the deep spreading root system of cultural difference and the ascendancy of one tribe upon the backs of another. Terry and I were delighted visiting the homogenous Tesco's in Castlebar to see a bare-midriffed Britney Spears look-alike call out in all the characteristic warmth of the broadest Mayo voice: "Mamaí, did ya get the brioche?" Mum is being brought to the Alzheimer's care facility in Knockthomas three days a week, where she gets her dinner and interacts with other people. She told me that it's a lovely place "and so clean – it must be run by Protestants."

Two months before the prostatectomy operation, in November, we went back to stay in Weimar for a long weekend. And on the Sunday morning, we decided to drive to the *Wallfahrt-skirche Vierzehnheiligen* for mass, to undertake a pilgrimage in order to pray for the strength needed to face this looming ordeal for both of us. In the fifteenth century, a herdsman had a vision of the Christ Child, surrounded by fourteen holy helpers. A mighty baroque basilica was built of ochre sandstone at the site on the open hillside, opposite Banz, the holy mountain of Franconia, and overlooking the Upper Main. The designs are by Balthasar Neumann. Because of the play of the light inside on the pillars and the refined stucco work, the interior is a riot of graceful swirling shapes, convex upon concave, so that it appears to be in perpetual motion; and yet, it's surprisingly restrained and elegant, with cool colours of blue and white picked out in gold leaf. The centrepiece and focal point in the church is a rococo pyramid to the Fourteen Auxiliary Saints, whose cult was fostered by the Dominicans.

We took our places in front of the high altar as the celebrant began the mass behind us, in the bay housing the altar to the Holy Helpers, the *Gnadenaltar* or Mercy Altar. When it came to the sermon, the celebrant used the motif of the Old Testament reading in the mass, "Hear, O Israel", to build a wonderful exhortation, though I was struck by the incongruity that there must be very few people of Israel left in the whole of Germany to listen to what he was saying. Again and again he'd revert to this motif, and he spoke softly, allowing the microphone pick up his mellifluous voice, which increased the sense of intimacy. Then out of the blue – he was speaking about globalisation – he launched a scud: gay unions are being proposed as an alternative to marriage and the family, he said. Not true: I don't want to be married, though I do want my union of twenty-five years to be recognised by the State, so that Terry and I can have protection under the law.

Can any human being in the light of the Holocaust, above

all a German with that particular weight of history on his shoulders, preach discrimination, eschew truth and deliberately play on people's fears? I was furious at the sleight of hand. I knew that I had to confront the celebrant immediately. My German isn't fluent, so in whispers I rehearsed a short phrase with Terry, who'd studied psychology in Bremen, which would get my point across: "Jews and homosexuals were murdered in Buchenwald." Hear, O Israel . . . At the consecration of the bread and wine, at that moment of the Saviour's crucifixion, I remembered the Jews and the homosexuals and all of those who died in terror at Buchenwald, and I was given a context for the medical operation that I was facing, and the extraordinary embrace of care and kindness, the respect that my suffering would elicit, both for me, and for Terry who would be my witness. I singled out the celebrant at communion and stood in his queue. I put out my hand and received the host from him, and then I said, "*Die Juden und die Homosexuellen waren im Buchenwald gemordet.*" The sentence should have been, "*Juden und Homosexuelle wurden in Buchenwald ermordet,*" but any German would've understood instantly what I was saying. So the priest did hear what I said. And gay was a homophone that inserted itself by default "*ge-mordet.*" I was in front of the priest, and I didn't have to raise my voice. I know how to use it, and as Terry is wont to say, "Shhh – you have a voice which carries."

I didn't see the blow coming, and I was knocked out of my standing by the priest: I found myself over on his right-hand side. But I did continue the sentence I'd begun until I had it completed. Holding the chalice in his left hand, the priest had cast me aside and beaten me out of the way with his right hand. There was nothing more to say – the people were receiving communion one after the other – so I turned and went back to my seat. I was shaking more with the shock of what

I'd done than with the effect of the celebrant's response to me. As I knelt down again in the seat, I thanked God for coming to me in communion, and I told Terry that the priest had struck me. That bungled speech action, my protest, seems to be part of the ongoing conversation between me and the father and the true expression of my unconscious desire as son for which I have to accept responsibility.

At the conclusion of the mass, the celebrant passed us by in a procession to the sacristy led by a cross bearer. He was a man in his forties, handsome, with a shock of well-coiffed grey hair, preceded by two young thurifers and two altar girls. He held his head to one side, hands joined in prayer, a little smile playing about his lips.

We drove away from there as quickly as we could, and I'd the ugly feeling that our car was being pursued down the mountainside by a posse of priests, or even by the police, and most probably fanned away from there by the ghosts of beatings past given to me by my father and the ghosts of those whose contribution was to dispossess others of their rightful inheritance. They shrieked and howled through the air, buffeting the car with screams of fury, wave upon wave. Eventually, after the longest time, we slowly gained ground, and their shrill cacophony began to fade into the distance. I was more than a little unhinged and very frightened, and I didn't relax until we'd crossed the Bavarian border back into Bach's Lutheran state of Thuringia. There was another man from another time who'd courageously spoken his truth: "I cannot and will not recant anything, for to go against conscience is neither right nor safe. Here I stand, I can do no other, so help me God. Amen."

On the way, Terry hurriedly rang Katherine Zappone and Ann Louise Gilligan at the Shanty, women who bravely, but unsuccessfully, brought the Irish State to court because they did want to have the reality of their Canadian marriage recognised.

These good, poised people, who shine the beacon of their keen intelligences on to the insatiable passion for ignorance and who can laugh heartily at a nonsense which isn't pernicious, have set up programmes in Tallaght for disadvantaged women and their children. The lunches they provided for the schoolgoers soon had the mammies knocking on the door asking, "What's spinach, and how do you cook it?" I gave them private tuition in how to do interviews with the media about their legal case. Terry and I took great joy in ticking off the boxes as they presented word perfect on the *Late Late Show* with Pat Kenny. They want the institution of marriage to be as "open" – a good Old English word meaning not closed or barred – to them in Ireland as it was in Canada. Terry left a message on their answering machine that Sunday saying, "I'm sitting here in the car beside a hero: you'd be proud of him!" I reflected that I was a hero, not only because of what I'd said, but because of the reality that I'd moved forward to say it, and to say it to the father.

When we arrived back in Ireland, I was very angry about the fact that I'd been struck. So I looked up this priest on the internet, and I recognised him from a photograph. I also saw that he was a Franciscan, and I subscribe to the prayer attributed to St Francis: "Lord, make me an instrument of your peace. Where there is hatred let me sow love; Where there is injury, pardon; where there is doubt, faith; where there is despair, hope; where there is darkness, light; where there is sadness, joy." I was determined to write him a letter by email, because I didn't want him to feel that he could get away with this without a further protest. The injury had moved on. Hopefully, I was continuing to shine a light in the darkness; at least, that was my intention.

I contacted my German friend Ursula for help. She was a tall, handsome woman, who spoke perfect English. She'd picked up something of a southern Irish accent from her husband, pronouncing "huge" as "youge". She had terrifying childhood memories of the war, running with her mother through streets of blazing houses, and had always suffered with her skin, as though a protective layer to her personality was burned away at that time. She married John McCarthy, the former geneticist at UCD, and a warm, soft-hearted man with a quick and clever mind which houses many compartments, who has a devilish sense of humour for the absurdities of life. When John retired at last, they sold their house in Dublin and began to build the modernistic house of their dreams in their former garden plot. They also bought a holiday home in New Zealand for visits to their grandchildren on the far side of the world.

Then, a hospital consultant looked across his desk at Ursula, and said, "I'm sorry to have to tell you that you have cancer of the pancreas."

I heard of this reality initially through John's sorrow, a conduit which the protective cushion of my rude health had blocked out at the time. Ursula underwent an operation, and the surgeon cut away what was life threatening. We met Ursula in the nursing home after surgery, her bravery etched into the tautness of her fine features. Her ebullient spirit reached out to soothe our fears and give the impression that the worst was behind her. During a respite in the harsh, follow-up regime of her recuperation, John and Ursula were given permission by the doctors to come and partake of Spain's abundance, to relax from their ordeal in the familiar, orderly, German community of La Mairena, near Marbella, which we've now made our own. As a gift to us, they bought for our terraced garden several large cacti, which Ursula planted into the thirsty soil with the gloved hands of the practised gardener. Two years on, the fruit of her loving and kindly intention continues to survive there despite the neglect of her absence, and blesses us with a blooming memory of her presence.

When they returned to Dublin, Ursula got such excellent results from the surgeon that they were cleared to visit New Zealand and embrace the growing up of their grandchildren for several months. But Ursula had another project there. In a late flowering of her spirit, she took photographs of the fossilised remains of a forest which is now washed by sea water, hinting at colour through the heightened light reflected off the Pacific. Her pictures are a song of praise to existence. They tell of origins and of endurance over time through her inspired and sensitive recognition.

Ursula had just returned from her mythical journey to the ends of the earth when I emailed her, and I asked her to write me a translation of my email into German, which she gladly did. However, I didn't understand that Ursula is a Lutheran, particularly as she hails from near Münster. She has since explained that her miner father was a blow-in. In her letter she employs the Lutheran term for the Eucharist.

To Fr Christoph Kreitmeir OFM, Vikar, Franziskaner-kloster, Vierzehnheiligen. And to his credit, Fr Christoph replied by return, although a close reading of his German gives the impression that he didn't spend an undue amount of time on it. He opens with a Bavarian greeting, to which I refer in my letter as being preferable, and writes: "*Grüss Gott* – God be with you. To make things easier, I inserted my answer in blue, writing it into your letter underneath. I also got your letter in the English original as well. Sincerely yours, P. Christoph Kreitmeir OFM (Wallfahrtsbüro–Vierzehnheiligen)."

MM: Dear Fr Christoph, I am the person you assaulted during Communion at the 10.30 Mass in Vierzehnheiligen on Sunday, November 3, 2006. The text of your sermon was "Hear, O Israel . . ." which you used as a motif throughout. It was beautifully crafted and delivered in hushed and modulated tones: truly a superb performance. When speaking about globalisation, you referred to homosexuality being put forward as an alternative to the family (forgive my paraphrase): your statement was mischievously untrue, and a displacement that scapegoats a tiny minority.

CK: Many thanks for your words of praise. Your assertion that my statement is wrong is a matter for interpretation. I am not distorting reality, and I am not scapegoating a minority. Please read the relevant texts of the Catholic Church on this theme. I could say more about it, but I will not do so in this context.

MM: During the Consecration, I reflected that Jesus had offered himself up in the bodies of the people of Israel and the thousands of homosexuals who died in Buchenwald, and I remembered their grief and terror.

CK: I find it remarkable that you focussed on one single sentence in my sermon. I'm sure there are reasons for that.

MM: So when I received communion, I confronted you and said, "Jews and homosexuals were murdered in Buchenwald." You held the chalice in your left hand, and without looking at me, struck me with your right hand so forcefully that I was cast aside. I am still shaken by the immediacy of your violent attack. However, I did finish my short sentence and then I walked away.

CK: As you surely know, *Abendmahl* is called Eucharist in the Catholic Church. Taking into account that very many people receive communion, it is not done that anybody would say anything to anybody before communion; therefore, I had to push you aside somewhat. I did that gently, but with determination. It is absolutely wrong of you to say that you were hit and thrown aside. That seems to be your subjective take on it. All the other people would have noticed, but the communion continued smoothly. That is proof that it can not have happened as you write about it. It happens again and again that people who are psychologically damaged (I do not refer to you) molest us priests during communion. Therefore I reacted to you in a determined but quiet way. It was not a violent assault, and now I am myself shaken that you see it as such.

MM: Had you looked me in the eye and heard me, with the chalice in one hand and the host in the other, you could have drawn on the other – Bavarian – tradition of invoking God's blessing on the both of us: "*Grüss Gott . . .*" It has the effect of directing speech into truth.

CK: Apparently you are not familiar with the giving out of communion in a Catholic service. We only say "The body of Christ," and the faithful answer "Amen."

MM: I have no idea why your rage is so near the surface, but I am worried that other people could be in danger of physical assault by you.

CK: My rage is not near the surface, and my action was considered. If you allege otherwise, I have to accept it. Certainly no other people are in danger; you need not worry. I am much sought-after as a pastor (carer of souls) and therapist.

MM: It is a matter which needs to be talked through.

CK: I have hereby dealt with this now. I ask you to accept it.

MM: *Grüss Gott*, Michael Murphy, Psychoanalyst.

CK: I wish God's blessing on you! P. Christoph Kreitmeir (Theologian, Psychologist and Psychotherapist, and Child Sociologist). P.S. I normally do not mention all my titles, but as you mention the Psychoanalyst, I wish to show you that I am an expert too.

God's blessing: I've been rendered holy by means of a religious rite and been given honour and glory through being sprinkled with sacrificial blood. The inspiring people I work with have shyly, over time, let me see their woundings to the spirit, the suffering that goes with the miracle of life. The two resemble the alternation of electrical current, a flickering which all of us bear sometimes with stoicism, more often with bellowings. And after being covered in droplets from their sweat and blood, they've initiated me into transcendence, a knowledge that pain possesses a power to transform us into gods.

Psychology regards the second wave of sowing harmony where previously there was discord to be the more important action in filling in the solid foundations of the personality, with hands raised, with the offer of humbled words that can live, flourish, to begin a cycle of redemption where previously there was bitterness. That gesture can be helped to grow if it's met with forgiveness. However, in my experience, an apology from the father is rarely forthcoming. The word "mortmain" comes to mind. It refers to ownership, and means the state or condition of lands or buildings, goods or chattels held inalienably by an ecclesiastical corporation, deriving from medieval Latin *mortua manus*, dead hand. I seem to have been marked yet again by a powerful dead hand which lacks the revolutionary, life-giving understanding of what it means to be an individual, inhabiting a place of equality before God, the co-creator.

I talked later to Ursula about Fr Christoph's reply. Her artistic soul could see instantly with a penetrative eye that can understand and invite to action. She warned me gently, "Michael, surely you can't be thinking of writing back to him. As far as he's concerned, the matter has been dealt with." And

then Ursula told me the bad news that she had cancerous sec-
ondaries in her ovaries, and she was still very weak at the
moment after her operation, although she and John had spent
four days relaxing down in a hotel in Mulranny, opposite
Mayo's holy mountain, Croagh Patrick. She was to begin
chemo in a fortnight.

Christoph Kreitmeir is my shadow, working within a system which leaves no room for error, no room for the sinner,
no room for the messiness of human feeling, and for the failure
inherent in being successfully human. He's me as
producer/director: the perfection of the programme at all
costs, whatever it takes: "To give and not to count the cost; to
fight and not to heed the wounds; to toil and not to seek for
rest . . ." That's the prayer of the obsessional soldier, a fanatic,
leading to the imperious triumph of the will. Such an entreaty
also has within it the fervour of the impotent child, who stands
upright, dry-eyed, unconditional before the capricious might
of the father, so tiny and dignified, barely hoping for an
embrace. As a man, I've to be careful to act constructively and
responsibly lest an unjust advantage be taken, in order that I
can keep a firm hold on my freedom of choice to do the next
right thing. In the poetic words of the patriot, and legal
defender of the 1798 United Irishmen, John Philpot Curran:
"The condition upon which God hath granted liberty to man
is eternal vigilance."

Part Fifteen: Prostate Cancer

Apparently on a whim, I thought I'd like to go back on air and soar with outstretched wings white against the blue of the sky during those summer months when the sun barely sets. But the timing of this gesture was suspicious, as if inside I realised that a final flourish were needed to express my emotions and ideas, the outflow of my being, one last time. Towards winter, with the yellow sunlight slanting low down on the horizon, my black reflection in the waters of the Atlantic in Clew Bay could be a phantom currach, scudding over the waves in that drowned, drumlin landscape. I didn't see that the shadow was growing bigger by the day, until just before Christmas in a fetch of the tide, it rose up from the depths, a terrifying, massive, black wave dragging with it the raging ocean that blotted out the light. I was dwarfed as it hung over me, pulsing oily and shimmering, poised with widespread and beating wings, the Angel of Death. With a gulp of his lungs, he'd swallowed the air and the colour, and held the nothingness for an eternity, before howling back his tortured intent, blasting silently into the face of God.

The voice failed me spectacularly one Saturday morning early, one week before the operation. My usual preparation for radio is to gently sing scales and do vocal exercises in the car on the way to work at five o'clock in the morning, so that the muscle of the voice is put through its paces and I can sound fully awake and ready for the day, hit the ground running on the first radio bulletin of the shift at six o'clock. But on this particular day the warm-up seemed to have no effect, and when I went on air, I could only make ugly, rasping sounds. For the first time in thirty-five years, the voice wouldn't work because of laryngitis, a *píachán* from which I'd never suffered before. Without any warning, I'd run out of road. Articulation and enunciation of the words was still there, the flow of air was there so that it was possible to make sounds in the mouth, but the voice box, the engine of power, had shut down.

I wrote an explanatory note for the director of Radio News, Michael Good, admitting that my voice, or rather the lack of one, was distracting from the bulletin and that I'd gone home. Declan Dunne, the chief sub, had no idea that I'd cancer, but I felt that the timing of this massive shunt into absence was uncanny and that anything of my previous life which had sustained me was being violently stripped away and taken from me, so that when the day for the operation arrived, I was being forced to face my God naked, humbled, dispossessed, and his judgement raking me was fierce. Without realising it, I'd crossed a line into absence. I was now standing in the way of my own key light and cancelling myself out.

At night, in room 312 of Vincent's Hospital, as I lay stretched out, hands over the covers, afraid to move in the bed lest I somehow disintegrate and become the snowflakes of ashes consigned to God riding the waves off Old Head in Mayo, the soundtrack in my ears was Bach. I'd occupy my mind with those sounds from the piano elicited by Glenn Gould until I fell into a drug-induced slumber. Occasionally I'd weep out loud, pegged down with spilling tears under the weight of the sadness, realising that life as I had known it up to now had come to an end. I was already dead and living in a space beyond death. I stood at the end of the pier, and the wan sunlight warmed my face as I looked across the blue-green sea chopped with white waves at Croagh Patrick, where the tiny white chapel encapsulating the spirit of Mayo was worn atop at an angle of defiance. And it all became peaceful, after the final nightly injection into the stomach: "This will be our secret," whispered a beautiful Indian nurse to me one night. She was a *gitana* from Ronda, who held the bottle of wine by the base, one hand behind her back and, with flamenco moves, had the liquid ejaculate into the glass from the far side of the table without spilling a drop.

When a surgeon ripped me open, he had to take down a mesh attached to the organs inside from a previous hernia operation, which prevented the spilling of my guts. As a result, it took four and a half hours to take out my prostate, which is a large gland about the size of a golf ball. It's a very serious operation to undergo, on the double as it were. As I recovered, I had a tube coming out of my penis which carried most of my urine, and I was wearing a pad held in place by a pair of gauze underpants, to soak up the remainder, because the urethra was healthily trying to bypass the tube, recognising it as something foreign in the body. There was a time in the hospital for several days after the operation when I'd to keep pacing the floor to get relief from the burning in my scrotum, and I couldn't sit down because of the pain in my mangled penis.

The pessimistic turn to "And how're you now?" rang true. First there was the cancer. "Your doctor may suggest surgery if the tumour is small and within the prostate gland. The aim of surgery is to remove the entire tumour and cure the cancer. Some men have no further problems after surgery for prostate cancer."

I felt terror at the thought of having the tumours removed,

five on one side and one on the other. Then there was the pain kept at bay by morphine, and the desperate physical sickness, partly an allergic reaction to Zydol, when I turned green in the bed and told the nurse I was going to die, insane from the punishing, fourteen days of hospital recovery, hours of standing in the bathroom being ministered to by caring young nurses who gently handled my tube-filled penis with plastic gloves as urine leaked down over everywhere, fitting on the wee-wee pads and the mesh tights, joking about David Beckham wearing them and helping me to fasten hospital smocks from behind, although Terry had ironed my smart German pyjamas, which remained folded away in the wardrobe, irrelevant.

"The urinary catheter will remain in place for about three weeks after the operation. You may experience bladder spasm while you have a catheter in place, but this is normal."

There was unremitting suffering with the tubes, the drain in my side from the wound deep within, guts phuttering as the tube was tugged out like a disembowelled intestine. The catheter seemed lodged at my groin, which was achingly painful, and issued down through my burning penis to the bag, agony when it was pulled or when the stand carrying the bag fell over, or worse, was tripped over, torn. I called that stand Señor Xolotl after the Mexican artist Frida Kahlo's companion, her chihuahua. He was the representative of her soul, who accompanied her through the underworld of suffering. He barked at the dark with the weapon of his voice and had no conception that he was so tiny.

"Most men are incontinent when the catheter is first removed. Usually this improves with time, but it can be frustrating."

It's still a misery without end of incontinence, of wetness and heavy, full pads of pungent urine. And there's been no improvement. When we visited our best friends, Barbara and

Tiernan, their daughter Carla's dog, a fourteen-month-old labrador called Honey, kept burying her face in my lap wanting to chew at my urine-soaked pad. Barbara saw my discomfiture as I fended her off, and to put me at ease assured me that Honey loves smelling behinds, warmly, generously reaching out with an equality that only served to emphasise difference.

"There are four main types of urinary incontinence: stress, urge, overflow and total."

Last thing before bed at night, there's the ceremony of the *accouchement*. Unlike the public ritual at the French court of the Sun King, this is done alone. Place the mats on the bathroom floor. Open the big plastic bag on the back of the door to take the wrapped up soaking pads. Have several pairs of mesh knickers ready in case they get wet with exploding spills, open up the inner pad to take the load and place it in the centre of the big, plastic purple incontinence pad to keep it all in, lest the wetness escape into the bed. Open the packet of wipes and pull some out to dry my scrotum and legs over the loo because of the drips, and open the other packet with the perfumed nappy sacks for the soaked pad as it comes off, and the antiseptic wipes to dry down the rim of the toilet bowl. Make sure there's nothing left on the floor, because if I've to bend down I'll spray urine, and if the purple pad is already on, the flaps will tear open, and I shall have to begin the ceremony all over again – not manifestations of obsession, just practicality.

Every night I renew a decision to accept the indignity of wearing ballooning purple pads to protect the bed, using baby cream for the sores, and endure the dribbling and agonising spurts, the *steall,* when I move, heightening the overwhelming truth that I never had any control over any aspect of my life anyway. Recently, I was talking on the phone to my friend Graham, the optometrist, who offered a new pair of sunglasses, and he said that he'd just the pair of black "butt-watchers", as he called them.

"I'm too old for that, Graham. I'm over sixty."

"Sure you're only a baby: aren't you still in nappies?"

Sharp humour, his laughter unwittingly driving home the difference between us. Sometimes I lie there on the bed like a corpse, unmoving, dry mouth open, staring at the ceiling, until the raging pain in my scrotum eases.

"Even though the treatment for cancer can have some unpleasant side-effects, many people manage to live a relatively normal life during treatment."

There's terrible suffering involved, upon which those honeyed words have no effect, and which are as misleading and useless as the American misnomers "collateral damage" and "extraordinary rendition," terms which cynically attack the hope for a better way of life.

The emotional low point was reached when my ship was scuttled by a *scadán,* a young student, who was kind enough to take the time to visit me in my hospital room for one and a half hours, and I just wasn't able. Breda, the elegant staff nurse, subsequently took charge and decreed, "Five minutes, if even that." I sat upright on the edge of an armchair – keep dealing with the pain, Michael – and listened and talked about skiing in France and surfing in Donegal. About one hour into the visit, this guy who plays rugby and is well used to changing rooms jerked his head and interjected without thinking, "Oh, cover yourself up."

The force of his words, the shock of them, sank me, and I felt shamed to my core. He'd made violent contact. The hospital smock which I was wearing had ridden up my legs. It exposed a truth which wasn't acceptable by me or by him on any level, and I'd difficulty holding my voice steady. The truth I'd grown up with, that had been beaten into my bones – if you reveal your true self, you'll be annihilated – overwhelmed me once again. The woman arrived with the sandwich for my tea, so I continued smiling and made a big play of having to eat it because they remove the tray so quickly and so on, and I sat upon the bed with my back half-turned to him, with the smock modestly protecting me from further glimpses of tubes. This is my personal space, and you've come into it to visit me, but I don't have any ownership over any part of the proceedings whatsoever, and you've seen through me to my vulnerable wounding, and you continue to sit there, calmly examining my discomfiture. In rugby terms, you've creased me and held on to my head, scrubbing my face all over with my urine-sodden nappy until the very skin, the slits that were my eyes and the hole of my mouth, that silent, yielding *mantachán*, were besmeared with shame and scalded with acid. And you appear to be unaware of what you've done. When you played against Blackrock College as a teenager and someone attempted to gouge your eyes out, you rightly complained to the referee. The uninterested and biased response of the Blackrock teacher was that if you weren't able for this level of competition, for winning at any cost, then you should give up rugby. Disillusioned with that adult's failure to protect you, you did at the time.

Terry breezed into the situation and generously offered fruit from a heaped up hamper that'd arrived via the internet from a client who works in a very responsible medical position, but who had suffered from vindictive bullying at the hands of her line manager. That man played a groundless complaint against her by the rule book in order to force her resignation. She was subsequently cleared of all allegations by a board of enquiry and promoted, but she still has to cope with the shattering after-effects of his casual and undermining cruelty, which was intentional, unlike the hapless reaction of this likable young man. There were many apples, oranges, pears, mandarins, plums, peaches on offer from her sympathy. He opened up his satchel and carefully put into it the centrepiece, a pineapple and the melon: "Thanks very much!" He then left to visit a former school friend in St Camillus' Ward, where I'd done my clinical training as a student psychoanalyst. Terry looked over at me, and he was very angry. I was exhausted.

The definition of truth derived from the Swiss psychoanalyst Carl Jung of expressing as much of the unbridled unconscious through the filter of conscious life as I can bear is probably the one that animates me the most, but I falter when I don't experience the good manners that derive from an empathy that has taken root. Like the gestures of a modern flamenco dancer, I'd wish to inaugurate new steps from the classically precise, conventional ones and try to live dangerously. The regulated and restrained *Jugendstil* furniture and fittings of the Nietzsche Archive in Weimar, his sister's house where the philosopher spent the last three years of his life descending into madness, were avant-garde at the time. And he wrote, "The secret of realising the greatest fruitfulness and the greatest enjoyment of existence is: to live dangerously." Except that from now on there can be no dissembling about the masculine function, because the doctors who did my plumbing have removed the prostate doughnut that secreted a liquid constituent of semen from underneath the cylinder of the bladder, and in the process, they've damaged the automatic functioning of the waterworks so that there's no signalling system left, just the constant drip, drip, drip of urine from a flaccid penis mouse.

Because of the operation to remove my prostate gland, I've stepped aside from myself. I'm worried about having to turn away from thoughts of sex because at the moment it causes physical pain in my penis. Never to factor sex into human interaction again because it's been physically rooted out surely must have a radical effect on my emotional outlook. Never again to be able to respond naturally to the patina of sexuality, or to have to deliberately abstract it from people, sounds to me like wreaking terrible violence. The paradigm of creativity has been taken from me; the potential that we take for granted and build our civilisation upon has been wilfully ended, to save my life. The question and answer session involved in trying to come to terms with that particular conversation has to be drenched in the truth-proving of Socratic irony, where the answer is known before the question is asked. It was a technique used by the senior broadcaster Gay Byrne on the *Late Late Show*, who from the first time that I saw him, concentrating, preparing backstage to introduce effortlessly before the cameras the acts at the Castlebar International Song Contest, I'd emulated. He later described me on air as his "favourite broadcaster". His endorsement signified that I'd arrived in career terms, but that's an aside from another time.

What are the further implications now of having prostate cancer? How is it possible for me to have sex if the penis never hardens? If every time it's approached there's no reaction from inside, no tightening of the scrotum, no lengthening of the shaft, no swelling of the glans? My penis has retreated back into itself like a snail into its shell, hidden within the undergrowth of damp hair at my crotch so that it has to be searched for: there's no signal which indicates where it is. "*Seilleachaí, seilleachaí púcaí*, put out your ho-orns . . ." And every time I reach in for it, spouts of urine fountain out wetting my clothes, spraying my shoes, the floor and the toilet bowl because it cannot be directed. To make love, to involve another in my mess, in the brutal shock of the unenvisaged, is unthinkable. As in the case of a helpless baby, the words don't exist which can beg the forgiveness of being acceptable in someone else's eyes.

Sometime during the fourteen days I was in hospital, my eighty-three-year-old aunt, a fiery redhead still, who was very shocked when she was told of my diagnosis over a Sunday dinner in our apartment, took the opportunity to have a go at Terry when he was alone one night. This is a woman who had to emigrate to New York from the narrow, inward-looking Ireland of the fifties, where she worked day and night as a private-duty nurse, and who sent her money home for our birthdays and bought clothes for us and fluffy American towels and drip-dry sheets, which she parcelled up in her small apartment in Woodside and sent home for our Christmases. It was she, and not my mother, who had courageously broken the silence surrounding the alcoholism in her own family. And the night my brother Tom was born, she confronted my father, who was well on, in the hallway: "Tommie, Sue would not like what you're doing on this day of all days." He brushed aside her protests and continued on his way, accepting a lift out to the Golf Club bar. My aunt argued with Terry in a phone call about whether I should convalesce in a nursing home, adamant that I should, using her trump card of, "Well, he's my nephew." Through that founding statement, which named a familial tie that to her credit she has maintained, my aunt was also posing the question of who Terry was, of what he was, what relationship he had with me, and goading him into giving her the opportunity of continuing on the conversation so that she could rob him of any validity.

Terry had visited me every day for the fourteen days I was in hospital and spent until late in the evening with me, bringing me little containers of chopped fruit to eat and yoghurts, flavoured waters, anti-bacterial wipes, anything that could help me and show me that I was loved. Now it was my champion who needed to be minded: even the quiet refuge that has been our home had turned against him, and the plumbing had come out in sympathy with my own. The cylinder in the hot press had burst open, and the water was pouring out. Terry was in bed when he heard the commotion, and he got up to see water gushing, flooding and spreading unremittingly over the floor. It had destroyed all of the towels and the linen, and was soaking into the carpets in all of the rooms. Terry was demented. But he organised a plumber, the insurance and new Irish from Latvia and Poland, who arrived with big machines to hoover up the water and enormous fans to dry out the carpets. When I arrived home from hospital, I was marooned in the bedroom, because there were huge hillocks of carpet being dried up every-where else about the apartment. Barbara arrived to muck in and carried six black sackloads of clothes off down to the laun-derette in Monkstown. She too has suffered dispossession through an *aguisín le huacht,* a codicil to a will. Terry and I can empathise with her bravery in continuing on regardless.

Out of respect for my aunt's long-standing kindness and rather than open himself up to defending his essential role as loving partner in my life, which still has neither legal status nor protection under the law, Terry was forced to say, "I'm termi-nating this phone call," in order not to hurt an elderly woman who is now in the frontline facing death as well. Predictably, the phone rang and rang, harassing him for the rest of the evening. But my aunt apologised humbly for her obtrusive out-burst a week later.

The suffering, while mostly bearable in any given half hour, was constantly present, and it has worn me down. Like truth, it's a layering, a stalagmite built from continual dripping. My testicles are sore, and particularly the tip of my penis, exquis-itely painful as if I jerked the tube by mistake. There's been this massive assault upon my sexuality which has turned can-cerous, so that doctors have had to go into my abdomen and pluck it out at the root, discarding the rest of my body like the rejected skin of a banana. I see now that the assault had begun, very many years ago.

Nothing in my life has been saved, to be considered of value. I just have these words with no sound, which I continue to type on to a screen. The repetition is soothing. I save them over and over, accumulating words that furnish within the dumb despair of their configuration an external distraction from feelings of futility. They pour out easily: I see hurt words to do with damage, certainly assault, hitting with force, words ostensibly inspired by the violence of cancer.

Twenty years ago I was at my brother's on Christmas day. My nephew was four years old, and he knelt at a stool with his back to the room, looking out through the glass sliding doors into the safety of the empty garden. And he played there with his Lego for the whole day, unmoving, solitary, while the adults' Christmas went on in the background. They tell me these days of emotional distress have to be gone through, before I too can venture through the glass screen and yoke myself to the words, inhabit them if ever it becomes safe to do so, in a garden where the protection that peace gives will no longer increase the awareness of pain, and emptiness will be a boon, flowering out of the dead earth like the surprising spring crocus, a harbinger of nature's renewal in which I too can find lodgings.

Part Sixteen: Three Women

Confirmation is a rite that admits a person who's been immersed in the mystery of God's love to full participation in the community to which he belongs. The ceremony also contains the ritual of manumission, *e manu mittere,* when the bishop strikes a candidate with his hand to free that person from servitude and send them forth. I returned from a short break in Spain four weeks after my operation for cancer to be the sponsor for my godchild at her confirmation. Terry had wanted me to stay on in Spain, but I pointed out that apart from her baptism, this was the only formal fathering duty I had to perform for my niece, and I wanted to fulfil it. So before coming home, we drove down into Gibraltar with Anna, our Danish friend who's lived in Spain for the past thirty years, and chose a delightful white watch as a confirmation gift.

Anna was adopted as a child, chosen and wanted. She's now a good-looking woman in her early forties, who dresses casually in shirts, slacks and cashmere sweaters. She has a gentleness about her that men still covet and try to take advantage of, but her cool exterior is animated by an astute mind that shines through her honey-brown eyes, which her generous heart can sometimes overrule. Like many of the women I know, Anna draws exuberantly on wells of youthful energy.

She was there at the apartment when we arrived and when we were leaving, to manhandle our cases up and down the steps: "Stop – you have stitches inside – you are not to bloody well do it!" Last summer she took possession of sixty huge palm trees, and she dug the hard Spanish ground around her property herself and planted each one of them into the red earth to form a guard of honour along her driveway. She lives in a modernist villa of wood and brick and glass, a Frank Lloyd Wright type of building, built over several levels, and which is unique in the south of Spain. Anna loves that house, and she has filled it with antiques, with art and with original pieces she has begged and bartered and bought.

"The taxman came to visit," she said delightedly, "and I'd no money in my account. He said, 'Where is all the money?' And I said I use it to live. And he didn't see that the dusty old table that he was writing on was seventeenth-century Spanish, and cost two million pesetas."

Anna had visited us in Dublin to lend support shortly after my operation, and Terry arranged for a friend of his, Mary MacEvaddy, to show Anna around her Irish home on the north side of the city, a Georgian mansion that Mary had restored.

"Micheal," she said, "you're looking remarkably well. I've been keeping up with your news from Terry, and I hear you've been through the mill."

Mary is a warm, giving woman, elegant, who wears couture and teeters about in the highest of heels. She's a busy entrepreneur, but that afternoon she gave us an Irish welcome with buttered wads of crumbling brown soda bread that she'd taken the time to bake for us, covered in layers of Howth smoked salmon. We walked the avenue banked with cheering daffodils, where she'd planted upwards of ten thousand bulbs.

"Didn't you know that I was once a farmer?"

Mary's husband is a Mayoman from Foxford, who told us the story of the massive Cuban mahogany dining table, at which the Talbot brothers had breakfasted on the morning of the battle of the Boyne and on which they were laid out by sunset. For dinner that evening in Anna's honour, Mary had chosen to wear an Irish tweed suit, whose rough earthiness was contrasted with the femininity of lace, barely visible within the pleats of the skirt. I asked for her observations on the Mayo people she's met down the years. By way of illustration, she shyly described to us a fellow townsman who hasn't spoken to his wife for the past twenty years, but who takes communion every Sunday.

"I think people from Mayo are concerned about appearances," she proffered across the table.

"Not to hear, not to see, and above all, not to say?"

"Precisely."

"But Mary," I argued, "those are the responses of a colonised people: 'To hell or to Connacht.' With good reason they've been fearful of taking their rightful place under the sun."

Anna was puzzled beside me at the serious turn in the conversation, so I explained to her how Catholic-owned land was confiscated by the English general, Cromwell, in the mid-seventeenth century and given to Protestant Scottish and English settlers, and that the defeated Irish were given the choice of death or of a new life of dispossession in their own country in the poorer province of Connacht. I warmed to my argument: "Anyway, in the Irish language the subject of a sentence is often hidden, and that's the language in which we still think: English is just an approximation, and we use it like that. But the piece which isn't visible, which is held in reserve, is the most valuable piece of the Mayo psyche, because it's in that silence that the truth of the subject speaks – I'm sounding like a pompous psychoanalyst, amn't I?" To laughter, I turned to Anna and said over the hubbub, "But you can see how such a complicated relationship with language – what's said and what's not said, both at the same time, and how we Irish speak in one language while thinking and meaning in another – how that facilitates dissent."

"What is Irish like?" asked Anna.

"It's a language based on being: having really doesn't agree with us."

Sitting bolt upright, Mary looked at me from the other side of the table, and I could see her evaluating for a moment, and then, "I grant you that," she said, nodding imperceptibly. Mary is a wise Irishwoman.

I remember when we climbed the cool, shaded steps under the sheltering blue and white tiled roof of the Chapelle du Rosaire of the Dominican nuns in Vence, conceived in his mind by an aging Matisse in the year that I was born, and entered into truth. It's a very tiny chapel, just fifteen metres long by six metres wide, shaped like an upside-down L, with the altar block in *pierre de rogne*, which has the texture of bread, angled in the corner and the nun's choir off to the left, the whole of the creation shining with light. There are two elements: colour in the stained-glass windows and black drawing on the white, ceramic tiles. Behind the altar depicted in glass is the tree of life, the cactus, the symbol of endurance, and it predominates. The paddle-like blooms of the flowers are lemon yellow, frosted and translucent. The stems are bottle green against an ultramarine blue sky, both colours clear and transparent. To the right, larger than life size, is a simple line drawing of St Dominic, but without the features of a face. We knelt there about five summers ago, sweating in the heat. As we contemplated the window, the hot Mediterranean sun burst through, projecting on to us colours of crimson and mauve, bathing us in ochre. And at once we were transfigured by the lightness of touch to become infinitely more than mere vegetal survivors in a desert. We were the live participants in a vision created by Matisse, the master.

"So this is what he meant," I whispered to Terry, and we were awestruck.

"It's good for us to be here," he smiled back.

I moved up to the altar and greeted St Dominic face to face, old friend that he was. He hung in the air like a dancer ascending, just above the ground as if slightly removed, his father's face looking to the left, filling out in an unbroken line of succession, his large left hand clasping the good news marked with a cross to his breast. It was striking that Matisse didn't see him with a right hand. My reflection superimposed itself on the glaze of the white tiles, and once more it was I, standing on terra firma, who was wearing the habit of Br Dominic.

That warm evening in the south of France as I wheeled into the kitchen balancing some empty dishes from the candle-lit dining table out on the terrace, Mary was turning around from the oven, and we met across the island as she laid down the baking dish holding a large sea bass, *un loup de mer,* the hound of the sea, *muir cú,* that she'd cooked in our honour. She's a beautiful woman, and she inhabits her lithe body as if making an entrance, and her big eyes are brown. "Michael," she said, "I want you to know how much it means to me to have you here in my home in the south of France. I've known the warmth of your voice so much over the years that you're like an old friend to me. And I'm delighted to be able to cook for you and Terry."

The gift of herself, a divine grace we celebrated over a meal of bread and wine, and a delicate, firm-fleshed fish from the Mediterranean that carries within itself the Murphy name: truly, it was a holy communion and also a valued verification of belonging.

We'd brought Mary a plumbago, whose pastel-blue flowers have always welcomed us into our home in Spain and which Monsieur Ted planted by Mary's doorway the next morning. As we stood in the garden and chatted about the plants he'd tended over many seasons, he revealed to me that he doesn't work outside, just inside where nobody from his village can see him. From the shock of my expression, he registered that I not only understood his dilemma, but that I could sympathise. He was suddenly embarrassed and muttered something about a private arrangement with Mary. I moved to rescue the situation.

"How valuable that is," I said, "to tend to a garden which is internal and which one only shows to people who are chosen. I'd be honoured if you would show me around."

And the gardener became a guide, leading me along unseen paths, pointing out his favourites among the many generous plants in Mary's garden. We stood side by side in a moment of fellow feeling, at one with the exuberant vegetation, listening to silence in the chirruping of flitting birds, the crickets, bells from St Paul de Vence. Then I shook his hand that was rough from manual labour, and we said *au revoir* each to the other, and I went out through the gates of the house and walked up into the village.

I rang Helen, that heartfelt friend from Spain, and told her that we were going to be in Gibraltar with Anna if she cared to meet up.

"Oh Michael, I would love to. Shall we meet halfway up the Rock?"

We sat out on the terrace of the Rock Hotel beneath the palm trees in somewhat faded colonial splendour and were served tea and hot scones with lashings of cream and strawberry jam as we watched the British paratroopers leap from an aeroplane circling in the blue sky and practice their jumps into

Algeciras Bay. It was Anna's treat. She'd just got her cheque for half of a debt, so it was a celebration, because we were meeting Helen for the first time in many months and had just bought the perfect watch for my young niece.

Helen lives very simply, gloriously, out in the *campo,* and her skin was brown from the sun. She's been advised not to put dyes in her hair, which deeply upsets her. We were chatting about cancer and the various effects it has, because Helen has had that cancerous tumour on the brain, Anna is recovering from breast cancer, and I was just over the prostatectomy operation. Both women agreed that life after cancer was completely different.

"There was a time I was so bored with life that I did a parachute jump."

"Did you, Helen?"

"Yes, in London, to kick start me into being, but not any more. Each day is a blessing."

Anna hesitated. "Always in the background there's a ticking clock. And I take it one day at a time," she said thoughtfully.

"Different half hours," I murmured, and it sounded quite depressed.

Helen rubbed my arm. "You'll get there."

And as we were leaving, descending the steps to reception, Helen lifted out from her capacious bag a plastic bottle.

"Michael, this is noni juice from Polynesia, and I want you to take it back to Ireland with you – can you do that? – and take one tablespoonful every day. It tastes vile, so you should cut it with orange juice. It's filled with vitamins and minerals, everything you need to make you well."

In honour of Our Lady of Solitude, whose tear-stained statue clothed in cream and scarlet I saw in a side chapel of the crumblingly baroque Iglesia de San Pedro up in Priego de

Cordoba, I ritually swallowed a tablespoon of this awful liquid at the kitchen sink every morning for a month. And although the taste was ugly, I was grateful that these three extraordinarily honourable women criss-cross the darkened rooms of my life with their concern, *deá-chroí,* good-hearted women who continue to weave with light from silver lanterns a hammock of support. Mary had brought me a body lotion with grape polyphenols from the south of France, "Your skin gets very dry with the medication, and this will neutralise the free radicals," she said, standing in the hall, immaculate, offering once more.

When I walked down the aisle in the Church of the Sacred Heart in Donnybrook, formal suit over the incontinence pad, I was met by my brother John, who said, "Mike, only family are allowed in the centre-aisle seats. But if you like, I'll sit with you in the side aisle." He went on to explain that his daughter's sponsor would be her eldest brother, who was sitting staring straight ahead beside her in the seat. I urged him to rejoin his family, and I took up my position elsewhere.

Part Seventeen: Recovery

It's the brightness that first astounds you in Spain. The quality of the light, particularly in those clear days in early March where the umbrella pines look painted on to the blue skies, is intense, as if at any moment the weight of the sky's pigment could slide and crumple on to the tops of the supportive trees. The gnarled, criss-cross pattern of the cork oak branches, green leaves dappled *sol y sombra*, sun and shade, frame panes of glittering blue cut glass, so that the grove where we descend the steps to our apartment becomes an outdoor church, alive with God's spirit.

La Mairena is located in a designated UNESCO world heritage site of protected forest, at the peak of Elviria's Monte Alto. It's referred to as "The Village Above". The apartment's vast terrace affords breathtaking views of the Mediterranean all the way around from the Sierra de Mijas to the Rock of Gibraltar. The complex was designed by the Chilean architect Melvin Villarroel, who was informed by the shapes and clustering of the *pueblos blancos*, the white villages of Andalusia. Our apartment has a private entrance, and it's open to summer breezes on three sides, so the experience is of living in a bungalow within a glade of tropical foliage, or even in a tree house that looks out over the tops of the Royal Oak pine trees and old-growth

cork trees that plunge in a steep slope to the sea. When Helen
came to visit and overnight with us, lending her support after
the operation, she remarked on the motto *"Dein ist nun das
Land"* which we'd traced out in navy, tiled lettering above the
hall door. The verse comes from a very old, traditional German
hymn, uttered with devotion down the centuries. A literal translation is "Thine is now the land," meaning we've entered into
the kingdom of God: that we've arrived.

Giving her the tour up our end of the coast, we called into
Mijas church as the wind blew fiercely through the massive
terracotta trunks of the palm trees, tearing at the fans of leaves
so that they clacked together in a finger snapping *jaleo,* to say
a Hail Mary and light a candle to the town's patron saint,
Nuestra Senora de la Pena. The church is built on the site of
the former Arab mosque and still has an impressive *Mudéhar*
tower, embodying the fusion of cultures that wash by us every
day in Andalusia. Inside, I was drowning in the silence, a *cante
grande* which turned shrill during those half hours of uncon-
trollable grief. I needed to reach out to her, to find out if the
abyss into which I'd been plunged would one day have some
boundaries and I could arrest my fall, sing *intermedio* and
make some effort at recovery from sorrow. The Virgin herself
resides in a little sanctuary to the side of the town, where she'd
appeared to children. When we called in to say hello to this
tiny figure in beautifully embroidered robes wearing a crown
of gold, there were a dozen freshly cut yellow roses in a vase
before the altar, with a message which I read aloud, left by a
woman on her golden wedding anniversary, in loving memory
of her husband, Terry.

"Oh don't." Helen pleaded, and she shook herself, hand
blocking the mouth, to escape being immersed in the expression of another's sadness at being left solitary. Leaving there,
buffeted by the wind and shining once more in the light of the

sun, she said that she could see herself living in Mijas. Eight years ago, we were christened "*nuevos Mijenos*" by the owner of a local restaurant, who gave a key ring to each of us newly arrived immigrants, with a portrait of *La Virgen de la Pena* engraved on the fob. The first night we'd taken up residence in Casa Alquimia, we'd locked ourselves out into the open air under the stars of heaven. So Mijas has remained our spiritual home, and we choose to live here in Spain at the pleasure of *La Virgen,* gathered safely beneath the folds of her cloak, her azure *cobijo.*

That short break in Spain following the prostatectomy was hard. Terry and I went to Macro in Malaga one afternoon to buy some towels and blankets for the apartment. I heard a scrabbling noise, as if pebbles were falling down behind the plaster in the walls, and then everything began to shake all around me. I hurried outside, and I could see the road ahead rolling up and down in the heat, as if somebody were shaking out a carpet. This was an earthquake.

I told Terry that I didn't think I'd survive the cancer, and I felt that I was going to die. I told him the depression I was experiencing was always held just to one side, and that at times it took centre stage. I didn't know if it was an effect of the operation I'd been through or whether it represented the inevitable truth of the masculine condition that there really is no point to any of it anyway, but I felt it too keenly for that question to be unanswerable. I was reciting a *caoineadh,* a lament at my own wake, and the weight of my words threw Terry into deep mourning. He was very shaken by them, because he didn't feel that there'd be any point in going on without me. Instinctively I patted him on the back, but I was down too deep to have any hope of rising to the surface. The edifice of support that we'd constructed together was collapsing in the liquefaction, and my despair was the cause of that.

The contract between life and me has been sundered, as much by the diagnosis of cancer, which introduces a fatal doubt, as by the invasive operation to remove my prostate, which has left me crazed with shock. I'm experiencing an emotional devastation out of all proportion to what's been done to me, which echoes and reverberates off past injuries. I can no longer trust life to continue on, the way you can be sure that the summer sun will shine in Spain tomorrow and that there'll be more of the blue sky. I've had my prostate gland removed, the surgeon has taken it out and thrown it away, and that's a position beyond rectification or recovery which has left me broken-hearted and incontinent. Every time I touch my penis, a dribble of urine drenches my fingers and soaks my pad. If by some miracle an erection were to occur, the overflow of urine precludes any sexual activity, which also serves to protect me from embarrassment and disgust, but I feel bereft. I've become an untouchable, the lowest caste which deals with the slops. I can enter the dance, a *fandango* or *malaguena*, and try out steps to pull myself together, but I can't obliterate the predicament I'm in: that my black Shadow will also try out another, different set of steps, raising the stakes, and so we go on back and forth with the follow-up hospital visits, back and forth *ad infinitum*. The loss transforms me into the category of being lacking, at constant risk of being judged the fool, of being mocked at by life: "My, that's a damp squib!" And there's no way out of this messy dilemma, which goes to the root of being a real man, of having lead in your pencil, and I don't measure up. I've no validity left.

The bill for another box of incontinence pads was €208 at the chemist, so I rang the local health centre in Stillorgan one Friday I was off recuperating. The nurse said to drop by, that she would help if she could. I stood in front of the receptionist and explained that my name was Michael Murphy and that

I'd just been on about the incontinence problem, but I couldn't remember the name of the woman I was talking to.

"Would it be Joan?" She rang Joan, and Joan appeared.

"I rang about the incontinence problem."

"Yes?"

"Was I talking to you?"

"No, I don't think so. Maybe you were talking to Beatrice?" Scottish accent. "He might have been talking to Beatrice."

The receptionist rang Beatrice: "Do sit down. Michael, while you're waiting."

There was a painter painting the door with slow strokes, up and down, who never took his eyes off the door.

"I've Michael Murphy here about an incontinence problem. Was he talking to you?" They had leaflets about prostate cancer up in a rack on the wall. Beatrice made an appearance.

I stood up. "Hello, I'm Michael Murphy, I rang you about the incontinence problem."

"I'm delighted to meet you, Michael." She shook my hand and I felt that she meant it. "Now, Michael, I haven't come across this problem before, but if I can help, I certainly will. We'll go down to this office through here." And she led the way. When we were installed, she said, "D'you mind if I fill out this form, Michael? Name . . . Date of birth . . . Nature of the problem, Michael . . . Next of kin?" I was intimately involved with a stranger, and all control was gone.

"Prostate cancer . . . Incontinence . . ." The details of my life were delivered in stark words, gilded by my voice. They hung in the air, like overseeing cherubs in a baroque basilica, in order to get a few free incontinence pads. Oh God! Oh God! Oh God! On my way out, the painter moved aside to let me pass, and this time as he searched my face we nodded knowingly to each other. I was carrying a black plastic goody bag overflowing with incontinence pads and the telephone number of a continence adviser in Dr Steeven's Hospital, whom I had had to wait for – "I've a gentleman here with an incontinence problem" – but who wasn't at work that day. Kindness from strangers. Oh God! Oh God! Oh God!

I find it strange sitting in the insulated comfort of the Lexus for those afternoon jaunts with Terry as I recover, looking out at people passing purposefully by. I've nothing in common with them any more. I feel like a ghost, living now in that other place beyond death. The wonder is that people take health as a given and can transfer the vigour it gives to them into the passionate soap opera of interactions which make up their lives. Increasingly, like my mother's hesitant reactions on the phone when I forget and touch on something meaningful, the television programme behind the glass seems to have nothing to do with me. Like her I tread on a *fóidín mearaí,* a sod of confusion, and momentarily lose my footing, but I can still see the show going on elsewhere in a black and white blizzard. Perhaps she realises this also, neither of us saying so in a conversation that's both present and absent. Maybe the momentous happening of cancer had already laid hold of me in that other arena of not being in my twenties any more. Sometime over the past year or so, when I stood at a Londis shop counter in the Sandyford Industrial Estate waiting to be served, I was continually passed over by the young, female shop assistant. She had a blank spot in her eye with which I corresponded. Instead of me, there was absence. I'd become a ghost. The Greeks have a word for it: *eidolon,* the hollow image.

Part Eighteen: My Mother

It was nineteen minutes past three of a Friday evening in Longford in the rain, and we were caught in the line of traffic heading west for the Patrick's weekend. Sheets of mist were driving by the gloomy mass of the cathedral, as new Irish laden with Lidl bags wrestled with the wind. When we crossed the Mayo border at Carracastle, Terry gave a "Yahoo – up May-oooh!" I looked at him. With twinkling eyes he pointed out it was sedate and decorous, in keeping with this moment of recovery: "a little restrained, but nothing fancy!"

The wildness of the scenery in the low, slanting March light through racing clouds, the yellow colours of the sedges, the furze, the open expanse from Neiphin Mountain on the right, Croagh Patrick straight ahead, the vastness of this empty plain of the yew trees on a sky road grazed by mist in the approach to Castlebar quickened my heart like the massed spring daffodils. I was also apprehensive, because this weekend was the first time I'd been home to Mayo since the operation, and it'd also be an opportunity to reconnect with Mum and to assess how her situation was progressing.

When Fintan, my youngest brother, arrived into the Mall, he'd a great welcome for me. He shook my hand and immediately referred to me as the *"pater familias,"* classic words descended from Indo-European. It was unexpected to see myself through his eyes. He explained to the fourth Thomas, our nephew, who hadn't studied Latin, nor had he heard it spoken in his short lifetime, that I was "the father of the family"! It was as though I were impelled into the spotlight as ambassador, a stand-in for my dead father. So we stood around the large mahogany dining table in the kitchen that later had seated the seven of us with three further places to be occupied, and I was hearing a version of myself being carried to my nephew through Fintan's words.

I exercised a protective, fathering function towards Fintan as a child. I remember the many times that I hooshed the *íochtar* up the back garden and out through the Green Bay Café into Flannery's field and safety to spare him beatings from my father: we've those in common. But I've no children, so I don't share with my brother on a daily basis the overwhelming, emotional experience of what it means to be a father. Now prostate cancer has interfered with the natural order, and definitively removed from me all future possibilities of generation. Nonetheless, he sees me occupying the symbolic function of father, inscribed in a patrilineal line of male descent. It's of a cultural order, as opposed to that of nature, mother to son, and I'd always regarded myself as a sort of cultural attaché to the family, because of living in the house next door. How odd a feeling to be a "*père-version,*" as the French say, with its overtones of being awry, of being turned the wrong way: left-handed. Fintan had acknowledged me as head of the household, despite being gelded. The *pater familias* had a greater freedom to act in Roman law, not granted to others, because the head of the household was free of parental guidance. He was considered to have come into his own freedom and was therefore a real man, *monus*, meaning the creature that possesses the continuity of remembrance.

When I rang Tom to say hello, he told me over the phone that he and his wife Mary had just finished cleaning the house on the Mall because my mother had got rid of the third home help. He sounded burdened. I surmise that Mum's difficulties with another woman in her home have to do with that replacement housekeeper who unexpectedly arrived into her childhood, indecently soon after the death of her mother. But when she again praised Tom and Mary later that evening for the work they did that day, I impatiently retorted, "They had to clean the house, Mum, because you got rid of the cleaner." She looked bewildered, and I could see that cause and effect, since it involves the future, no longer exist for her, and I deeply regretted the sudden eruption of my guilty resentment, which has become as pointless as the unremembered past, a past which never happened.

She returned to the subject again and again, but because I didn't know the names of these women either, I couldn't explain to her what I was talking about, so the both of us were lost in the cold blizzard of a nonsensical world of my own making, where the futile direction of the residual words just made matters worse. It was a frustrating and humbling experience, and it gave me a lacerating glimpse of how important the currency of memory is. She didn't mention to me again the subject of the home help, but I'd seen in her eyes that she was stricken by my remark, a hurting which was as incomprehensible to her as the lonely and baffling world in which she now finds herself living.

No sexual relationship following the prostatectomy will be a loss, although I didn't talk with my brothers about the limits that have now been reached; everybody just wants me to get well. I feel neutral about not being able to perform an action that has reconciled me to life and that was a compensation for the eternal lack in my being. When I revisit those sentences, judgements handed down, and begin to live continuously within them, I find that it's the future tense which has become irrelevant. Present time absorbs me fully, almost like a child for whom talk of an envisaged future belongs to the insight of parental speculation. Cancer has clarified the otherness of that future, which was definitively excised by the surgeon's knife at the moment that he cut away my cancerous prostate. Similarly, the guarantee of ongoing meaning within the family conversation that my mother's interest and the archive of her memory underpinned has evaporated. The future arrived for her one day in her eighties, and she too began to live in the present time of a beyond. Many times she'll turn to me across the dining table and ask, "Have I done everything, Michael?" It's a question to do with the writing of her will and the distribution of the silver, the furniture of her life and her money, which has escaped from her comprehension entirely. Latterly she's only concerned with the few notes and coins in the three purses which keep disappearing from the drawer in the kitchen as she loses them to various leather handbags.

"You've done everything, Mum," I answer, touching her shoulder or grasping her cold hand to reassure her with my warmth, not yet ebbing.

But I also hear the wider question in her confession, and I understand too well the unanswerable predicament of asking forgiveness of God for what she's failed to do. In his place I ache to relieve the quavering anxiety of this elderly woman and to tell her truthfully that, "You've done more than enough in your life, Mum, to earn an unstinting absolution." But her powerful question accesses directly that internal room from my childhood, a place seething with pain, and I remember her betrayal of me in relation to her husband, and I feel rage once again as the kitchen goes up in flames. It's not a question of seeing my father as a rival for her affection. I want to reproach her with my own question as to how she could have given me up for an adoption by my grandmother next door. In moments of lucidity, I surmise that maybe it was the only means she had of protecting me, and in the way that she upheld the law of the father, which from a child's experience I knew to be murderous, she was making sure that I'd survive to enjoy the future that she was handing on, in the only manner that was possible for her at the time and that he'd agree to. And now she's asking me to forgive her.

Mum was in great spirits, though. She's become extremely tractable. When we went over to The Creel in Westport for lunch, I asked her about her "classes" as she calls them, where she goes to the Alzheimer's Care Society three days a week. She said she likes them, and that Tom brings her down and brings her back, and that the meal is always very good. They got a piano for her, although it needs to be tuned. "And they know all the Irish songs from the book that John got me for Christmas." It surprises me how much I'm attuned to her. I'd helped her into the restaurant; she was leaning on to me for shelter against the wind while Terry parked the car. When he entered with his walking stick, a whack of wind snatched the door out of his hand and slammed it shut. He said we both turned and looked at him with identical expressions: you don't make noise.

"I didn't make the noise – the door did!" he yelled at us, and he sat down annoyed, poking his stick on to the fourth chair so that it fell off and clattered on to the tiled floor. I picked it up for him and tried to humour him with a grin. I've inherited a lot of my mother's attitudes and ways of looking at the world. I see expressions on her face against pain that I'd use, ways of breathing. And I've a constant fear that she be not discommoded, which is not just to do with her age: a knot in my stomach, a negative, hand gesture of the palm flat to the floor, chopping it sideways. Over the years I've got much better at dealing with that devastation. I remember Fr Finnegan, the Jungian analyst, telling me that he'd a ring on his finger that he used to twist, just to steady himself and give him a breathing space in his mother's company. What must it have been like for me as a child whenever I returned from my granny's, eyes popping out of my head, curling a lock of my hair at my forehead, scanning the room like a satellite receiver for the mood, for an area of safety and freedom from hidden landmines.

The clouds hung low down on Croagh Patrick, and the sea was a tawny colour, choppy in the wind, as we continued on past Lecanvy over to Old Head. She asked a few times who was singing, and I said Cecilia Bartoli: track one "*Il tenero momento*", the tender moment, the prize of so much love. After a particularly difficult passage in which Bartoli invested the vocal line with deep emotion, displaying wonderful breath control, "Isn't she marvellous," she exclaimed. We pulled up on the pier. There were two brave souls walking the beach way over in the distance, so we sat in the car and watched the waves splash on to the rocks and up the sand. The tide was in. "Oh look at those . . ." she said, indicating towards the horizon with a crooked finger, "what d'you call them?"

"Buoys."

". . . bobbing in the water." She was silent, and we listened to the trio: track nine "*Soave sia il vento*", may the wind be gentle, may the waves be calm. She turned around to me in the back seat, wonderingly. "Is that Mozart?"

"Yes, Mum." Very soon now the tide will be on the turn.

Terry drove us down to the evening mass, and the polished benches in the Church of the Holy Rosary were surprisingly empty for Patrick's Day, washed with the light spilling out from the sanctuary. The smell was the familiar mixture of beeswax from burning candles with a touch of incense. The gleaming white marble of the high altar was bare of flowers during this Lenten season, and the statues were draped in the purple cloths that Pat Jordan, the sacristan, would grumblingly cover them in using tall ladders, so that I wasn't able to recall them or decide which was which from the shape of their disguise: St Joseph, or maybe the Sacred Heart? But though it was a surprise, the sight was familiar, and there was a comfort in the way that its predictability reminded me of the satisfied expectations. We knelt into the seat, which we had to ourselves, two thirds of the way down the centre aisle, opposite the stained glass window of St Dominic in the left bay. The magic ritual of changing tenses in the liturgical seasons, the priest wearing silk vestments of green this morning and a purple chasuble tonight, the ceremonies that I knew by heart from having participated in them down the years and from having served them on those altar steps as a boy, still have the power to evoke awe and to console. Today was Laetare Sunday, a joyful, sweet-filled moment in the bleak season of penitence. The powerful voice of the parish priest rolling off the altar like wind-blown clouds off the Atlantic; his English warm with western intonations, pronunciations, swept us along. He presented for our reflection the ideals contained in what he termed "perhaps the greatest gospel story, the parable of the Prodigal Son, the sinner who's welcomed back unconditionally into his home by the father who loves him (while the elder brother holds back, and doesn't go inside in the house to celebrate) because" and he quoted the gospel, " 'this son of mine was dead and has come back to life; he was lost and is found,' " roundly off the tongue.

Jesus had no father and desperately tried to place himself, position himself in relation to the silence, the absence, the gap, the paradox, the fading, the hole, the chasm, the abyss, the rupture, the fracture. He must have been terrified, hoping against hope that God might hear, drowning in his own blood, without the heavens opening in a yellow gash across the magenta sky and the mighty right hand of the Father like a thunderbolt reaching down to pluck him off the cross and massage him back to life between thumb and forefinger, kneading the raised figure on the cross at the end of a rosary beads, covering over the statue with his purple imprint. The ghastly horror of the suffocation, the obliteration, the ebbing away of hope. The Father had no intention of coming to the aid of his son. I trailed my mother up the aisle for communion and received the host into my hand from Fr Curran, then steered her frail figure back to the seat. My prayer of thanksgiving was for the inestimable value that she's still with us, kneeling quietly beside me before an empty, Lenten tabernacle.

I put Mum sitting at the piano, and my brother Tom did a duet with her on the high notes as she rattled off the songs on her list, starting with "Roll Out the Barrel" and "Side by Side". We all tried to sing "The Robin's Return" ("Doodle-idyll doodle-idyll doodle-idyll doodle-idyll dum dum dum dum dumb!"), but we couldn't quite get it on the second round of doodle-idylls; "Harbour Lights", and what was an Al Jolson medley: "Toot-Toot Tootsie Goodbye", "Swannee", "California Here I Come". I reminded her that she rewrote the words of "California" for a Christmas pantomime that she accompanied with the orchestra down in the Town Hall: "Welcome to our pantomime, at this happy New Year's time . . ." That year I played Sukie, the cat: it was *Dick Whittington*. We sang along, Terry reading the paper at the kitchen table and me taking some photographs of the proceedings. At one stage Mum did a right-hand flourish up the piano and nearly toppled over. There was general hilarity as we joked about Tom constructing a wooden railing to keep her upright: "I still have the carpenter's set I got from Santy out in the garage."

She appeared puzzled by one song on her list, and asked, "What's 'Galway Bay'?"

"A place or state of rest where some souls suffer for a time, before . . ." I contributed, recalling the Old Green Catechism definition of purgatory. We laughed out loud with the surprise, and it obviously connected with her, because she had to hold her head in her hands with mirth; she couldn't speak for the laughing: "Ohhh, I have to go to the toilet." And we howled with laughter. There was a similar occurrence at a harbour restaurant in Cabopino when she was out on holidays in Spain with Terry and me. For dessert they presented her with an enormous Knickerbocker Glory topped off with paper umbrellas and sparklers. Everyone was laughing at the joy of it, and I said, "We had a great night – we got sick an' everything." The photographs show her helpless with laughter. We even had to try and explain the joke to the English party at the next table: lost in translation.

I came into the kitchen at around a quarter to eleven prior to going up to bed, and Mum was distracted at the table with a handbag. "I've no money," she said. "I keep money in this handbag and I don't have it."

"You got your pension the other day, and you've over a hundred, Mum."

"But I always had money in this bag before. If I wanted to go and get my hair done . . ." She was distressed. The car had left the road, suddenly.

"Tom knows where it is – he told me. So we'll ask him tomorrow when he comes in."

"He told you?"

"Yes he did, Mum, and he told me that you have over a hundred."

"Maybe there's no need to ask him so." Please don't tell him.

"I assure you, Mum, that there's money. It's probably upstairs, and we'll get it in the morning. Look, I'll go up now and I'll get your red tablet, and you can take it before we go to bed. Is that all right? And I'll bring up your glass of water for you."

"Why should I take a tablet?"

"The tablet isn't for you, Mum, it's for Tom – to keep him from getting cranky."

We dissolved into laughter, recognising his conscientiousness as her primary carer.

Back in Dublin, I woke with a dream about me being on top of a deep blue lorry in a depot that had yellow writing all along its side, making an impossible effort at crawling towards the front to escape through some lid, it seemed like. Death was there invading the bedroom, in his cloak and hood, unmoving. Shortly after Terry left for work, I got up, took off the incontinence pad, showered, put on the day one and had breakfast. About an hour later in the kitchen, Death reached forward with icy fingers which went in through my chest wall, and he grasped my heart in his right hand, holding it firmly. It was horrifying and a shock. Nothing was said between us, but Death was looking at me as my heart pulsed in his hand. I remembered the surgeon's words that the cancer "was attached", and I understood for the first time that there was every likelihood, there was every certainty, that the cancer will show up again one day. I would have to ask the surgeon a question about this when I met him on Monday morning next. It was no longer a matter of a feeling, but of fact, devoid of speculation. Death rearranged his bony fingers, and ever so slightly he massaged my heart, ruminatively. With no feeling he reversed his arm out of my chest and held on to my heart like a priest holding a chalice. I could see it beating in his grasp. Later in the morning when I was working with analysands, I realised the hand was no longer there and that the hooded figure was on the far side of the room, head bowed, still. Different half-hours. Was I able for this? Or so bone weary and fatigued, not really able to pack up the laptop and carry it and the case and walk out in the rain, even though Terry had left an umbrella beside my jacket, to stand at the bus stop for it to take me home?

The first meeting with David Mulvin was arranged for a quarter past eight. He'd just come back from a consultant's meeting in Europe where they'd talked about the same operation and the different rates of healing among their patients. He felt I should be further along in the continence stakes, but obviously the urinary tract infection would set back the healing. The sphincter was lazy and is now having to do work that the prostate previously helped with. And he referred me on to a physiotherapist, who'd help in showing me how to get those pelvic floor muscles working. When he was writing the note, I asked him about the word "attached". At first he didn't understand what I meant, but he looked at his notes and saw that a tumour at the right posterior was attached to the outer layer of the prostate. I remembered he'd told me that he got as much of the prostate as he possibly could, and he now offered assurance that he expected me to see at least fifteen years free from cancer. Our friend Donal, a financier, had warned us to listen for the magical number "fifteen years", which was the immortal figure from an actuarial table, signifying of great age.

Terry was with me, and he underlined what was said: "Are you relieved?" In the car afterwards I told Terry that I hadn't heard David say that.

"He said it twice, Michael."

"So keep March the twenty-sixth free, fifteen years hence, is that it?"

"What do you mean?"

"2022 is the date of my death: I'll be seventy-four." I reflected that a discreet change had occurred, which I hadn't felt happening, but I was resting differently inside. David wrote out a prescription to help with the ongoing bladder problems, shook hands and said he'd set up a meeting in three months' time, for which I should come prepared with the prostate specific antigen test results from a blood sample. That meeting would be at the end of June, six months from the time that I had the radical prostatectomy and one year since the whole process had begun.

Part Nineteen: Artistry

There's a simple, vaulted window which gives on to my world in Spain. It frames the blackened upper branches of a Royal Oak tree, gnarled with crusty lichens. The cascade of small green leaves interspersed with the occasional yellow one undulates ceaselessly before such a luminous pale blue sky that at times the picture appears monochrome, a chiaroscuro, and becomes the blinding fretwork of glass which speckled Nasrid kings amidst the darkened salons of the Alhambra palace. Then my spirit flows out through those pinpoints of light to play in the kingdom of the wind, sharpened with the shock of snow from the Sierra Nevada. I tumble and twist, soaring like an eagle on the thermals of rising air, then free-fall with outstretched arms until it comes time to repeat the cycle. And the wind is whispering to me over and over, "I have always remembered . . ."

Out of the blackness, myriads of words like ghostly beings appear, and I can recognise huddled together their families, the etymologies that have been moulded by all of them over the centuries and shall continue to mould their descendants on into the future. They're the stars strewn across the night skies firing rapidly, then dying successively. But the breadth and the depth of this vision of eternity astonishes me. And I too am

being illuminated, a participant in the wind's mighty kaleido-
scopic display. I'm writing those shining words as they arrive,
but there's a stronger sense that I'm the one who's going to be
given written expression here, a voice transposed into the
heightened, harsher Spanish daylight, words to be whittled
away to the clouds of dust blown about by the cutting levanter,
but which make the thinness of the wind become visible.

The storytelling speech that I learned from my mother –
"Once upon a time . . ." – cradled on her knee with a book
which she held open in her hands, out among the wildflowers
and bees in the sunshine of our back garden, following the
words as she voiced the fairy tales of the first Danish person
who had my trust, Hans Christian Andersen, enabled me to
make sense of my world through naming, placing, inventing
and setting free my imagination. Words wove a *ciseán,* a wick-
er basket, protective strands which swirled about me in the
beaks of the active, colourful little finches that fly and swoop,
interweaving within the forest of bright green trees outside the
curved windows of the eyrie where I write, their spirit linking
heaven and earth, redolent of both: *entre el cielo y la tierra.*
But they also set up an unconditional trust in the imaginative
reality I was experiencing, constructed out of printed words
animated by the pouring flow of my mother's intonation, and
which relied on the warmth of a lap to buoy me up. This was
the font where I learned to believe without question in the
well-wishing of others and in the immediate truth of their
words.

The limits of my language are the limits of my world,
according to Wittgenstein, who lived in Ireland for a while, so
he too was held in the embrace of the comfortable, warm tones
of Irish voices. That's why Irish is so important to me as a language, because it names from my immediate environment
what otherwise wouldn't exist and contributes nuances of

meaning which catch the alternation of light and shade in the Mayo countryside from scudding clouds blown by westerlies. I also like German as a language, because the sense is in the construction: you add bits on like Lego. Freud could overhear in his consulting rooms what wasn't being said in the way that the words and sentences were put together, a skill that I've developed for English within the *temenos* of the psychoanalytic session. I like French for its analytical precision. The French verb *manier* means to model or fashion with the hand, and that's what I do with the building blocks of words: I can construct a spiritual safe house with words where I can belong without being constantly called out.

The writing of this book and the calling on the rich European heritage of words that it evokes is the taking possession at long last of an architectural masterpiece, whose foundations were hollowed out for me once upon a time in a Mayo garden by my mother. These days, when we stroll companionably beneath the leafy chestnut trees around the Mall and she's bothered, lost for words, it is I who hand them back to her, so that our conversation can be carried on for just that little bit longer, before she finally retreats inside and closes the hall door for ever, draining my past of relevance. Bathed in the autumn gold of her spirit, which has begun to flicker and fall to earth with the onset of the chill winds, crumbling to dust underfoot, I understand that I'd been commissioned to build that masterpiece in the long-distant past. We stop to rest and laugh heartily together at a deft caricature of one of my brothers. I bend down and examine the lifetime of service etched into the furrows on her face. I can see more and more clearly that she's given to me the gift of a living foundation stone, upon which she's traced her signature.

"You really should write a book, Michael," she tells me, acknowledging with her eyes that she'd have a hand in the writing of it. It'd be a book that could be crammed with the words which are abandoning her, words that she could peruse and savour at her leisure, reacquainting herself once more with those friends from a world that has packed up and left without her, puzzling "I don't know anybody in Castlebar any more." It'd be a geography book where she could find in the exuberant child's play of the words' combinations a narrative thread which would lead her back into the centre of the familial labyrinth. It would also be a history book of the dreaming spirit in which she could find her place once again, as in the Corpus Christi procession, walking beneath an embroidered canopy of golden words on carpets of strewn rose petals to an altar banked with flowers, lupins, peony roses, constructed at the middle of the Mall. She created me – "This is my body; this is my blood . . ." – so that now I can create her: "In the beginning was the word . . ." It's the carrying forward of an eternal presence on this earth, our turn under the sun, within a myth-making tradition of familial storytelling to which my mother has given her blessing.

This writing, the rolling swell of feeling from my overflowing heart down through my arms into the fingers of my hands, quarantines outside in the bawnogue, in the smallest paddock, the residual cancerous tumours that have been constructed inside me by sixty years of dammed-up internalisation, without ever thinking to vet other people's words. Some of their expressions turned out to be inassimilable foreign bodies that lodged themselves in my prostate, poisoning my being. They've targeted my generative organs and sabotaged my creativity, shaming, humiliating, forbidding, disregarding, belittling, being careless of, withholding and all the while assailing my freedom to be. This is a late expression of my soul that has helped me to stay alive and to grow, expanding and deepening the parameters of my being despite the encroaching cancer of impediments, limits that I admit to having once accepted. Those aspects of this book which sing of innermost things, beautiful things, truth-telling at last, would be suppressed by those who have as much right to breathe God's air as I do, because they judge that my take on life is unacceptable or is too honest, even hurtful to others. Neither do they understand the way that I can move unhindered from one thought to another, as a word or an idea sparks off a feeling, giving to myself the freedom to run away with an emotional layering and speak figuratively, so that the happenings of my past can allegorise the tensions in this present moment as I recover from cancer. My soaring, overarching song should not be heard, or at least be of so high a pitch that only the dogs in the country-side off in Spain are pained by the miracle of it, so that they can howl in unison, street to street, and drown out my voice; an acquiescing surrogate to deflect attention from the deadly silence that always surrounds abusers. You should not, ought not, must not, will not put into words of whatever language what has not yet been spoken, lest something new be created to crawl upon this earth. But I'm saying that the cancer has been a positive catalyst which has propelled me into a beyond of handing back the shame that never belonged to me in the first place, where I no longer have the choice to live a diminished life, confined within the boundaries of a pen which, at the very least, is set by the controlling forbearance of another. Nobody should have to tolerate that abuse for a moment. At last, at long last, I'm able to claim the freedom to become what I always was.

Before Kieran's death from cancer, a battering down of the door in the early morning, a too solid slice of reality which was impossible to stomach, he told me that he was wakened one morning by a crashing about in his front lounge, and he appealed to the guardians of the peace for help. It was a bird that had entered his house by way of the chimney, spreading black soot everywhere: the Morrigan, the war goddess, the battle crow that presages death, the apparition of fate that sits on the shoulder of the dying hero, Cuchulainn, whose statue is in the General Post Office in O'Connell Street.

At that time I'd a dream that my dead father knocked on the door of our house in Rathgar. When I opened the door to him, he was standing there looking younger than I remember, wearing a white raincoat, like in those photographs of Albert Camus, or maybe the coat came from the gangster movies starring Humphrey Bogart, which was Dad's era. I fell back against the wall in shock, but he passed me by going on down the hall, and I crumpled on to the floor with relief. He'd come for somebody, but he passed his eldest son by. With hindsight, I could see and I understood that it wasn't yet my turn, a summons which he'd announce to me one day.

I learned to swim up the lake. There was a rope in the water up from the diving board to prevent us heading towards the swally hole, in whose murky blackness Bernard Brady from Kie's class was drowned. I pushed through the murmuring throng in the hospital morgue, and I saw him laid out flat in a white coffin, unmoving, and his mother was weeping inconsolably over his head, bobbing up and down in the treacherous waters of her grief, trying to raise him, stroking the cow's lick of fair hair at his forehead.

"Holy Mary, mother of God, pray for us sinners, now and at the hour of our death."

The order in words that corresponds to the rope, which keeps me safe within its submerged boundaries, has been intertwined down the centuries by my ancestors on both sides. As a child I could hear them all speaking in the voices of my father and my mother, choosing for them their words, pulling at their accents, contributing colour, a successive shaping like

Michael Roche, the potter, a friend of ours from Enniscorthy, gives to his clay when it's pliable and running with water. If the good manners of the grammar that I know so well are breached, then the world implodes, and as a child I'm at grave risk of being sucked under and clasped by the grasping tentacles of reeds in an adult's embrace, gasping for breath and crying because I don't understand what's happening. If words are misused to hurt, mispronounced, they turn speech inside out, leaving me solitary with the bleakest incomprehension. I've no voice with which to fight back, just bubbles of air that rise to the surface and disperse unseen, signalling to myself that I'm being betrayed. On the other hand, the experience of swimming alone among the drumlin islands in the bluest of water, washed clean with the warmth of Mayo's Hiberno-English pronunciation, the mountains of the Neiphin Beg range and Corraun white at the line of the horizon, then rising blue and fawn in the sun like a renaissance reredos is a triptych: I-er-land. This gives me such rich personal enjoyment in prevailing with the clarity of the enunciation that I lead the De La Salle flageolet band, arms outstretched at the turns, in a triumphant march around the Mall. And yet a man follows along on the footpath by the hotel in a mocking exaggeration of my walk, showing me that I raise my right leg higher than I do my left, like *Bocaidí* Bathgate from Castle Street, who was crippled.

It was Fr Shannon who taught me the Latinate pronunciation in sixth class in the national school: "*Introibo ad altare Dei*".

"*Ad de-um qui lae-ti-fi-cat ju-ven-tu-tem me-am . . .*" and I came first in the class even then, with flawless responses to all of it, winning from him a coloured comic book that explained the liturgical architecture of the mass. I'm unafraid of the broadest, Latinate "a", which the poet, Desmond Egan, uses in his tenderly loving description on the death of his father:

> the night nurse tightening bedclothes
> leaned down to ask is there
> anything you want Tom?
> A fan! I barely caught his last words
> the bottom of that old humour
> its irony partly mocking himself
> Athlone to the bitter end . . .

Donal, who advises us in financial matters, remembers watching me on the television news as a youngster in Dalkey. He was sitting on his hunkers, in a shabby room that was clothed in three different kinds of wallpaper with linoleum on the floor, and his brothers and sisters were watching with him. His mother told him over his shoulder that I'd received an award for reading the *News for the Deaf*. I've always valued what I regarded as the irony inherent in receiving that award. I was a person rewarded for not being heard, for being silent. I was being encouraged to live up to the award, which was given to me for being seen and not heard. It chimed with the injunctions I'd internalised as a child. But I harvested inspiration from those courageous people, who gave me the courage in turn to shoulder the responsibility of making a presence out of absence. I'm grateful for having received an accolade from a group who overtly acknowledge from moment to moment that communication poses challenges. They gave me the confidence to stand over a construction that I can believe in, and that has never let me down when I was allowed the freedom to animate my own response: the laws of language and the privilege of speech.

It was the beard, which was designed by a fellow-Mayoman, Alf O'Reilly from Westport, the head of the Graphic and Design Department in RTÉ, that helped to emphasise my enunciation of the words, making it easier for people who are deaf to understand me. I met him once on the pier at Old Head shortly before he and his Morris Minor disappeared without a trace. Donal used to read the *News for the Deaf*, following me word for word as the printed words went up the screen and disappeared into my chest, so that I incarnated the illustration of how words written by others are incorporated and given back through speech. He said that I resembled the picture of the Sacred Heart, looking down from the wall in the kitchen, which had words written across Him: "The heart of Jesus pleading."

As a child I puzzled over what the word "pleading" meant. I imagined it must be the surname of Jesus. The derivation is from the Latin *placere*, to please, which is what I thought I was doing by being myself as a child. But a deaf ear was turned to the advocate when the Father sacrificed me for the thirty pieces of silver, turning the holy picture to the wall.

"If I give you half-a-crown and send you over to Hanley's for the paper which costs tuppence, what change d'you bring me back?"

The rules of maths! It was a nightly ritual that had no possible ending.

"Answer me."

Terrorised against the wall under the light switch at the far end of the kitchen, hemmed in by his massive bulk as he flayed me with his words, in my panic I was never able to guess the correct form of speech with which to answer what I believed was a bizarre game of chance, because the rules of raising children had gone out the kitchen window and up the back garden to form treacherous, mucky cow-pats near the gate of Flannery's field. I was now exposed. There was no correct answer. A man in his mid-forties would interrogate me until I almost wet myself in fright like a pup in training.

"If I give you two shillings . . ." The questioning would begin again. "If I give you a ten shilling note . . ."

He was standing on top of a stone wall with red braces over his white shirt, garters holding up the cuffs of his shirt, and hurling rocks down on top of me until I crumpled under the weight of the cairn being built. That was the moment I knew I was a failure, invalid, standing on bockety legs. There are signposts, inadequate explanations, pointing the way to ruined, bronze-age monuments of stone on the top of hills all over Ireland. Fairy forts, long overgrown. They're the memorials to children who were buried alive beneath them, and at dusk those lost souls emerge from deep underground to play. You can catch a reflection of them capering about in the streaks of mist on the greenest hillsides, and in the *sí gaoithe,* the flurries of wind that toss wisps of hay into the air.

I've a dream that recurs in times of stress that I walk into the sitting room to turn on the television, and out of the corner of my eye, standing to my right in the middle of the carpet, is an enormous, black bull, flicking his tail. His head turns, and he looks at me with blazing, yellow eyes. He opens his mouth, crinkling back his lips to expose his teeth, and instead of bellowing, he hisses at me in delight. Panicked, in slow motion as I reverse and lean to go, he launches himself into an upward and forward charge.

Paradoxically, I truly learned to swim in that kitchen; effortlessly, joyfully and iridescently soar. In my imagination I became a Richard Strauss song in front of the unseeing eyes of my father, who couldn't hear that I was singing in that night, like Hans Anderson's little mermaid beneath the surface glass of the darkening waves gazing up at the prince, and had become a little white angel twinkling in the night sky: *duine le Dia,* literally, a person with God, a nascent fool. "May the souls of the faithful departed rest in peace. Amen." The little mermaid had split in two, and in every step that she took with her new legs, it was as if knives were shooting up through her. The surgeon had used a perineal approach. From deep within, a *Herzensbildung* was being put in place.

There's an excited hush in the *tablao*. The percussive strumming of the acoustic guitar, interspersed with the knocking, *golpe,* is already keeping the beat, waiting for me to join in. I've to concentrate wholly on the beat within, *compass,* if I'm to improvise under the influence of *duende.* From the intermingling of the both beats, within and without, there resolves a third that sets off in my soul a new beginning. I can pace out a pilgrim path in a new and more trustworthy direction. I can hold my head high, proudly, and deliver a virtuoso performance of abandonment to the *duende,* of allowing the *duende* lead towards the attainment of a truth that cannot but astonish.

It's within, to be shared only with the very few, who are of my quiet constituency. In such a setting, I can venture a *copla* or two, my song suspended on the high wire of their intimacy. And they can urge me further, in the knowledge that this heartfelt cry is not entertainment. I turn deeply within and engage with the *duende,* who floods into all corners of my being so that I can stand possessed. As I walk out across that invisible wire releasing the *quejido,* my voice enfolds us in a lament which comes up from the depths of my soul, reverberating within the community of those few souls who can hear, a liberating song that pierces into the impossible, the hopeless, the solitude, and peels it back like the skin of an orange.

When the consultant urologist, David Mulvin, said that "the prostate is attached", he meant that the cancer had penetrated into that outer layer. He took it out and looked at it in his gloved hand. I can hear bubbling in the blood that wells up through fountains first built by the Visigoths, Mozarabic song, hymns from Jewish synagogues, plaints from the Moriscos, an unbroken musical flow animated by the dispossessed, the marginalised, the exiled, the oppressed, the silenced, the solitary, the disinherited. In the song that I dance with a rattle of heels, tonal patterns appear to turn summersaults in a whirl of upright arms, like the civilisations overthrown successively in Spain, swinging out on to the rhythms of the time, all of them present now in a rush of feeling. They balance in that intermediate space between ecstasy and despair, inviting those sudden, expressive arm movements, *brazadas,* from prisoners fearful of being held at the pleasure of authority, from Jews hated for being chosen by God, from reviled gay men constantly at risk of domination by bullies, and despised *gitanos* blackened from living in the street outside their corner house open to extremes, all of them awkward in the freedom of their release. The song that I sing is their song, so ancient and the same: the truth of pain.

Before dawn in those cold winter mornings when I served in St Mary's Priory in Tallaght, a Dominican brother would walk the length of the long corridor to knock on my door and waken me: "*Benedicamus Domino.*"

And I'd call out in response, "*Deo gratias.*" I'd awaken with a feeling of thankfulness, an attitude set by the first two words I uttered that early morning, and a determination to uphold once more the burden of the day. I've taken the cockleshell and make the long and arduous pilgrimage to the Cathedral of Santiago de Compostela, built on top of a Roman necropolis. A guide wakes me from an exhausted sleep, knocking on the door of the hospice with an eight foot stave. This is followed by the cry "*Outraia,*" meaning "Forward with courage!" I offered that word to my client, Helen, when she'd completed her analysis, and she presented me in turn with a small silver bowl for rice, a gift from her, an offering for the nourishment she intuitively perceived I needed to receive from others and that cancer would lead me on to accept with humility and gratefulness. It all had to be as it was: there could've been no escape from what was to be accomplished. So step once more into those stout sandals, drape the heavy cape around weary shoulders, put on the broad-brimmed felt hat turned up jauntily in the front and emblazoned with scallop shells, and carry that staff for support and for protection. Somewhere within the inevitability of the ancient journey towards Compostela, the cathedral of the cemetery in *finis terrae*, at the ends of the earth, is the freedom that I'm grateful for.

Part Twenty: Martin and Ursula

Anna phoned Terry from Spain to say that she'd be having lunch with Martin on Friday next in the Art Cafe in Elviria, if we wanted to drop by and meet him when we arrived. "But he's unpredictable," she said, "and might not want to speak."

So we came down the mountain, and walked into the little restaurant at about two o'clock. We spied Anna in at the back, and we went over and sat at the next table, said hello. The tall man opposite her was laboriously eating a Caesar salad. His skin had a grey pallor, a whiteness which was grey, *básaire*, and he looked gaunt and very ill indeed.

"Martin, these are my friends just arrived from Ireland – Mike and Terry."

He raised his head and nodded. Martin was an artist who was dying of cancer, and the doctors had given him at most two or three months. He'd always lived for today and made no provision for the future. He lectured in the art school in Malaga for very little money, and over the years when he and Anna had argued about the rent for his apartment, he'd paid her in pictures, which were beautiful. Many of them were of the women who'd loved him and whom he had loved, which was evident from the paints he'd chosen and the brush work with which he'd rendered them so intimately, so deftly. Those women who had served him as an artist were exposed on the walls of Anna's house. There's a particular series of a nude woman with long, curling black hair which she uses as an adornment, by the waters of a pool, whose milky skin is palpably sexual, whose wet eyes and mouth issue an invitation to touch, to stroke, to graze with pursed lips, and then to possess her as violently as the Catholic Church took possession of the great mosque at Cordoba, a *Besetzung* which culminated in a state of being possessed. She evokes guilt because she's forbidden to me: her wanting is for the artist.

We own a large watercolour by Martin entitled *French Honeysuckle – spring – Bolonia, 1996:* a mass of purples, reds, yellows, greens and white, sweet-smelling flowers from the meadows through which Helen wends her way to the beach, which hangs in La Mairena. In his neat, black handwriting, Martin carefully noted on the back of the frame "L. *Hedysarum coronarium,* a robust herbaceous plant which grows in Mediterranean regions." When Anna was trying to raise money for Martin's treatment, she sold it to us. I guess she must have paid out a lot of her own money to cover his treatment fees in hospital, and when she could no longer afford it, she brought him home.

"The doctors said he's going to bloody die anyway, so why should I keep on paying? He's got family back in Scotland, let them take care of him, only he doesn't want to go back there. Bloody typical of Martin. Am I obliged to continue to look after him – I'm his landlady, for Chrissakes?"

And she'd exasperatedly run her hand through her greying, wavy hair, little points of red colouring her fine, Scandinavian cheekbones.

I looked across at Martin, at the courageous effort he was making to eat his meal. I was remembering the four brothers who happened to be in Dublin on the same afternoon. We went over to visit Kie, who was eating his lunch on a tray in the sitting room of his home in Mount Anville. He didn't get up. We sat on the floor around him making conversation, laughing and joking with him as we used to do, and he'd lift a plastic plum-pudding bowl and gently get sick into it, and then continue on the conversation. He was really waiting to die.

We ordered egg Benedict and *dos cafés americanos*. Anna chatted with us about art, and we ventured that Martin's soul was visible in his artwork and that we could appreciate that. He smiled wistfully, but seemed pleased. Anna was there to try and organise an exhibition of Martin's work on the walls of the café with the owner, a woman from London who'd recently been to Dublin. She also owned the flower shop next door, so before Terry and I left, we bought a bouquet of summer flowers for Martin, which we gave to him. That evening Anna phoned us up to say how much Martin had enjoyed our visit and that he'd chosen a painting for us of a statue that he'd painted in a park in Santiago in Chile, and which she had for us. It's a sombre world of greys and greens, with just one vivid splash of purple, a flower in the background, which serves to illuminate the canvas.

Noeleen had introduced us to the *objets trouvés* world of second-hand shops on the Costa, so on one of our regular pottering forays down past Estepona, we came across a small, art deco plaster cast of a man, seated on a suitcase with his head raised in anticipation. We brought it home with us and cemented it into place among the scarlet geraniums on top of a low wall outside the door to our apartment. Like the swallows, we come and go so regularly that the figurine became invested with the transience that we've increasingly learned to live with. As we descend through the grove of trees, we can see him sitting silently on his suitcase, lit by a splash of sunlight, *en attendant.* Inevitably, we've come to refer to him as Martin. He watches over our arrivals and departures, the being present and absent, like a guardian angel who crosses the great divide.

I met David Douglas loping along Morehampton Road on his way to work, earphones on, iPod in hand, and he stopped to ask me how I was. David is a handsome man, with clear brown eyes under the peaked cap that engage with you head on, and he was just back from visiting Cordoba, a city which he'd loved, so he was tanned. We chatted about his experiences there. And then I mentioned to him about my friend Ursula and the photographs she'd taken in New Zealand.

"David, she's a photographer blessed with an artist's eye, and she's taken these amazing photographs in New Zealand of a two hundred million year old forest which has endured for so long that it has solidified into stone, washed over by the sea. Her pictures are breathtaking."

He said directly, "I'll go out and visit her and look at the photographs, and if they're good enough, we'll hold an exhibition in the gallery." I searched his eyes. "Get her to ring me," he said.

Ursula was delighted when next I spoke with her, "I've an exhibition arranged for New Zealand in December, but because we are locked into the present three-week cycle of the chemo, I don't know whether we will be able to travel or whether the chemo will do its work." There is definitely a southern Irish sing-song to her voice, overlaid with a German correctness. We'd been talking about their home in New Zealand, and John McCarthy was twinkling. He said he'd come across a lovely word: "mindfulness", which comes from the Old English word for memory.

Terry interjected that, "It sounds very Protestant."

"Did I tell you, John, that I've discovered my great, great grandmother, Mary Jane Wylie, was the daughter of an

Anglican clergyman in Randalstown? One-sixteenth Protestant: interpreting the scriptures for myself."

He chuckled at me, a knowing glint of mischief in his eye.

"Sorry, John: mindfulness . . ."

"It means living in the present. Mindfulness. A very serviceable word. Heeding what's going on around you: being careful of it. That's the way we live now. Maybe in the autumn, but we've no plans to go to New Zealand while Ursula is undergoing chemo."

"It knocks me for six. For about a week afterwards, I lie flat on my back, Michael. I've no energy whatsoever. But by the third week, I'm good." Ursula seemed to have lost weight, but she was lively. At different times during the meal, while the other was talking to Terry, they both spoke about death.

John said, "I've talked to friends at Fitzwilliam tennis club who've lost partners, or who've separated, and they all said you get on with it. I tell myself not to go there – that's why mindfulness is a good word." He was holding back the tears. "But of course, you inevitably do . . .," and his voice trailed off.

Ursula said, "The prognosis for pancreatic cancer isn't very good, you know, Michael. Prostate cancer is one of the lucky ones. So we're taking it day by day, and we enjoy the sunny weather in the patio garden at lunchtime, and we go for a walk when we can, when I'm feeling good in that third week." And then she looked into my eyes, "You go into those dark places, Michael, that I try to keep at a step removed, trying to keep on this side of the river Styx, for as long as I can."

We rang Ursula from Spain to find out how she'd got on with David Douglas.

"We seemed to get on very well. But I've no idea whether he thought the photographs were good enough to show in an exhibition."

When I'd spoken to John earlier, I'd warned him that David was very much of today's fearless generation, who've an eye towards the future where everything is for ever possible. "He's a cool businessman, John, very much aware of the bottom line. And perhaps he lacks reverence."

David had sent a text message: "Hi M & T. Went excellent. She's a great bird. Gonna try and arrange some sort of show within next few months. It was a real pleasure to meet her + John. Gas pair!" When David's company emailed her about the forthcoming arrangements for an exhibition in August, Ursula was in hospital with pneumonia.

But she did have her exhibition in David's gallery. That night she wore her heels, and even visited a hairdresser to have her hair put up for the occasion. And everybody came. Ursula was in such good form throwing her party, proudly showing her guests the photographs that she'd taken at Curio Bay in the South Island of New Zealand which graced the walls of the gallery, shyly posing for Conor Ó Mearáin's photographs, awkward in front of a lens. David judged the opening a tremendous success, and it was a time of joy for Ursula. The shortest time afterwards, she was to die an unimaginably awful death from cancer. The living hell of her final days revived those memories of her beginnings in Germany, when she was running terrified through collapsing streets of burning houses, clasped in her mother's arms, under attack from the aeroplanes roaring overhead. Only this time it was John who supported her. He kept a constant vigil at Ursula's bedside throughout the horror. Each night when he'd leave the hospital, he'd pray that a merciful God would take her to Himself in love. And early on the following morning, he'd hurry back, praying that Ursula would still be alive for even one extra day.

At Ursula's request, I gave the eulogy to an intimate group of German and Irish friends, who gathered to remember her life and to sing her favourite hymns at St Finian's Lutheran Church, when the last September leaves clung on to autumn's boughs, still green along the Adelaide Road in Dublin. I pointed out that Ursula had kept her word: she endured to keep on this side of the river Styx for as long as she was able. As in her photographs of those great trees that had fallen some millions of years before, those traces of her presence were all she had to offer in the twilight days at season's change, but Ursula had offered all, in love.

Part Twenty-one: Poetry

I received a postcard with a black and white portrait of Des by Wilhelm Föckersperger on the front, the emphasis on the dark, quizzical eyes, entitled "Desmond Egan, poet." In clear handwriting on the back, it read

Dear Michael,

Both Viv and I were delighted to hear your voice back reading the News – properly for a change. I'd left messages and tried to contact you, including at work – to no response and we thought you'd gone abroad. Welcome back! I hope we get to meet again, soon. Viv is going through chemo and it's tough but she's bearing up and we hope all will be well. I am scribbling away as usual, writing poems that nobody reads. God bless, Des.

Oh, poor Viv: I hadn't known. I'm so sorry.

When I was writing my M.Phil. thesis in psychoanalytic studies for Trinity College, I chose to examine the question of the father through a sequence of poems that Des had written called *A Song for My Father*. I interviewed him in his back garden in Kildare, sheltered by the privet, one hot summer afternoon. On that day there was a spirit of liveliness about the place. White butterflies flitted among the veronica and lavender in the sunshine, and fragrance wafted from the sweet pea. The dogs fought on the gravel at Des's knee for his attention, and a jackass occasionally poked his head over the fence from the next field to listen to the murmur of voices. Neither Viv nor I displayed symptoms of the ordeal we were to face, the burden of the fatigue, the draining away of hope, the broken-heartedness. She'd prepared a delicious lunch of home-made breads and salads. Then she left the two of us alone, and we drank deep of the richest Rioja from a case that Des had brought home with him following a lecture tour in Spain. He'd taught in Newbridge College after I'd left, and we both had spent time in seminaries. I asked him which question exercised him more: a question about relationships or a question about being? He had no hesitation in saying that the question about being is what permeates his work. So the hard disc in his computer is also that of the obsessional.

I marvelled that Des had the ability to write a sequence about his father, that call of the blood, which is full of tender feelings of acceptance towards him that could arch over the intellectual difference between them: ". . . like it or lump it he was himself . . . he'd walk by all their groves in Elysium to the spot where Kerrigan . . . Pakie and the others were drinking tea chatting about Athlone . . ." He wrote about his relationship with his father from a perspective beyond death of "no more season tickets . . . no more fixture lists . . . no more following him out . . ." It's shiningly clear that Des loved him: ". . . in the intensive care unit where he lay dying, for the first time since I put on long trousers I kissed my father." The concluding poem is an epitaph which echoes Horace, written at McKenna's monument in Cornamagh cemetery: "Tom Egan does not lie here . . . not his warmth . . . not his laugh . . . not his spirit . . . nor our love more lasting than granite," the absence of his father redeemed by a present tense of lasting love in which both are involved, and which continues, holding both of them in an embrace where life and death are equivalent.

The first time Des read aloud those poems in public was at a reading he gave in Naas with me and Eileen Dunne, my newscaster colleague and pal. We supported him and gave him comfort that evening, because he'd found it an intense and emotional experience. The words which Des spoke, which stand in for his father on the page, had the effect of resurrecting him in the Athlone tones of his own voice and in the intrusive echoes in his ears from the familiar voices of his newscaster friends, who stood on either side of him like the two thieves. It was both the being and alienation in the relationship all at once, a distressing crucifixion in which he was torn, and which drew sympathetic applause from the audience, unconsciously attuned to the dilemma. They stood at the foot of that cross and overheard the chilling father question, "Why hast thou forsaken me?" in words which rent the veil of the temple in two.

If I were to interrogate my own father, it is I who withheld recognition for the longest time. I blame myself for this reactionary stance, while the truth is that Dad forfeited my allegiance by the beatings he handed out before my brothers saw the light of day. The guilty spew he covered me in still clings to the hairs of my head and to my raiment. I remember my confirmation suit, the first time that I wore long trousers. When I was being fitted for it, my father was on the other side of the curtain in the shop with his back to me, engrossed in his chat with the draper. I was helplessly being felt up in the darkened booth by the young shop assistant, too frightened to move or to say anything, appalled that this too early induction into the world of adulthood should be visited on me yet again.

And always I felt that the suit my father paid for smelled of vomit in sunlight. I believed that I was the one who smelled.

Once upon a time, a father betrayed his son and left him forlorn. That position next door at his granny's became for the son an impregnable landing place, where he was able to haul himself out of the fast flowing stream of his father's wanting, to wait for what the stars would bring. An unspoken barrier imprisoned them both, and they served their time. When it was over, the hurt of the past no longer seemed to matter. The son was astonished to discover a wellspring of love for the father that had remained hidden deep within and bubbled to the surface now in a life-giving stream that washed away the *dríodar,* the detritus. So that truthfully I was able to say, "I always loved my father." And from far away, the father would hear those words as a laying on of hands, *asserere in libertatem* which would set him free.

We stood in the centre of Germany, in Würzburg, in the square before the Cathedral of St Killian, which had been reconstructed after the devastation of the war. Within the German hubbub, we heard behind us the lilt of a familiar voice. The poems of Desmond Egan have so penetrated into my unconscious that I can hear borrowings I've held on to as my own. We turned around, and there he was, filling the air with his presence. Des had just arrived to do a poetry reading at the university. The encounter was a coincidence brought about by a fellow Irishman from Cavan, St Killian, that I regret not having taken advantage of, because I could've contributed the second voice at his reading, a counterpoint that'd create a texture to his work which Des has always intended. As it turned out, I wasn't present, and the resonating absence sings to me in an epic that I continue to carry, music that I swim in, a swally hole in which I endlessly drown silently.

When I walked into the Thomaskirche in Leipzig, a posy

of flowers was thrown on to the large, dark-bronze tablature which marks Bach's final resting place before the high altar of the church where he worked as cantor. Those few flowers looked incidental, an afterthought like the last piece of music that Bach wrote before he died. The comprehensive work that had occupied him during his ultimate decade, *The Art of Fugue*, was already at the engravers when he added a quadruple fugue in his own hand, which valiantly broke new ground at the highest level of achievement, even as he was digging out the sods of his own grave in St John's cemetery, six paces from the south door. A kaleidoscope of shimmering chord progressions on the organ follow one another without seeming to achieve rest. The fugue is, in fact, unfinished: it breaks off after two hundred and thirty-nine measures. Nothingness is given a place and forms a part of this complex score. The implications of the interplay of so many dimensions, the integration of textures – both present and absent – is brought by Bach to a completion that can always comprehend potential, irresolution and the retrospection given by an arbitrary end point. For me it's an expression in musical terms of the freedom that I strive for and fight for and defend. Those final notes echo in the air, having already explored pathways of possibility to which I would have wanted to contribute what ending, which resolution, and there's none. So first time around I berate myself for having sunk into the defensive pit of incomprehension, then check myself, matching what's in those notes with what I hear and don't hear together, setting free my soul to soar openly like the outstretched cross in the vault above the high altar, and there's no body. It's so personal an expression that in the third theme, the *kapellmeister* constructs a subject on the musical letters of his family name, which links him on to the identifying chain of his forefathers: B and H are the German note names for B-flat and B-natural. The music is open and abstract, written by a master drawing on all of his experience, who's inexorably moving beyond the known parameters of creation. Glenn Gould characterised this final contrapunctus as "the most extraordinary piece that a human mind ever conceived." And even with his spectacular keyboard technique, Gould was daunted by the thought of playing it. Eventually he gave it an elegiac interpretation.

Johann Sebastian Bach had taken his thought processes on instrumental counterpoint to the farthest end of human endeavour, so that it redounds to astonish me. This man, who was blind following an unsuccessful operation for cataracts, who spent his life within the confines of a provincial, Lutheran state, was able to express himself in sounds so universal in scope as to span generations, which affirm for ever the music that makes up the soul of mankind. Like the offering of dying flowers strewn on a tomb before an altar, a spot of colour brilliantly defying the darkness, Bach's unfinished fugue is a masterpiece which contributes an afterthought of gratitude and remembrance, tying together life and death, presence and absence within the same bunch: *soli deo gloria*.

Part Twenty-two: Love

Terry had been ringing Anna in Spain on a regular basis to find out how she was coping with the chemo. They were able to save her breast without surgery, but there were times when Anna had holed up at home in her vast house in Elviria when Ian was in England, not wanting to talk to anybody. Occasionally on those winter evenings, she was able to unburden herself to Terry. Cancer was an unwelcome guest who was exhausting company. And she too spoke about the breach of contract with life, the divorce she wanted nothing from, but which left her depressed and miserable and which she wanted to put behind her as quickly as possible, but whose interwoven threads take time to unpick.

"Are you going to buy the watch?" she asked.

Terry was unsure. "We gave a commitment to Lars that we were going to buy the bed from him."

"Fuck the bed – buy the Cartier!"

> We lost Christmas on the Costa del Sol,
> The windy coast. It was closed: "No peoples . . ."
> An English couple hanging on to Santa hats
> And bottle trophies from a garage supermarket
> Supported one another.

At lunch alone, we looked
And silently fleeing Bing Crosby's "White Christmas"
Stammering tips in the pizzeria in Elviria
Escaped to where?
¡*Feliz navidad*!

Christmas dinner was held in La Mairena. Anna and Ian were there, and Michael and Johanna Roche from Kiltrea Bridge Pottery had made it down that morning on the train from Sevilla. Piercing blue Christmas lights draped all around the terrace signalled our presence to a constellation of empty urbanisations. We stood out there in the eerie silence of the mountain top, wrapped up against the cold, laughing and talking, sipping sekt in the clear air as the sun went down behind the sea. We lay underneath the Christmas tree of a darkening Spanish sky, looking up through the magic of the glittering starlight. I felt I was alone among the scattered presents, having been handed the gift of a foreshortened perspective. Michael questioned me with great interest about prostate cancer, because his father had died from the disease, and he wanted to understand the effect of the loss.

I was profoundly sad. The loss I felt came from an understanding that I was dying, certainly. But the effect of this particular loss was to open up a chasm between me and other people of which only I was aware. So that when I shook hands with Michael and touched his shoulder, felt the warmth of his sudden embrace, huge potter's arms pulling me to him, or kissed Johanna on both cheeks admiring her forcefulness, I worried that the glacial feel of my hands, of my lips, would leave scorch marks on their bodies. And I scanned their eyes, admiring that sparkle. I felt reassured that they hadn't grasped that I was already dead.

"Mike," Kie had called me to him from his hospital bed as I was going out the door of his room, "enjoy your life."

"Thanks, Kie, I will." And I turned on my heel and left him. It was the start of a conversation that I never had with him, could never have with him. I knelt down on to the cold ground of the corridor outside his closed door, grief-stricken. My brother was gone. When Tatters Chambers died, Anne and Eleanor Chambers, Frank and Maureen Pelly, Kie and I formed a procession, and we held a funeral for him up in Granny's garden. He'd played a part in all of our adventures, trailing us behind, and now we reverently brought him with us on a tray through the wet grass, preceded by a lighted candle. We dug a hole, not very deep, in the ground beneath arching flower stems with flame-coloured trumpets, a spreading clump of montbretia, and we laid his white little body with the gold patch at his ear on to the crumbling earth. There was a tin box with a lid on it, into which we each put something valuable: a pink plastic rosary beads so he could say his prayers, a photograph of the Chambers so that he could remember them, a coloured glass marble to play with, a penny if he wanted to buy anything and some slab toffee for when he got hungry. We placed the box beside him in the grave so that he would be all right, and then we covered him over and patted him down. John Joe from next door has since built a patio in the garden, but I know that he's still there. And sometimes I can make out his outline in the clouds or in a pattern of stars in the night sky, and I'm able to draw the shape of my smaller companion who'd give me the paw, filling in the colour so that he comes alive once again in my heart.

During the banter over the Christmas dinner, Anna expostulating and Michael boisterously trying to rein her in, Johanna turned to Ian and asked with an American directness that brought everybody up short, "Are you divorced?"

Ian is a bluff, genial Englishman, about twenty years Anna's senior, who's been living with her for the past three years. And Johanna's question was evoked by his statement, "We're trying to sell our house in Elviria." Ian started a tor-turous, lumbering explanation about the property interests he and his wife Pam in England had together.

Johanna cut in, "So you're not divorced?"

"No, not exactly."

"And in any settlement, Pam could be entitled to half of any property you have in Spain?"

"Well, yes, if you put it like that, I suppose she could."

Anna wasn't uncomfortable with the turn in the conversa-tion. She moved to clear the table while Terry set up the plum puddings we'd brought down in the suitcase. The divorce with Allen taught her the finality of being replaced. The uncoupling was a shock which had emptied her spirit so that she could barely breathe. But the encouragement of friends telling her they could see her coming back to herself, that they admired her bravery, helped her along the first few steps of a road that she hadn't chosen. She glanced back over her shoulder and grazed her nose off a barrier that had never been part of her upbringing, that left her no space, that stripped her of possi-bilities and made a mockery of what she had hoped would be her past. Every type of cancer does that.

When we were leaving them back to the train station in Malaga, I tried once again to put Michael in the picture. "I just know that it's over."

"What do you mean – it's over? Life is over – what?"

I am telling you now, Michael, that the loss comes from the shame of being repudiated and from the knowledge that there's no way back. The irreparable nature of this loss is made worse by the fact that the wound heals over eventually, unnaturally, because something was taken which has left an unseen cavity inside. There's solitude in keeping the secret, that private pact with someone else who knows. But any public explanation that's acceptable fails in the attempt, because it tells a story from someone else's point of view who's no longer involved. I see it as a motiveless crime. It's a forbidding which has ring-fenced off another future. I certainly experienced it as an assault, but I'm actually assailed by an absence, which has won out. And I've lost. No resolve, no mustering of bravery, no courageous act on my part can lift and overturn that final judgement. Once it was handed down, it will continue to determine destiny. So it's over, Michael. It's been accomplished, and it's over.

I was little when Dr Mongey died, and I pushed open his hall door at the Mall and walked into the surgery where he was laid out on a bed, with many candles being lighted around him by his daughter Mary Rose. His head looked cream and still, and I knelt down beside him to say a prayer, and then I ran out. I skipped all the way home because I was frightened by the strangeness of what I'd seen, and the scuff of my sandals on the footpath was a loud and comforting noise, telling me that I was alive.

Terry and I were present at his bedside when Vincent Hanley died. He was Terry's best friend, who'd lived with Terry in his mother's house in Hatch Street; indeed, a lot of the humour that Vincent used as a broadcaster on air – Fab Vinny – I recognise as having come from Terry. He'd also been the lively presenter of a summer series that I'd produced for RTÉ Two television. Vincent was the first person whom I saw die before my eyes. I remember a conversation I had with him about God in those final weeks when he was very sick and dying of Aids. I said that Jung knew God existed, because at a certain point in the analysis, he'd come across what he termed the "*Imago Dei,*" which each person had within them. Vincent simply said, "I knew it." It seemed as if the sun were moving rapidly through the branches of trees, slowly dappling his body from his feet up to the crown of his head, while Vincent breathed his last. The nurse lit a candle, and his brother Fergus, Bill Hughes, the producer, Terry and I linked arms to form a supportive arcade around the bed, a viaduct for the sorrow we were feeling, and we prayed out loud an Our Father, a Hail Mary and a Glory Be, to speed Vincent on his way as his body was transformed and his spirit left each of us bereaved in the hospital room lit by the flickering light.

When Vincent scored his first success in broadcasting, he rewarded himself with a Cartier tank watch from his earnings, a discreet expression of his success. He proudly showed it to me on his wrist up in the small RTÉ canteen the day that he'd bought it in Weirs. And that was the watch that Vincent had willed to Terry. Years later a screw had loosened on the bar that held the strap in place, and when Terry was in Washington DC delivering a lecture on the Irish experience of treating abuser priests for the Granada Institute, he surmised that the watch must have fallen off his wrist in a taxi. It was a very big loss, and Terry could never bring himself to replace Vincent's watch with another.

Once again, under the watchful eye of a uniformed armed guard, Terry was looking at a tank watch in the Cartier shop in Marbella when his eye was drawn to an exceptionally beautiful timepiece which was on display by itself in a reinforced glass case over Carmen's shoulder. As she unlocked it, she explained that this particular watch was from the *collection privée*, that only a limited number were made, and that it was a contemporary take on the tank of 1931; not the same, but an advance on what had gone before. She placed the watch on a small velvet tray and offered it for Terry's appraisal. As he picked up this beautiful gold object, the work of skilled craftsmen, and weighed it in his palm, Carmen pointed out what was really exceptional: the movement was a mechanism in rectangular format, created exclusively for the tank à vis, which was visible through the transparent crystal back. Terry was overwhelmed by its beauty and delicacy, the ingeniousness of the watch, and he parted with it reluctantly and talked about it often. I wanted him to possess the tank à vis, because while the watch would remind him of Vincent and his broadcasting days, it would in addition be the gift that I was buying for him, and that I was giving to him. This timepiece would be a Te Deum, a canticle of thanksgiving for having proved stalwart during a desperate period of testing. I could trust his being there with a solid support at a time when I was struck down with cancer and needed propping up with the unconditional giving of his practical help and emotional encouragement. For the first time in my life, I was given to understand that whatever I was feeling at any moment of the day was of value and need not be glossed over. Whatever I had to say was heard by him, gratefully. The tank à vis would be an eternal keepsake, the physical expression of a golden saying that Terry would have when I'm dead, a daily reminder of the time when he had once been loved in return.

I couldn't have undergone the operation and its aftermath on my own without Terry's dedicated support: such survival wouldn't have been possible on my own. I know that over the twenty-five years we've saved each other, but this time has been exceptional, summoning in Terry an unyielding response of hope, a *volontarisme* of actively pushing beneficence. Terry is aware that I think I'm going to die. Is there any other way of dealing with what I understood as a child was the father's death wish for me and the place he'd hollowed out for me in his wanting so that it had become a living limestone sarcophagus, eating away at my flesh like the cancer?

So is that it, Death? Is it in relation to you that I've been having these conversations about male cancer? Is it facing you that I've these arguments about borrowed time, about surviving six more years? Just as I argued with that young nurse in the hospital at five in the afternoon about whether I could have a second Ponstan when I was maddened with pain. Then I drew upon my days as a producer/director to take charge and said that the painkiller wasn't working, that the pain barrier had been breached and another way forward had to be found. What way forward is there with you, because I've never been able to find it? What manner or style of dress are you wearing today? I've met you in so many guises throughout my career that I can draw your lineament with facility. At the reception you're charming and at ease socially with others, but when I come into your presence, you look away and take the first opportunity to escape. And yet, you give the impression that you know me too well. If I engage you in conversation, you look down at me as if you don't rate me, more irritation than contempt that I should be occupying your attention when there are others with whom you clearly want to spend your time. You don't want to engage with me at all. You possess the power to encourage me and smooth my way, but you don't wish to extend that benevolence to me. Indeed, you wish me harm.

So in your consulting room where there's nobody else to see, when you sit opposite me dressed up as Death, with that long hood concealing your empty face, I know then that you've no escape, no more than I have, and that you must deal with me. But you're closed off: there's nothing I can say that will achieve anything. You'll take my best proposal, thank me for it and immediately stand up and cross the room to put it in the file with all the others in the cabinet behind me, then shake my hand and hold the door open for me on the way out. What if I were to turn my body to you and suddenly dance on your carpeted floor my heartfelt belief that flamenco music is about the movement of feeling that starts with overwhelming grief and through finding the resources within so that I can liberate myself, comes to a climax in a glorious, noisy celebration of the joy and happiness of living? What if I were suddenly to pierce the suffocating silence in your room and appeal to you in song so that you could help encourage my euphoria, that ability to endure which I need so badly and which you could respond to by giving even a little? You'd stare at me blankly while continuing to ambiguously hold open the door before you shut it, and I'd be made to feel embarrassed, shamed about my distasteful truth, the messiness of human feeling which so obviously lacks decorum. What if I were to dance a final turn, stamp my feet, one arm raised, whip my head around in slow-motion – "*Thart ort*" – so that the perspiration dripping from the pain in my soul and gathered on the end of my locks would surge across the room, slashing you in a crimson gash across the front of your habit? Yes, I feel the passion of anger. But you're practised and at all times in charge within your sphere of influence. It's very clear that I've to be in charge elsewhere, always elsewhere, if ever I'm to sing *cante chico*, that uplifting finale to the whole of my life, a shout of defiance against the inevitable, a cry that will travel for ever off into the vast, blackness of the universe, so that even when I'm gone, the music of my voice will continue on by way of valediction, to say that at one time I was here, to say that for the shortest flicker of light I too mattered to someone.

And, I bought the watch for Terry.

Part Twenty-three: Endurance

Towards the end of a sultry June, one year and a half after the prostatectomy, sunlight brightening the sheen on grassy meadows which leaked yellow under slabs of massed clouds, Terry had driven my mother and me through green archways, leafy lanes in Leitrim, the foliage bursting with summer abundance around the Lakeland, to take her back to Ballinamore, the small, straggling town where she'd spent her childhood. As we slowly walked the streets that hot summer afternoon, the threat of a sudden shower building in the humid air, the *brothall*, my mother discovered a plaque on the wall of what had been the Railway Hotel, commemorating her mama's father, Philip McGauran, who had founded the local branch of the Gaelic Athletic Association there in his home. Further down we stopped and took photographs outside the derelict house in the Main Street where she was brought up, as she familiarised herself with changed shop fronts.

"You know the house goes way back: there were seven bedrooms. Were the Cryans always over there, or was that the McLoughlins' house?" She was thinking aloud and asking me, one of her childhood companions from over eighty years ago.

"That was the McLoughlins' house," interjected a woman passing. By coincidence, it turned out to be her cousin, Molly

McGauran from Tarmon, who was thrilled to meet my mother once again. As they reminisced, Molly reminded her, "You spent all your summer holidays out in our house in Tarmon, or in Whiterock with the O'Beirnes, and in Castleroggy with the Creamers."

My mother turned and introduced us: "I have five sons," she said, "Terry and Michael, John, Tom and Fintan." The moment of inscription slipped by so fast we almost missed it. Her unconscious mistake and the erroneous nature of it was a proclamation delivered on the steps of the family home. I glanced at the four empty upstairs windows and thought I caught a glimpse of people pulling back into the shadows who'd witnessed her declaration. The conversation continued on between the two women, but my mother had made an acknowledgement which honoured Terry's constant presence in her life over these past twenty-three years, the holidays he gave her in Spain, the Christmases in Dublin he celebrated with her around his table, the place of honour he accorded to my mother at his own mother's funeral when he asked her to do the readings. Now she'd made a place for him in there with me, her two adoptive sons, as she rearranged the canopy and welcomed the two of us back home.

When Molly parted from her regretfully, I put a stout arm around my mother's gathering confusion and guided her over to visit the modern library building, newly opened across the street. Inside the cool order of the displays, there was a whole section at the back devoted to local interest, so I asked the librarian whether there was anything on file about my mother's grandfather, Charles O'Beirne. She put up a roll of microfilm on the computer for us of stories which were printed in the *Leitrim Advertiser*, where we found that Papa's father is immortalised. It details his attendance at several meetings of the Land League all over the county: Mohill, Proughlish,

Cloone, at Carrick-on-Shannon where he spoke, Ballinamore of course and Kiltoghart. Those reports were there for all to see. We sat at the table side by side, chatting to each other and going through the papers. The jigsaw pieces of a picture began to interlock and coalesce, and we made out something that neither of us knew. The revelation was about what had actually befallen her grandfather and his family over a century and a quarter before.

They knocked on his door at eight o'clock in the morning, on the first Friday of June in 1881, and invaded his general merchant's premises at Main Street, Ballinamore, the house in which my mother was born and reared. Charles O'Beirne, a member of the executive of the Land League, was arrested by the Royal Irish Constabulary under the Coercion Act, which permitted internment without trial. He was one of six people from Ballinamore who were arrested on that day, the third of June. Since nobody in the town would make available a horse or car to take them to Dromad railway station, the police were forced to frogmarch the prisoners up the street and to detain them in the barracks for several hours while they telegraphed Mohill and Carrick-on-Shannon for reinforcements, fearing that a rescue attempt would be made. When the 80th Foot Regiment eventually marched into town with horses and cars from Mohill, Lieutenant Daubeny found an excitable crowd of over a thousand people assembled outside the barracks, vigorously protesting the arrests. The military manoeuvred the milling crowds of people into the lower part of the town and positioned a double line of soldiery across the road. They then brought out the prisoners one by one and placed them in the cars before the eyes of their bereft families and fellow townspeople, who watched helplessly, held at a safe distance. No drivers could be found to drive the cars, so the reins had to be taken by some of the constables themselves, and the convoy set off for Dromad railway station by a circuitous route through Cloone, in order to foil any risk of an ambush. The Ballinamore brass band led the crowd and accompanied Charles O'Beirne and the five other men every step of their journey to Dromad, playing Irish martial airs to keep up their spirits, to demonstrate the loudest participation in their protest and to give them a heroic send-off, as befits people who are distinguished by their integrity. The half-past five train slowly pulled out of the station taking the prisoners away to Galway Gaol, and the brass band continued to play, saluting their courage from the end of the platform with the crowd, who were cheering them on lustily. "Hip-hip hurrah, hip-hip hurrah, hip-hip, hurrah." As the train disappeared from view trailing clouds of steam, thirty Queen's Bays summoned from Longford galloped up to enforce the peace, to restore the status quo, to disperse dissent. But the Ballinamore brass band played on.

The story doesn't end there. The *Leitrim Advertiser* documents that towards the end of February of the following year, my mother's grandfather refused his release from Galway Gaol because of the unacceptable conditions in which he and his fellow prisoners were being kept by the authorities. The experience of prison had revealed to him the depth of his resolve to fight tyranny in all of its many guises, and despite the apparent futility of his gesture, he was emerging defiant. The powers that be had divested him of the love of his family, the security of his home and his livelihood, the support of his standing in the community, but he was proving to all of them that they were unable to rob him of his spirit. Because he had spoken out again, this Irish patriot was held at the pleasure of Her Imperial Majesty for a further three months. He suffered punishing torture on the treadmill, until his eventual release in May of 1882. Altogether, Charles had undergone eleven months' hard labour bearing witness to the unshakable truth of what he believed in. The O'Beirne family suffered the consequences of his sacrifice, and they took pride in the soaring achievement of his spirit, which endures.

I stood with my mother on the top of the hill next to the sixth-century stones of Feenagh Abbey, surrounded by the Celtic crosses of all those who are buried in the churchyard. We didn't find the family grave, but we said out loud a decade of the rosary so that all might hear the summons in our voices and recognise themselves in the strewn rose petals of our tones and accents, to rest in peace that we had continued on and had returned to this hallowed place another time to remember. Billowing clouds were blowing across the sun so that we were swept with passing shadows. The countryside round about was alive with the handlings of the wind, caressing, ruffling, smoothing. I held up my mother's hand as we carefully picked our way among the dead, like two ballet dancers taking a final curtain call. She didn't look back as we headed on the road towards Castlebar in the release of the rain, on the familiar journey she'd undertaken many's the time to boarding school, and finally to what became for her a Mayo lifetime. When we stopped for an ice cream in Charlestown after crossing the border, she looked across at me with the sparkling, bright-blue eyes of the O'Beirnes and said simply, "Thank you, Michael, for a wonderful day. And thank you, Terry."

He pressed with his right hand around my groin area, and each time there was a gentle spurt of urine from my shrivelled penis out over the fingers of his left hand.

"I see what you mean," he said, as he turned to wash. "You can cover yourself up, Michael. And how many pads would you get through in a day?"

"Five or six."

"And you're stopping the urine in mid-flow?"

"The physio said it's better to close your back passage as if you're about to break wind and to hold it for twelve seconds, three times lying down, three times sitting and three times standing, and I do those exercises twice a day."

"And there's been no improvement?"

"Well maybe at night."

"That's because there's no pressure. But I would have expected you to be further along the road by now. How long is it since the operation?" He leafed through his notes. "Six months. Let's give it another three months. Come back to me in September, and if there's been no progress, we can think of inserting an artificial sphincter. This has a button that you can press, and it voids the bladder for about a minute. And here, I'll give you a prescription for patches, which will quieten down the bladder." He was writing on his pad. "And I want you to ask the physio for electrical stimulation. She'll get you a probe which you can put into your anus. It's attached to a machine, and the electrical pulses will stimulate the muscles of the pelvic floor. Do that for about thirty minutes every day." He saw the incredulous look on my face. "It's a neat machine, about the size of a wallet," he explained.

"Thank you," I said.

One of the effects of the cancer is that I've no protection any more, none. I'm an open book. As a parting shot, a client may say, "And you're going away for three weeks? You obviously don't care very much about your clients," feeling without, angry at being abandoned. Clients' reactions are transferential, and they're also part of an ongoing process of change, but the words that they use are sometimes designed to slaughter, and the lack of reaching out they demonstrate can hurt me now. I'm available in the analytic arena for an assassin to strike a lethal blow without warning. I don't believe that

Manolete caught out of the corner of his eye the fact that the bull's right horn would gore when the pass was completed.

Each night, I take out this little machine which works with batteries, about the size of a full wallet. It has a small probe attached to it with wires. I cover this in gel and push it up into my back passage. Then I regulate the controls until I feel a vibration. This stimulation directly affects the hammock of pelvic floor muscle. It causes an uncomfortable feeling inside of continual spasms, and making the time available to use it privately is a nuisance that I could do without, but hopefully the procedure will enable me to gain some control over the leaking of urine. I leave the electrical probe in position for thirty minutes, and then I pull it out and wipe it clean of the smeared excrement with bacterial wipes, so that it is ready for the next day. Perhaps that cleansing is a metaphor too far; nevertheless, it's now a part of my daily reality. The machine hasn't made any difference to the overflow of urine as far as I can tell. Sometimes I get so wet that the pad fills up heavily under my crotch and the urine spreads out into my trousers, and I've to take a bath and wash my clothes. But I spat into the palm of fate for luck when I chose to have the operation. I clasped that bony hand in both of mine, bargaining for help with my recovery, so I've no complaints.

"Don't you recognise me, Michael?"

As I let go and glance up, with his right hand, he's pulling the hood back off his head, shaking loose the locks of long, greasy, grey hair. I see through the swirling gloom that he's standing tall in a tethered boat on a fast flowing river. Then he turns around his face towards me, the face of a jackal, and examines my soul with the deadest of yellowing eyes.

He crinkles back his lips into a smile of anticipation, "That's it," he reminds me, "that's the boy."

Part Twenty-four:
The Mooney Show

When I was very little, Mum said one afternoon, "Come on, Michael, and we'll go for a stroll." She said that I replied, "And what'll we do with the stroll when we get it?" Even at that early age I was listening to the literal meaning of what she was saying. I was following the rules, and yet the sentence blew up in my face. For me, language as a paradigm of structure has always marked out difference, but a difference that signalled a lack of understanding that inverted communication so that a barrier was thrown up against me. My response to my mother was a spontaneous, cleverly constructed question by a precocious three-year-old designed to regain control of the ball in the linguistic field and to sidestep incomprehension. When I was in my forties and undergoing analysis with Helen Sheehan, I always dreaded those unexpected tackles of the unconscious, the Freudian slips of the tongue that spectacularly felled my speech before it could score the conscious try, because those internal landmines were reminiscent of the linguistic relationships with my peers.

I used to sit upright in the bed running with sweat, from versions of the same nightmare, when the microphone in studio goes live and I've been given to read an empty, blank script. Sometimes in my dreams there's no script, and I'm live on air when each broadcasting second feels like an eternity. It's the moment of death, referred to in the business as "dead air," when I run out of words. It's also the moment of terrified awareness that there's nothing left to say, a terror which increases exponentially as the seconds tick away, when hooded Death faces me down with malicious laughter from the other side of the microphone desk.

It happened to me on television, the night the chief sub editor Dan O'Shea failed to come back from Madigan's pub and Rory O'Connor, the assistant head of news, stood in for him and fed the main evening *Nine O'Clock News* sheet by sheet under the studio door, which meant I'd to read the entire half-hour bulletin sight unseen, with the underlying anxiety of not being sure that the following words would arrive on time. During the *Six-Thirty News* on radio, which was split in two by a commercial break at six forty-five, I began a bulletin with the second half scripts, so that the words arrived unexpectedly before their time. When I came to the first insert, a report recorded by a journalist, the sound-man waved his arms: he didn't have it set up. I apologised and went into the second story and cued the insert. Again, frantic arm waving from the sound operator through the glass. Third report, same story. After four consecutive apologies, I explained that we were experiencing technical difficulties and that I was returning the broadcast to the presentation studio, where the panicked voice of the announcer introduced the record permanently on standby – "Let's take this opportunity to listen to one of Dvorak's Slavonic Dances" – until we sorted out the problems in communication. The chief sub that night, David Pate, who was kicking the walls on both sides of the control room with temper, requested a transfer to a radio station in Canada and emigrated.

The nightmares ceased when I determined that if ever this were to occur again, I'd turn around and face the fear that was pursuing me. I'd take myself out from behind the platitudinous screen of words to deliberately expose myself on air by naming the experience, by putting it into words of my own choosing, by saying so live on air. And almost two years after the prostatectomy operation, I succeeded in my endeavour on Derek Mooney's afternoon radio show.

At that time of year in November, sunrise in Spain is at eight o'clock. It's preceded by an hour-long overture, a progressive brightening of yellow, orange and pink hues at the horizon, which extend upwards into a clear blue sky. I was standing out on the terrace of La Mairena wrapped in a blanket, pondering Derek Mooney's interview of the day before and that question which had brought me into the unknown territory of a new world. From the balcony, I listened to the voice of the wind, hoarse with a heavy cold, as it sifted through the conifers, which stubbled the hills below with the blackest green. Then a pinpoint of gleaming red, east-southeast, rose quickly out of the sea, and was transformed into a blinding disc. Instinctively I responded to the radiant energy with raised arms and open palms, as the sun lit a wide, golden pathway across the Mediterranean Sea to Fuengirola. A little to the right and due south, the Rif Mountains of Morocco sailed into view, to hover over the horizon like clouds of pastel blue supporting a purple sky. It was an amazing sight, because they must be a hundred and forty kilometres away. The nearest peak would be Monte Hacho in the autonomous Spanish city of Ceuta, and a little further to the west and four times its size, Jebel Musa. The Pillars of Hercules appear as a support on the Spanish coat of arms, with the motto *Plus Ultra,* indicating Spain's openness to the rest of the world beyond the straits of Gibraltar.

That question: "You know I have to ask you this," and brutally, "Is there any lead in your pencil?"

It was the difficult question for which ostensibly I should have prepared, but somehow I thought that the interviewer would stick to generalities about prostate cancer and not make it so personal a matter.

Behind glass in the darkened control room, Jim Lockhart, the radio producer, had leaped out of his chair. "Oh he shouldn't have said that!"

"But he'd agreed to come on and answer whatever questions," mollified my partner Terry, who was seated behind him. "Oh, I beg your pardon, I thought you were referring to Michael: I've misunderstood you. The tension has me up to high doh."

When I was caught up in a car crash outside the gates of Terenure College, I seemed to be bathed in light so that the world outside the windscreen appeared in shadow. All I could see was the dashboard and the doors begin to close in gradually around me, inch by inch. I was aware of a creaking noise, but it was similar to the way that the pain was held in the middle distance when I'd been high on morphine after the cancer operation. Idly in the extended time-frame I wondered whether the car would continue to move in on top of me until I'd be crushed to death. The question had been released into the studio, and it was hanging there in the air. I looked across at Derek Mooney, one earphone can to his ear, the other off, and he was waiting for a reply. Is there any lead in my pencil? The question referred to the liquid constituent of semen, so the technical answer was no. But Derek was really asking me whether I was an alpha male following the radical prostatectomy or whether I considered myself relegated to the second division. Derek's question sounded insolent, but he'd put it to me as a good journalist is bound to do. And he borrowed the words which I'd indicated were out there in the reservoir of language. So why was I experiencing his approach as an assault? I flinched when he expelled the words through his smiling mouth. He innocently talked about this soft, blackish graphite, which derives from the Greek verb *to write,* painting a picture with the most delicate brush strokes, while at the same time he was transferring it to an action that it doesn't denote in order to imply a resemblance. His thinking on view was that since the word pencil derives from the Latin *peniculus* meaning little tail, it's analogous to my penis. He'd now arrived at a different portrait altogether, and to my mind it was modernistic and crude, lacked grace, and was devoid of feeling. "You know I have to ask you this," and brutally, "Are you still able to fuck?"

Well, am I? Instinctively, I feel such knowledge is private and is never elicited so explicitly, and never in so public a forum. This was the first time that such a question had ever been asked of me, and I was live on air. My whole life as a broadcaster and as a psychoanalyst has been about putting the world of the imagination into words, about telling the truth. I was very calm, and I took a deep breath: "No, Derek, I don't have any lead in my pencil."

A cascade of dammed up emotion thundered forth and knocked me sideways. Treacherously, I was being overthrown by a torrent of grief of which I'd been unaware until this very moment of burning astonishment, and I was drowning now in words that had invoked my loss. Death the Destroyer on his rearing horse, raised sword in hand, was loosed and in the ascendant, and I was vanquished. The supreme iconoclast, who'd cut down my erect phallus in a single sweep, was trampling in my domain through the debris of what had once been my honour and human dignity.

Derek said, "I'm feeling bad now that I asked you that question."

I cleared my throat in an attempt to regain my composure and to continue with the interview. I reassured him that it vindicated the purpose of breaking the taboo of male silence which surrounds the totem of prostate cancer: "We're two men who are talking about the effects of the disease. And I hope that today I may have done some good."

Jim, the producer, entered the studio during the ad break. He was tearful as he said goodbye, and he put his arm around my shoulder. Terry and I left immediately, and we took a plane to Spain early the following morning.

While ruminating over the interview, I speculated that Derek would for ever be known for having asked that one question. It was another forty-eight hours before the horrifying impact of my revelation stared me in the face. *The Sunday Independent* had run with an edited version of the interview, and it was emailed out, together with the "nice photograph" from the archives that had been taken some twenty years before. That evening as I watched the telly in Spain, the enormity of what I'd divulged weighed me down, and I felt deeply ashamed.

When I was shocked at the way Fr Flanagan in Newbridge had used pure slabs of colour, he'd advised me then, "Paint with broad strokes, and boldly, Michael." He'd led me through the doors into further rooms that I hadn't known existed. Writing this book has been like that. Each step I take leads on to new positions, new perspectives and further choices that ask me for the unfaltering courage to breach defensive walls of silence and to say it out clearly. My words are like a Trojan horse, which carries the truth through enemy lines to wait for its unknown and subversive conclusion. It will be an ending, determined by those who can hear.

"But it's the only direction to follow, isn't it?"

After the radio interview, Terry and I had gone to the Stillorgan Orchard for a bite to eat. Ironically, "D'you know what *still organ* is in German? *Mickey marbh*," teased Terry in the car. A dead prick: a fool.

When Valerie arrived with two hot plates of food to our table, she said, "Mr Murphy, I sat down with my husband and listened to you on the radio this afternoon. You were really brave. I had a breast removed four years ago."

"Oh, Valerie, I'm very sorry."

"I'm fine now. But I'm always at my husband to go to the doctor and have the test done, and he never will. But after he heard you speak about it on the radio, he agreed. We rang the doctor when you were finished, and he has an appointment for Monday morning."

"Isn't that great news."

"It really is, because I've always been worried about him. And well done. I told him that you come in to me at least once a week." Then to the two of us, "Enjoy your meal."

Part Twenty-five: The Bullfight

There's a renaissance palace in Cordoba whose architecture, with its mix of styles, pays homage to Andalusia's tangled past. The Palacio de los Páez also houses artefacts from that rich archaeological heritage. Among the Roman sculptures on display in the archaeological museum, sheltered between two elegant patios, is a compact statue of the Aryan deity Mithra, from the second century.

Roman soldiers in Iberia venerated him as the god of victory and heavenly light, *Sol Invictus,* who vanquishes the lunar powers of darkness. The sandy, white marble shows the bullfighter, Mithra Tauroctonus, in the act of slaying the primordial bull. What's unique about this image is that it locates the bullfight in Spain almost two thousand years ago and gives to the *corrida,* the battle between man and beast, as well as a history, a genealogy that recognises its divine nature.

Mithra has thrown himself sideways on to the back of the bull, and after a terrifying ride holding on, the opening steps in this *paso doble,* he has wrestled it crashing to its knees. With the fingers of his left hand he pulls back the bull's muzzle, raising the head so that it's in the humiliating position of being open-mouthed, bellowing with pain and fright, under his control, while his right plunges down the dagger into the bull's neck, severing the carotid artery, so that it screams. Head held high, Mithra gazes proudly over his right shoulder, which serves to amplify his lethal gesture. I can hear him cry in triumph, "Behold!" not deigning to look down at the dangerous bull held by him in a life or death struggle. "Behold!" challenging us into wonder and awe at his bravado, while from underneath a scorpion stings the bull's testicles in a deathly grip. "Behold!" man's best friend and counterpart, a dog, and bound to the cycle of renewal through the shedding of its skin, a snake, are initiated into this ritual of the *taurobolium,* the bull sacrifice. Drenched in the bull's pumping gore, they drink and are nourished by the spilling of the blood. "Out of death . . ."

> ". . . comes life."
> "Out of violence and pain . . ."
> ". . . life."
> "Out of terror and fright . . ."
> ". . . life"
> "As Taurus at the vernal equinox,"
> "So Scorpio at the autumnal."
> "See and affirm that I am Mithra,"
> "*Ave!*"
> "Imbued with the power of life and of death."
> "*Ave!*"
> "These two are one and the same."
> "*Ave atque vale!*"

In the gathering heat of the Guadalquivir basin, I answered the invitation in Mithra's look and went out beyond myself to hold his gaze for a split second longer than I should have. A message was passed in a bolt of lightening, ricocheting back in time from the Christian era to that of the Greeks, who fashioned the image and gave Mithra Alexander's face, the Phrygian cap of liberty and the flowing garb of the Iranians. There was a flicker of desire from hero to hero, Mithra the archangel, the greatest of an order of angels, like St Michael, the archangel, who is like unto God. The sun exploded with blinding light, and it was dancing in the sky. Flamenco artists with flowing skirts and even step, male and female with arching back, come forward in an unbroken line and form a circle, raising arms and striking attitudes that privilege the look, all the while moving soundlessly round and round, now forming a circle within a circle, like the lines drawn around the yellow sand of a bullfighting arena. In a patio in Cordoba, goldfish darting in a pool surrounded by the stumps of roman pillars, my skin was being scalded, and I had to put on my sunglasses and move back into the shade.

Red is the colour of Marbella's mountain
Scrawled in God's fresh blood beneath the blue veined
    sky
An outing covenant danced in black
With clacking heels across this tract of plain.
The flourish of a final turn reveals
A red-emblazoned serpent shimmering.

Red is the colour of God's signature
Slumbering under a clear blue sky,
A red mountain mantra inscribed across
The talisman of a reflecting frieze
Evoking the latent voice of God.
A ruby red rioja from the juice of blackened grapes.

Red is the *muleta* trailed by God across the sand
A red flamenco frock swirling like the wild levante
Plunging to the hilt to the heart the sword
A roaring gush of vivid red unfurling

Cruel as the reddest sun that rises suddenly
Searing those stamping footsteps into the black bull's
   skin.

Red is the colour of Marbella's mountain
Kohled black eyes shaded behind mantilla grilles.
The far-off gaze of God is straight and proud unwavering
A red paper flower flies to earth from out of this dancer's
   hair
And is kicked to the side in a flounce of strutting skirts.
It creates the red arena for the inevitable ending
Of a final dance with God, a dance with Death.

Guessing at the strength I drew from the allegory of the Spanish bullfight and what it has meant to me during this time of testing, Anna had arranged as a surprise that we'd join a group of bullfighting aficionados outside the bullring in Fuengirola at midday on Sunday, where two air-conditioned coaches would pick up the verbally boisterous, raucous assembly and drive all of us to Sevilla. A local boy, Ismael Cuevas, was being presented for the first time in the most prestigious *plaza de toros* of Andalusia, La Maestranza. It was a joyful coincidence that Ismael's name has been used in general for an outcast, and that even the biblical description of Ismael says, "every man's hand will be against him." But now, his fellow townspeople were going on an outing to lend him their support. The journey took three hours on an empty motorway lined with pink oleanders. Our procession was through hectares of olive trees stubbling the white earth as far as the eye could see, and sometimes it was the fields of frilled yellow sunflowers carpeting the front of an isolated white *finca* which crowded together and peered impassively at our convoy as we excitedly passed by.

We were disgorged like a trumpet blast into the heavy heat

of Sevilla in front of the bullring's Puerta del Príncipe, where triumphant bullfighters are carried shoulder high by their adoring fans, as peaked policemen swooping in on motorbikes cleared a passage for the van carrying the *novilleros*. They were gorgeously attired, flashing gold and silver, as they were hustled up an alleyway through the milling throng and into the arena. The white façade, outlined with red, was blinding in the light. Through the cries of the men and women hawking bottles of icy water, stepping over one bottle rolling on the cobbles, as money and tickets changed hands, we followed Anna through the jostle, asking which entrance gate, which row, and with hundreds of others sailed through the baroque embellishments arching the wide doorways, down through the echoing vaulted ceilings, then the climb up, up into the scorching air and up into the tiers of bricked seats like the Romans did in Iberia two thousand years before, until we took our places and became part of the fluttering, colourful display around the yellow sand, the human corolla surrounding a giant, expectant sunflower.

At precisely five in the afternoon, the red gates swung open on the far side of the arena, the brass band struck up its cheerful *paso doble,* and the ceremonial parade of the three *novilleros* with their teams emerged, plumes waving in the breeze, and carrying a short cloak over their left arms, crossed through waves of rapturous applause to stand with the bailiffs dressed in seventeenth-century costume and to present before the *Presidente.* Ismael Cuevas from Fuengirola is just seventeen years old, the youngest and least experienced of the three, and he cut a slight figure, boxed into his tightly drawn satin suit of lights, which glittered scarlet and gold when struck by the rays of the sun.

It was he who walked alone across the arena, and in a male gesture of defiance, knelt with splayed knees and open cape in

264

front of the doorway which barred the entry of the bulls to welcome the *negro listón* into the ring. Cuevas nodded, and the gate was opened. There was silence while the sunlight lit the gap, visible and empty. Then a black bull, four hundred and ninety-five kilos of muscle, thundered down, head weaving to an intake of breath from the superstitious crowd, and he charged the swirling cape, flashing magenta and yellow, the colours of death, while Cuevas scrambled to safety. After the mounted picador had twice thrust his lance into the bull's neck, who repeatedly raked with his horns the cladding and the clanking iron stirrups on the blinded horse, forcing it over against the wood, the *Presidente* laid a white handkerchief over the edge of his velvet covered table, and two trumpeters sitting opposite in the sun, sheltering beneath a red umbrella, sounded out the fanfare for the second *tercio*.

Cuevas was his own *banderillero,* a tiny figure dancing forward on the tips of his toes, displaying with outstretched arms to the bull the upright flags he held, first the right, then the left, showing to him the glittering plumb line of his slender body, goading him; then a final run at an angle across the charge of the bull to plunge with great skill and to thunderous applause three sets of these colourful long darts into the back of the bull himself, who responded by shaking his head and bucking, trying to dislodge the barbs, which now hung down like a necklace of bright blue ribbons, drenching his back in blood.

The trumpets sounded for the *tercio de muerte*. Ismael marched into the ring, draping his red cape over a curved sword to face the bellowing bull, and with the skilful continuity of his passes, right-handed expanding the cloth, left-handed *natural,* trains him to be under his control. The bull is built like a juggernaut, with the hind legs moving easily around the carriage of the head, which is supported by the front legs, oftentimes raking the sand in rage. What I wasn't prepared for in this *novillada* was the fright which the flurry of the charging bull evokes, the aggression with which he hooks with his horns at the cape around the vulnerable body of the matador. Cuevas faces this angry, static bull, heaving in the heat, trickling urine on to the sand. Arching his back, he thrust his body forward, rippling in the sunlight, settling his leather pumps into the sand, and openly took up his position, waving down to his right-hand side the cape, challenging the bull to charge. "*Toro, toro*," I heard him call to the bull over the murmur of the crowd, inching his body forward. "*Toro, toro*," caressing with his voice. And the bull charged at the cape, thundering forward, reversing his head to try and hook it, but Cuevas deftly repositioned, and the bull charged the cape again. Forward and back man and beast went many times in this dramatic ballet, as the red cape became smaller and the interval between it and the slender, arched body holding it lessened. The brass band began to play, softly supporting with its popular two-beat tunes the skill of the passes, the grace displayed by this young *torero* under pressure now, who's stepping it out with Death in the arena. He carried the weight of the crowd's expectations on his young shoulders unflinchingly. Cuevas seemed to be using his weaving body as an alternate to attract the bull. I could see from the bull's head that it was learning quickly, moving from the cape to the bullfighter's body and back again; then a final charge at the cape and a whirl around Cuevas, dwarfed and obliterated by the massive size of the animal. And Cuevas walked away from the heaving bull having put his life on the line, dragging the cape behind him, pounding the air with his golden right hand in a gesture of triumph, which was rewarded by the thunderous applause of the crowd.

Ismael Cuevas from Fuengirola was finally handed the sword in the *plaza de primera de Sevilla* before his family of supporters, and he walked with steady steps out across the sand until he stood before the bull and they could see into each other's eyes. The excited crowd was hushed. He was a young artist, so he held the sword out before him, measuring the distance between the animal and himself, while at the same time, he sentenced the bull to death. Man and beast, they'd both fought bravely, but the time had come for Ismael Cuevas to inflict death on our behalf, and to triumph over it.

There was a period of tense immobility, in which the *torero* and the bull compelled the crowd not to breathe by their insupportable presence. I could hear the siffling of the wind. It was the moment of truth, *el momento de la verdad*. Together now both charged; Cuevas leaning over the bull's horns and plunging down the sword to the hilt between the cervical vertebrae into the bull's heart, blazing with blood, as two screaming swallows choose that moment of the kill to dive-bomb Anna, Terry and me so that we duck down in shock. It was all over so fast. The bull was immediately surrounded and distracted by the colours of the waving cloaks of the *peones,* one footman on the right, another on the left, back again until the beast fell to its knees and keeled over. A *cachetero* delivered the coup de grace at the back of the head using a *puntilla,* and he died within thirty seconds. The brass band was playing, the crowd rising to honour the bull, and Cuevas, having gratified our blood lust, had walked away.

The crowd was on its feet waving white handkerchiefs at the judge, who was a hard judge, not swayed by their preferences. After the bull was dragged away behind a harnessed team of jingling mules wearing red and white flags fluttering in the sudden breeze, attendants clacking whips and running alongside them urging them to go faster, Cuevas did a lap of honour around the arena with his team, relaxed now and smiling, throwing back up into the crowd the hats and the flowers that were thrown for him to touch, and then moving back into the centre of the arena, holding out his astrakhan hat in a wide circle, as it quickly filled up with plaudits and salutations, acknowledging those who had come to see him courageously overcome death at five in the afternoon. And he didn't disappoint them. Today, Ismael Cuevas became a matador, a killer of bulls in La Maestranza, and for today, within the presence of this day, Ismael Cuevas is immortal.

We were among the last to leave the arena, with the cushions being hurled through the air from the top tiers of seats by teams of cleaners. As we walked slowly over the cobblestones, we passed by a white van emblazoned *"Carnes Gomez"* busily receiving the carcase of a bull, hind feet tied together, from a forklift travelling backwards at speed, then reversing forward swinging the upside-down bull into the back. Terry spotted the two buses waiting down by the Torre del Oro, from where cruises along the Guadalquivir traditionally depart. It was a tired, subdued company, still sweating from the heat, that immediately set off in the heavy lines of traffic moving endlessly along the wide, tree-lined avenue named after the explorer *par excellence* Christopher Columbus, then veering off right along a narrow overpass in the direction of the Granada and Malaga motorway. The driver began to play Diana Navarro through the speaker system, and the lilt of her familiar voice was reassuring. We mustered up the energy to hum along, after what was an exhausting, tension-filled day.

There was a pit stop after midnight at a barn-like restaurant outside Estepa, which was geared to cater for busloads of day trippers. As we were finishing our coffees, the sliding doors opened, and Ismael Cuevas walked in, and his father was with him. They both were immediately surrounded by well-wishers. The noise and excitement was overpowering, with undersized women reaching up to kiss Ismael on both cheeks, men slapping him on the back, calling out greetings, all desirous of having something of their young hero. I stood up, and the man who was embracing him and Cuevas himself became aware of my camera, and they turned their heads to give me radiant smiles. Through the viewfinder I was able to focus up and look Ismael in the eyes, to take his measure. I could see that his youthful vigour had banished fear to the outer rims of the iris of eyes of crystal, which were dancing with his happiness and delight at being and walking once more among his people. Anna took the camera from me and motioned me to go in and stand beside Cuevas. I pushed through the tumult until I stood shoulder to shoulder with him. He was taller than I was, and his fair hair being rubbed by his supporters was standing out like *clúmh,* the softest down. He smiled at me with perfect white teeth, then turned for the camera leaning back into my shoulder, and I put my arm around his waist and rested my hand on his hip. He smelled of the freshly laundered cotton in his white shirt, big squares outlined in pink, and his body was warm to my touch. He was secure in himself. The camera flashed, and I thanked Cuevas, shaking his smooth hand, holding him briefly by the elbow. A look passed, of respect, admiration, a goodbye, and then he was gone, being pursued down by the counters, his attention being demanded by his fans.

The photograph of me standing beside Cuevas wasn't there in my camera: I searched for it many times. But on the bus home seated beside Terry, I had the extraordinary sensation that Cuevas was still in my arms. I looked down wonderingly and checked, slowly rubbing my finger along the very tips of the hairs of my right arm which still sensed him, his youth, his strength, the turn of his head with the laughing eyes and welcoming spirit, his bravery in the face of death. I knew that he was still here, inhabiting the space where I'd cradled him round such a short time before, and I was filled with awe. My fellow-passengers were oblivious to this sacred miracle of the La Maestranza matador, which was happening now in their midst. Their drowsiness wasn't penetrated by the white stars which were rising, releasing up from my seat to find their places in the soft cavern of the night sky, the light intensifying, gradually spreading out until it became a field of stars, a *campus stellae*, bathing his people in grace. It wasn't given to them to see or to hear the changes that were occurring, the searing golden whiteness of the heavens opening, beckoning, and Cuevas climbing the steps of a rainbow *ar shlí na fírinne*, on the pathway of truth. I could hear the massed choirs, the trumpet blasts, the choruses rolling over and over, ". . . *Cum Sancto Spiritu, in gloria Dei Patris*": the *Gloria in excelsis* from Bach's *B Minor Mass*. In his glittering *traje de luces*, Cuevas was gesturing in a circle with his hat so that we were drenched in sparkling colours, the spilling over of kisses blown by the wind, in the music that overflows in loving souls. *Adios*, go with God. He was consumed by such a fierce radiance, that in an instant he was gone too soon, leaving behind his hollow shape, a cavity in my arm, the aching hum of the engine continuing on relentlessly and the headlights raking the roadway, lighting but dimly the way ahead.

I have told it like it is, what I have seen and what I have heard. I have said it, and my saying is true. Because of the cancer, there's no longer any space available to hide in; neither is there any time left over for being silent. I have told the truth to save my life.

And you, gentle reader, now that you've heard my story, "And how're you *now*?"

www.michaelmurphyauthor.com

If you've enjoyed reading this book, then please tell others about it and recommend it to your friends. And if you'd like to say how this book has affected you, then please write a review or leave your comments on the accompanying website: www.michaelmurphyauthor.com.

To increase your enjoyment, the website features photographs of some of the people who've appeared in this book. You can also hear short extracts read in Michael Murphy's voice. You'll be able to see there how the book has been received by the literary critics. The website gives news of the latest book readings around the country, the proceeds of which go towards the Irish Cancer Society, where you'll also have an opportunity to meet Michael Murphy and to discuss this memoir with him.

Thank you for extending the kindness of your interest and your support to one of the many people who've been touched by cancer.

For expert information, support and advice about prostate cancer, talk to a specialist nurse in confidence at the National Cancer Information Service (Freefone 1800 200 700 and open Monday–Thursday 9am–7pm and Fridays 9am–5pm), email prostate@irishcancer.ie or visit www.cancer.ie/prostate.

Acknowledgements

I want to thank those who took the trouble to read the various drafts of this book. They are Hedwig Ast, who was always available to instruct me in the finer points of German; Dr Olga Cox-Cameron, whose husband died of cancer; Donal Leahy; Rosemary Liddy, who has also suffered from cancer; Professor John McCarthy and Mary MacEvaddy. Muireann Noonan was unwavering in her support of this book: she told me that she did not like the central character in the first draft, but I appreciated her vote of confidence in passing on the third draft to her mother. Others to be thanked include Dr Patrick Randall, Dermot Ronaldson, and Dr Katherine Zappone and Dr Ann Louise Gilligan, who engaged in an email correspondence during their summer vacation. I hope you can see how your considered critiques have influenced the finished work.

An immeasurable debt of gratitude goes to our loving friends Anna, Helen and Ursula. They were the cancer survivors who have supported and encouraged Terry and me with weekly phone calls, and whose generous contributions formed an essential part of my own recovery.

Geraldine Boyle, Jeanne and Aisling with Philip MacDermott facilitated the book's publication, as did Yvonne Byrne. Sadie Power's acts of kindness and Gerry Byrne acting as our Noah during the flood helped us to survive. Conor Ó Mearáin took the beautifully insightful photographs for the cover and for David Douglas's brilliant website, and he impressed us all with his gentle intelligence when dealing with divas, and divo. My literary agent, Emma Walsh, gave unstinting, continuing support to Terry and to me, and Steve MacDonogh was courageous enough to publish this book.

A special thank you must go to every individual with whom I have been privileged to work psychoanalytically. Since you inhabit the dream, you are necessarily represented in this book, but subject to condensation, displacement and revision. You have taught me what I know about human nature, and you have left me in awe of the human spirit, which alone endures. It is important to state clearly that any people depicted here to give the flavour of an analytic session are products of my imagination.

I want to acknowledge the honour that Mrs Mary Robinson has accorded this book by supplying the foreword. I feel privileged and grateful. Mayo people the world over are proud to claim her as one of our own, but Mary Robinson belongs to the world, which is a better place because of who she is: *dea-chroí*.

Finally, a heartfelt thank you to everybody who sent letters, cards (Finola wrote every week) and good wishes to Terry and to me during this time of anguish. Ann Dempsey was one of those good people who prayed for me. Your kindness was a beacon of hope which kept the two of us trudging ever onwards during the darkest of days, which, thankfully, are becoming fewer.

Rath Dé oraibh.